And It's Goodnight From Him . . .

Ronnie Corbett OBE has worked in the entertainment industry since the 1950s. He rose to prominence in the 1960s with his regular appearance on *The Frost Report*, where he met Ronnie Barker. Together, they formed *The Two Ronnies*, which went on to run for sixteen years. Ronnie Corbett has been happily married to Anne for more than forty years. They have two daughters and live near Croydon.

David Nobbs has written sixteen novels and several television series including *The Fall and Rise of Reginald Perrin*, *A Bit of A Do* and *Love on a Branch Line*. He has also written for many top comedians including Tommy Cooper, Ken Dodd, Les Dawson – and, of course, The Two Ronnies. He lives in North Yorkshire with his wife Susan.

And It's Goodnight From Him . . .

The Autobiography of the Two Ronnies

RONNIE CORBETT
with DAVID NOBBS

MICHAEL JOSEPH
an imprint of
PENGUIN BOOKS

MICHAEL JOSEPH

Published by the Penguin Group
Penguin Books Ltd, 80 Strand, London WC2R ORL, England
Penguin Group (USA) Inc., 375 Hudson Street, New York, New York 10014, USA
Penguin Group (Canada), 90 Eglinton Avenue East, Suite 700, Toronto, Ontario, Canada M4P 2Y3
(a division of Pearson Penguin Canada Inc.)
Penguin Ireland, 25 St Stephen's Green, Dublin 2, Ireland (a division of Penguin Books Ltd)
Penguin Group (Australia), 250 Camberwell Road,
Camberwell, Victoria 3124, Australia (a division of Pearson Australia Group Pty Ltd)
Penguin Books India Pvt Ltd, 11 Community Centre, Panchsheel Park, New Delhi – 110 017, India
Penguin Group (NZ), cnr Airborne and Rosedale Roads, Albany, Auckland 1310, New Zealand
(a division of Pearson New Zealand Ltd)
Penguin Books (South Africa) (Pty) Ltd, 24 Sturdee Avenue, Rosebank, Johannesburg 2196, South Africa

Penguin Books Ltd, Registered Offices: 80 Strand, London WC2R ORL, England

www.penguin.com

First published 2006
1

Copyright © Ronnie Corbett, 2006

The moral right of the author has been asserted

Set in 12/14.75 pt Monotype Bembo
Typeset by Rowland Phototypesetting Ltd, Bury St Edmunds, Suffolk
Printed in Great Britain by Clays Ltd, St Ives plc

A CIP catalogue record for this book is available from the British Library

HARDBACK
ISBN-13: 978-0-718-14964-2
ISBN-10: 0-718-14964-5

TRADE PAPERBACK
ISBN-13: 978-0-718-14996-3
ISBN-10: 0-718-14996-3

For dear Ron, a great friend and colleague who is deeply missed, and for Joy, who has borne her loss so bravely and supported this book so thoroughly

I would, personally, like to thank David Nobbs for lending this book his truly light touch and splendid way with words.

Ronnie Corbett

'Same again, please.'

Those were almost the first words that Ronnie Barker ever said to me. Not quite, obviously, because if he hadn't ordered a drink from me already, I could hardly have known what he meant by 'Same again, please.' But, sadly, I can't remember his very first words to me as I can't remember what he was drinking at that first meeting. It *was* a very long time ago.

It was 1963, in fact, the year of the Profumo Affair, in which John Profumo, Secretary of State for War in the Conservative government, confessed that he had lied to the House of Commons and had had an affair with Christine Keeler, call girl and model. Profumo resigned and, later in the year, largely as a result of this scandal, his Prime Minister, Harold Macmillan, was also forced to resign. It was the year of the Great Train Robbery, when the Scotland to London Post Office express was ambushed near Cheddington and robbed of £2.5 million. It was also the year in which President John F. Kennedy was assassinated. It was a momentous year in the world.

Ronnie was thirty-three, and I was a year younger. He was beginning to establish himself as a character actor in the West End and on radio, and I was working as a barman between jobs. Somehow, that seems an appropriate beginning. If we'd done a sketch about our first meeting, that was the way it would have been cast.

My life at that time was very busy. During the day I was running the stores at the Victory Club in Edgware Road, which was owned by Mecca Ballrooms. I had my lunch and tea there, and at five thirty I drove my little bullnose Morris to the Buckstone Club, where I had my supper and ran the bar until after midnight. And the theatrical term for that is 'resting'! Sometimes I was resting almost to the point of exhaustion.

The Buckstone Club was in a basement in Suffolk Street, right behind the stage door of the Haymarket Theatre, and was frequented by all sorts of theatrical luminaries – Sean Connery, Stanley Baker, John Gielgud, Edith Evans and many others. They felt safe from the public there, though not necessarily from the critics. The famous critic Kenneth Tynan – the first man to use a certain four-letter word on television, a word banned then and almost compulsory now – was a regular, in his velvet jacket, holding his cigarette artily between the wrong fingers. It's strange what one remembers.

Ronnie B. struck me at those early meetings as a very pleasant, easy person, very comfortable with himself. I realized later, when I got to know him better, that he sometimes found it difficult to be comfortable with every Tom, Dick or Harry. In fact he was quite shy. But in the Buckstone Club, in the company of his peers, he felt quite easy and at home. He was always quite smartly dressed, often in a Glen Urquhart suit, but I don't think he was actually particularly interested in clothes, certainly not as interested as I am. He didn't share my feeling for colours and textures of materials. His style was a bit conservative.

Ronnie was playing a French gangster in the long-running musical *Irma La Douce* – too long-running for his liking. He was trapped in it for two years and came to hate it and felt guilty about hating it when he was in regular work in such a precarious profession. He used to come in occasionally in the evenings, but our first meeting was at lunchtime. I did sometimes work the lunchtime shift. Ronnie was recording the very popular radio comedy *The Navy Lark* round the corner at the Paris Theatre and used to come in for a light lunch with his wife, Joy, who always accompanied him when he was doing shows with an audience.

One of the many coincidences that seemed to stalk our lives was that I already knew Joy, who was a stage manager. She had stage-managed a pantomime I had done in Bromley. So Ronnie knew about my career, just as I knew about his, and there was plenty to chat about as I served him his drinks. Was there anything more than that, some intimation about future happenings, some feeling that our first meeting was, for us at least, one more momentous event in that year of momentous events? None whatsoever.

Ronnie and I actually had only one remotely serious argument in our lives, and very few disagreements, but, ironically, one of the disagreements involves this very first meeting. He always claimed that I was standing on a box in order to see over the bar. Later he embroidered the story and said I had two boxes, one marked 'AGNES' and the other 'CHAMP'. It took him a while to work out that they were a champagne box cut in half. That sounds to me like a bit of typical Ronnie B. word play. Possibly he came to believe that I'd been standing on a box, but I promise you, I swear to you, hand on knee, that I wasn't. I didn't need to. It was a very low bar. Besides, I would have needed a whole row of boxes running the length of the bar, otherwise I would have been disappearing from view and popping up again all over the place. What did he think I was, a comedian?

The Buckstone Club was a cheery place, compact, almost scruffy in the best London traditions. In its poky dining room two delightful waitresses, Nancy from Ireland and Bianca from Austria, served light lunches, afternoon teas for actors

3

between matinees and evening performances and very good suppers. It was one of the most enjoyable of all my jobs, not least because it's intimately associated for me with the two most important people in my adult life. Not only Ronnie, my colleague and great friend, but also Anne, my lovely wife. Anne was five foot eight and appearing on stage with the Crazy Gang. I was naturally a little nervous about asking her out. The Buckstone Club provided a safe haven, where I was known, and we did much of our courtship there.

Our profession is an insecure one, and I didn't dare commit myself to Anne until I had got myself properly established. Little did I know then that the man in the Glen Urquhart suit would help me get established beyond my wildest dreams, and that, before ten years had passed, *The Two Ronnies* would be a huge hit on BBC1 on Saturday evenings, and the BBC bosses would be echoing those words of Ronnie Barker in the Buckstone Club.

'Same again, please.'

Three years after my first meeting with Ronnie Barker, David Frost invited me to tea at a much grander place than the Buckstone Club. The Methodist minister's son from Raunds in Northamptonshire had been propelled by the success of *That Was the Week That Was* into a lifestyle in which it was natural for him to have tea at the Ritz. Only two people have ever invited me to tea at the Ritz. The second was much more surprising. Of which more anon.

Over the cucumber sandwiches, David put an immensely appealing proposition to me. He wanted me to appear in his new show, *The Frost Report*. *TW3* had been a sensation, a live satirical show that had made TV instant and exciting and more talked about than it had ever been. David's follow-up to it would be a major television event, and to be a part of it would represent a huge leap in my career.

The idea was that I would team up with two other actors, one of whom was Ronnie Barker. Ronnie was a much more well-known figure than me, through his stage performances and his work on two extremely successful and long-running radio shows, *The Navy Lark* and *Variety Playhouse*. He had been suggested by the producer, Jimmy Gilbert.

The third actor was not at all well known. David knew him from the Cambridge Footlights, and he was currently in Canada with a university show, *Second City Review*. His name was John Cleese.

David had seen me performing with Danny La Rue at Winston's, a London night club. In those days the West End was packed with night clubs that put on proper little shows, slightly satirical, quite witty, a bit naughty, certainly glamorous, with lovely girls who would come on from *The Talk of the Town* or from musicals, and would be doing two jobs, and a nice little trio would play, and they would be specially written by people like Bryan Blackburn and Barry Cryer in his early days. Winston's was one of the best of these clubs, and I had a very happy time there. David used to visit with his girlfriend, the actress and dancer Jenny Logan. Apparently he saw me and . . . no, I'll rephrase that. I may be small but I'm not that small. He must have seen me. What I should have said is that apparently he liked what he saw. I say 'apparently' because he didn't talk to me and tell me, so the invitation for cucumber sandwiches came as a complete surprise.

There was an enormous snag, however. I was appearing in a new West End musical, *Twang*, at the Shaftesbury Theatre. Unless it closed, I wouldn't be able to do *The Frost Report*. Dick Vosburgh, later to become one of our regular and most brilliant writers, told me that he had urged Jimmy Gilbert to go and see me in *Twang*, in which I was playing the part of Will Scarlett. What Dick liked about my performance was that I was playing my part truthfully in a show in which, he thought, many of the cast were not.

David already felt that *Twang* wouldn't run, and that I would become available. In fact he must have been pretty certain, or I don't think he would have given me that tea. But how could it possibly fail? It was written by Lionel Bart, who had achieved massive successes with *Fings Ain't Wot They Used T'Be* and *Oliver*. It was directed by Joan Littlewood, who had become a legend in her own rehearsal time with huge hits like *Oh What a Lovely War*. It was designed by Oliver Messel and choreographed by Paddy Stone – great talents both.

As the King of Siam with Danny La Rue.

But Lionel Bart's reworking of the Robin Hood legend *did* fail. It failed famously, spectacularly, dispiritingly. It was a right old mess, and the more people changed it and tried to save it, the more it became an even righter old mess. It just about ruined Lionel Bart, who had pumped enormous amounts of his own money into it.

There is a huge element of chance in an actor's life. If *Twang* had not failed, I would never have done *The Frost Report* and I wouldn't be writing this book. There are also many difficult emotional moments. I could not possibly want a play in which I was appearing to fail, especially when I admired its author and knew how much it meant to him. Being part of a failure is a horrible experience. But we all knew that there was a great deal wrong with the show, and I

Very, very young! Winston's Club.

suppose I must have hoped that, if it was going to fail, it would fail quickly enough for me to be able to do *The Frost Report*. It did, and I would have to say, in retrospect, that its failure was as important to my career as any of my successes. At the time I took no pleasure from it, but I couldn't regret it either.

Each programme of *The Frost Report* was on a different subject – politics, authority, religion, class, the countryside, etc. The script was created in a rather unusual way. First Antony Jay, a very clever man who later wrote *Yes, Minister* with Jonathan Lynn, wrote a thoughtful, incisive essay on the subject of the week. Then the writers and actors gleefully removed most of the thoughtfulness and incisiveness, turning it into a funny series. That isn't quite fair. The show did contain some biting satirical material, and was never less than intelligent, and often very, very funny. We had some very clever writers, including Barry Cryer, Dick Vosburgh, Neil Shand, Graham Chapman, Michael Palin, Terry Jones and Eric Idle. The last four, with John Cleese, were later of course to become the stars of *Monty Python's Flying Circus*.

The format of the show was basically very simple: a continuous monologue by David, interspersed with one-liners, quickies and sketches from John, Ronnie, Sheila Steafel and me, and two musical numbers, one from the great Tom Lehrer, the other from the delightful Julie Felix.

Ronnie and I got on well from the start. There was an immediate comfort between us. It wasn't spectacular. There was a sensible reserve in our relationship. It was, if you like, the beginning of a very British friendship.

People forget that John Cleese first tried out his silly walks on *The Frost Report*, and I did a filmed item, probably long forgotten now, in which I came upon a sign which said, 'Do Not Walk On The Grass', so I danced on the grass, hopped

on the grass, jumped on the grass, did everything but walk on the grass. But one item that everybody remembers is the class sketch, written by a very clever Glaswegian writer named John Law, who died tragically young.

The three of us stood side by side, in front of a bare background. John Cleese stood on the left of the screen, wearing a bowler hat. Ronnie B. stood in the middle in a trilby. I stood to the right, in a cloth cap and muffler. The sight of the three of us, John so tall and I so short and Ronnie rather plump in the middle (I mean the middle of the three of us, not the middle of himself – well, that too, I suppose), was intrinsically funny. Indeed, writing in the *Listener*, that distinguished author Anthony Burgess – creator of *The Clockwork Orange* and much much else – said, 'Funny singly, the men are funnier still together, and part of their funniness derives from grotesque physical contrast – the very tall, the medium chubby, the very small. They are a kind of visual epigram made out of the intellectual fact of human variety. This epigram is also a paradigm for conjugating social statements – about class, chiefly – with great neatness.' I felt like phoning my dad in Scotland and saying, 'I've made it, Dad. Not only am I an epigram, I'm also a paradigm.'

All that did rather suggest the question, 'Were we chosen not for our talent, but for our height?' I'd like to think not, but, in any case, it hardly matters now.

'I look down on him,' began John, looking down on Ronnie B., 'because I am upper class.'

'I look up to him,' said Ronnie B., looking up at John, 'because he is upper class. But I look down on him . . .' he indicated me '. . . because he is lower class. I am middle class.'

'I know my place,' I said. 'I look up to them both. But I don't look up to him . . .' I looked up at Ronnie B. '. . . as much as I look up to him . . .' I looked up at John even more. '. . . 'cos he has innate breeding.'

'I have innate breeding, but I have not got any money,' said John. 'So sometimes I look up to him.'

He bent his knees and looked up at Ronnie B.

'I still look up to him,' said Ronnie B., looking up at John, 'because, although I have money, I am vulgar. But I am not as vulgar as him . . .' he indicated me '. . . so I still look down on him.'

'I know my place,' I said. 'I look up to both of them. But, while I am poor, I am industrious, honest and trustworthy. Had I the inclination, I could look down on them. But I don't.'

'We all know our place,' said Ronnie B., 'but what do we get out of it?'

'I get a feeling of superiority over them,' said John, indicating us both.

'I get a feeling of inferiority from him,' said Ronnie B., looking up at John, 'but a feeling of superiority over him.'

He looked down on me.

'I get a pain in the back of my neck,' I said.

I quote this sketch in full again because it has gone down as a classic, and because John Law deserves to be remembered.

I've sometimes been asked if I think that sketch represented any truth in the relationships between Ron, myself and John Cleese. There was a sense in which Ron and I felt like natural allies. Not that we didn't get on with John; there was no enmity, none whatsoever, but there was a feeling that there was a kind of fence between him and us. Was this due to class? I don't actually think so. Class isn't very important in our profession. I think education was the significant factor.

Ronnie and I had not gone beyond grammar school, while John Cleese and most of the writers had been to university. There was a feeling that people like John and Graham Chapman had got nice degrees on other subjects and were rather playing at our game, seeing how they liked it: 'We may stay on or we may go back to medicine or something.' Later I think they all got more serious about it, but at the time it was just slightly annoying to Ron and me; we thought, 'Hang on a minute. This is our livelihood, which we've been working at for seventeen years.'

I think the relevant fact about the class sketch, from the point of view of my relationship with Ronnie, was that it would have been possible for John Cleese to have looked down on us (I'm not saying that he did, I don't think for a moment that he did, I'm only saying that it would have been possible), but it wouldn't have been possible for either Ronnie

or me to have looked down on each other. Our backgrounds were too similar. We had too much in common.

It's time to look at our backgrounds. I'll start with mine, because obviously I know it in more detail, and, sadly, Ron isn't around to fill in the details about his.

3

I was born in Edinburgh on 4 December 1930. The only unusual thing about this event was that they left a swab in my poor dear mother. I was told about this so often that I almost began to believe that it was my fault.

All my grandparents were Scottish, although my maternal grandparents emigrated to London in search of work. My granddad was a policeman, a station sergeant in Upper Norwood and Gypsy Hill, not far from where I live now. I never met him or my grandmother, who was cook-housekeeper in a big house in Upper Belgrave Street. She loved the theatre and used to queue for the cheap seats at West End theatres, so maybe I got some of my desire to be an actor from her.

They returned to Edinburgh just before my mother, Anne, was born. She was educated at Boroughmuir School, where she was in the same class as that brilliantly funny character actor Alastair Sim. Before her marriage she worked on the switchboard and in the accounts department at the head office of John Menzies, the bookseller. She was quite bookish and loved poetry. Whisper it softly, but I think there was a feeling in her family that she married slightly beneath her. There was a lot of that sort of whispering in those far-off days.

My dad, who was called William, was a baker. He had tremendously high standards. Everything had to be just so, and he would make extremely detailed preparations before he began baking. There is more than a bit of him in me. In fact I thoroughly enjoy making bread and cakes, and when I do I set my stall out just as thoroughly as he did. I like to feel that he would approve if he could see me. He was a short man – just five foot six – and he had great energy. He was strict, even a bit severe, but never intimidating. He instilled in me a great desire to impress him, and a knowledge that it wouldn't be easy to do so. But he also had a great sense of humour, the tough Scottish kind that stared disaster in the face and laughed at it. He was very gregarious and loved to blether (a great Scottish word) with friends on street corners. He was also a very keen and pretty good golfer. I inherited the enthusiasm, but was never as good as him. Golf, baking, humour, pride and high standards – not a bad legacy to leave to your son.

I always felt close to my dad, but he was fundamentally reserved, despite his chattiness on minor matters, and there was one thing about which I never spoke to him in depth. He lied about his age in order to fight in the First World War, and actually took part in the Battle of the Somme at the age of sixteen and a half. He came back from the war without injury, but I have often wondered what effect it had on him mentally. It was over twelve years before I was born, and although he spoke occasionally about the terrible things that he had seen, I don't think he was able to let me fully into his heart about them.

I had a brother, Allan, six years younger than me and much taller, and a sister, Margaret, ten years my junior. Allan studied law at Edinburgh University and then went into the restaurant business, ending up running a very successful fish restaurant in Leith with his wife Jen. Margaret married a dentist from the US Air Force, and went to live in Florida.

I would say that on the whole I had a happy childhood, but my very first memory is far from happy. It was of almost drowning when I was three, in a paddling pool at the Step

From left to right: Allan, Margaret and me.

Rock in St Andrews, one of those natural pools which the water comes into at high tide. I very clearly remember the feeling of being under the water and seeing somebody coming to my rescue. I can still see the reflection of people through the crystal-clear water. I wasn't under for long, but it was quite frightening. My mother and father must have been in a terrible state because I was the first and they'd been married for six and a bit years and thought that perhaps they couldn't have a child until I came along. Anyway, it hasn't left me with any fear of water whatsoever and the area around the Step Rock was soon to be the scene of an altogether happier memory.

I took part in a pierrot show, when I was five and a bit, at the nearby Step Rock Pavilion. There was a pierrot show every afternoon, in the open air, outside the Pavilion, with a talent contest, and I sang a Bud Flanagan song and won first prize. It always seemed very odd to me that at St Andrews, so close to the Royal and Ancient Golf Club, the prize was a cricket bat.

I felt as though I made no mark at all at my first school, the James Gillespie School for Boys. When I moved on to the Royal High School, I did rather better, showing enough spirit to join the literary society and the debating society and go to all the school dances. Unfortunately, though, that's where my initiative ended. I joined, I went, but I didn't speak or dance.

I have to say that where girls were concerned, my height was a problem. It takes courage to approach girls who are much taller than you are. I used to try to judge, as I approached a line of seated girls, which ones would be the shortest when they stood up, but most of the time it was irrelevant, as they refused to stand up. I suppose it's the opposite of being stood up. I was constantly sat down by girls.

James Gillespie School for Boys. The class of 1936.
I'm sitting fourth from the left on the front row.

17

I felt that nobody wanted to dance with me, that they dreaded my approach.

Apart from that, strangely enough, I don't recall my height being a problem. I don't remember ever being bullied or mocked because I was so short, so maybe I was a bit stronger or a bit funnier or a bit more popular than I thought. I don't think that, apart from those wretched dances, I was as sensitive about my height as could have been expected. It was my Aunt Nell, not me, who paid two guineas and sent away for a course on How To Become Taller. This involved stretching exercises and positive thinking. I had to recite, 'Every day and in every way I'm getting taller and taller.' It was a waste of Aunt Nell's two precious guineas. Well, you can see that. All we were left with was a series of marks on the kitchen wall, each much too close to the preceding mark. I simply stopped growing at five foot one and a half inches. I was examined by doctors, who found that there was nothing wrong with me, I was just little. And perfectly formed, I'm tempted to add.

Aunt Nell was a lovely lady. She was beautiful, and she was kind. She married late in life and hated it. The marriage lasted less than a year. After it had ended she devoted her life to us and became like a second mother to me. She used to call me 'my little Rodie-Podie'. She may not have succeeded where my height was concerned, but she was very influential in another way. She was a tailor, and she made, or altered to my size, all my clothes, almost all of which needed altering, because I was so small. She gave me an interest in clothes and she taught me how important it was, because I was small, to look immaculate at all times. My uncle was also a tailor, and my father was a bit of a dresser too. He knew the value of buying a £25 suit, because it would last thirty years, whereas the £8 one wouldn't last two minutes. I learnt that lesson well. I am always careful about my clothes. It's not so easy to mock a small man if he looks smart and stylish. I have always felt that I know what clothes suit me, that I have a very clear idea of what style and what colours to wear – I particularly like pastel colours, light blue, duck-egg blue, although I sometimes enjoy wearing really strong colours. I dress in my own style, virtually unaffected by the passing trends and fashions.

How different life was in Britain in the years before and during and indeed immediately after the Second World War. How much narrower were our horizons. For our holidays we went to St Andrews almost every year. Ten days before the holiday, our huge trunks would be packed and roped up and sent on to the digs where we were to stay. We shared our holiday with other families, and our entertainment in the evenings would consist of taking a wee walk round the old town and, if we were very lucky, having a pennyworth of chips. I can still see myself going to church on Sundays in my Royal Stuart kilt, lovat-green sweater and brown brogues, and walking in the afternoon, still in our best clothes, over the Braid Hills, with their wide views over the Firth of Forth. I can picture, as if it were yesterday, the maroon and grey crocodile that walked from our school to the baths for our swimming lessons.

I was growing up, yet I was still a child. In my teens I took to going on tough adventure holidays, but I didn't always stick to the toughness and the adventure. I went on a skiing course in the Cairngorms, long before skiing was a popular pursuit in Britain. I went youth hostelling until I found that my bike was too heavily laden for me to be able to push it up hills. One winter four of us rented a miner's cottage on Raasay, a small, thinly populated island off Skye. I think we intended to test our stamina hiking in rough country in harsh weather, but in the event we spent most of our days huddled round a peat fire eating buttered toast.

A car was still a luxury, and Dad didn't have one until 1948, when he was fifty. In fact we both learnt to drive at the same time, taught by his brother, Geordie. I passed my test first time, but he didn't. I tried not to look too smug, sitting beside him as he drove with his L-plates on. We were stopped by a policeman, who asked Dad for his licence. It was provisional of course, and I must have looked about fourteen. The policeman was naturally very suspicious. It was a great moment as I handed him my full licence, and saw him pass it back to me shame-facedly and walk away without speaking.

The worst memory of my childhood involves my dad. He had been baking manager at McVitie and Guest. He had run Mackie's bakery. Then he ran the Lothian school meals service. The service was reorganized, and he found himself redundant. He became a caretaker in a big school, and he did that until he retired. I don't know why his career ended so ingloriously, but I do know that it hurt him very deeply, so deeply that he destroyed all his recipe books, all twenty-eight of them, each one written in his fine handwriting, and containing all the secrets that he had learnt. It wasn't exactly that he was embittered. That's too strong. The correct word to describe his feelings is, I think, that he was scunnered. That's a great Scottish word, and like all the best words there is no exact translation, but I suppose it means that he was sick to the back teeth with the world of baking. He would still bake in later life when it suited him, and when he came to stay with us for a fortnight we couldn't keep him out of the kitchen, but it was sad that he felt this professional disillusion. I think the experience and my memory of it has helped me never to count my chickens.

The best memory of my childhood, on the other hand, was when I was given the part of the wicked aunt in the

St Catherine-in-the-Grange church youth club production of *Babes in the Wood*. I had performed before. I had won my cricket bat at St Andrews. I had appeared in a concert for the war effort – to be more precise, for the Spitfire Fund, wearing a dressing gown and carrying a candle and singing a Christopher Robin song. At the Lyceum Theatre? Not quite. On the flat roof of the air-raid shelter in the communal garden at the back of our tenement. I don't want to boast, but I seem to recall that I raised almost £9. I was aware of having at least a bit of musical talent. I had taken piano lessons, eventually becoming good enough to play the organ in church.

But this was different. This was the real thing. I loved it. The minister, Tom Maxwell, told my mother, 'I think you ought to know that something quite remarkable is going on at rehearsals. Little Ron is being wonderful as the wicked aunt.' I can sense the surprise behind his use of the word 'remarkable', but he was a kind man, and I can't resent it, and it was, in a way, my very first review. I wish they had all been as flattering.

This single event changed my life. I knew now what I wanted to be. I wanted to be an actor. It wasn't just a case of being stage-struck. It was far more precise than that. I knew, in an instant, what kind of actor I wanted to be. I wanted to be a comic actor. I wanted to be a sophisticated light comedian, who would appear in Noël Coward's plays wearing a Scotts lightweight felt hat, which seemed to me to be the acme of sophistication.

I began going to the Lyceum and the King's Theatre every week, regardless of what was on. My mum and dad, unlike so many mums and dads, didn't recoil from my strange ambition. They didn't say, 'Listen, lad, baking's your destiny. You belong in the world of yeast. There's wholemeal bread and eclairs in your blood.' They encouraged me to join the Glover

Turner Robertson School in George Street in Edinburgh, where I began to learn my trade and was taught how to lose my Scottish accent – a necessity in those days when BBC English still ruled.

I hung around stage doors, hoping for autographs. Sometimes I even managed to walk alongside quite well-known actors on their way back to their hotels. The word I used for this is 'escort', but I have a feeling that their description might have been 'tag along'. I'm amazed now that I had the cheek to do it and amazed that they didn't all tell me to buzz off. Among those actors who failed to shake me off was Kenneth Connor, later to star in the *Carry On* . . . films.

I left school at seventeen with seven Higher Leaving Certificates. My father would have liked me to go to university, and my younger brother did go, but I'd had enough of school and learning in that way. I didn't feel there was any point in it for me, since I knew now what I wanted to do with my life.

It was all very well knowing what I wanted to do, but doing it was another matter. I had to earn a living, and started applying for jobs which I no longer really wanted. I sat a Civil Service exam, to try to be an officer in the Civil Service, and I missed it by about two places, so I found myself working as a clerical officer in the Ministry of Agriculture in Edinburgh. I don't think it would have made much difference to my life if I'd passed the exam. I had no intention of making a long-term career in the Civil Service.

Even animal foods were rationed in those austere days after the war. We issued coupons for proteins and cereals for farrowing sows and milk herds, and organized the wages for Polish ex-servicemen who helped farmers in the Borders with their harvest.

During my eighteen months with the Ministry of Agricul-

On the front row again, third from left.

ture I made no attempt to turn my theatrical dream into reality. I decided that I needed to get National Service out of the way first. I was actually looking forward to it. I had been very happy growing up in Edinburgh, but now I wanted to get away and begin to explore the world. I passed the medical despite a deviated septum and attacks of asthmatic bronchitis and I am so pleased that I did. I was one of those people who got enormous benefit from National Service.

I joined the RAF in 1949. I applied to be trained for a commission, was accepted for officer selection and passed out as a pilot officer at Spitalgate, near Cranwell. My military career may not have been startling – the only time I stepped into a plane was when a fellow officer took me for rides in a Tiger Moth, and because I was five foot one and a half inches the station commander at RAF Weeton suggested that I wear my full number-one dress at all times, for fear that experienced old hands might mistake me for a cadet – but being accepted as an officer despite my lack of height, not to mention my deviated septum, gave me a confidence which I had never felt before and have never lost since. I can't say that I had yet realized that my lack of height could be a great advantage to me, but I can claim that, while I might still on occasions be sensitive on the subject, I would never again be seriously worried by it.

I had my first real romantic encounter during my National Service, with a nursing sister whom I met when I was in hospital with asthmatic bronchitis. It was a very innocent romance. Those were very innocent days. Well, for me they were, anyway. I can still see her auburn hair but I can't remember her name. We both went on leave at the same time, and our train split up at Carlisle. My bit went to Edinburgh, and hers to Blackpool. My brief encounter was very touching, very painful, but nobody ever made a film of it. I blame the title – *Uncoupling at Carlisle*. Besides, we did actually meet up again after my demob. I took her to the Palladium to see Danny Kaye. We had a lovely evening, but that was the end of it. Reality was not as exciting as memory for me, and probably for her as well.

I suppose the most exotic place I got to during my National Service was Hornchurch. Not, on the face of it, much use socially. 'When I was in Hornchurch' doesn't trip off the tongue of an old military man very impressively. But my time there was in fact important to me. I made friends for the first time, real friends, lasting friends, friends who didn't give a damn about my deviated septum. One of them was the actor Edward Hardwicke, son of Sir Cedric Hardwicke, one of our great theatrical knights. Edward introduced me to a glamorous London world, and it was to London that I went, in 1951, after my National Service, with £97 in my savings account. He also introduced me to his mother, the actress Helena

Pickard, known to everyone as Pixie. She opened doors for me, doors into glamorous society and doors into much less glamorous work. I had small parts in films, often small in both senses. My very first proper job was as president of the Glasgow University students' union in *You're Only Young Twice*. This was followed by *Top of the Form* and *Fun at St Fanny's*, which was about as good as the title suggests.

The nation was becoming tired of post-war austerity. There was a feeling that Clement Attlee's Labour government had done its job of building a more socialist society; 1951 saw the Conservatives under Sir Winston Churchill back in power. Certainly the London that I was lucky enough to move in showed few signs of austerity. Any austerity was reserved for me and my early career.

I loved living in London and was determined to make it there and not have to return to Edinburgh in defeat. And I was lucky to have started my London life in style. I spent six months in the basement of Pixie's beautiful town house in St John's Wood. She even had a butler, a very posh butler. Edward and I sat at dinner, listening to the conversation of important writers and actors, Ralph Richardson and J. B. Priestley among them. She took us to the opening night of Noël Coward's show at the Café de Paris. Heady days.

I couldn't stay with Pixie for ever and moved, for 37 shillings a week, to another room in St John's Wood, in a basement at garden level at the back, in a house owned by another actress, Mary Merrall. She was the stepmother of Valentine Dyall, the Man in Black in the radio series *Appointment with Fear*. She was having a very stormy relationship with an Irish rogue named Chris. Also in the house were Mabbie Lonsdale, daughter of the well-known playwright Frederick Lonsdale, and her husband, the playwright Rodney

Ackland, who was very gay, though Mabbie never seemed to resent his boyfriends.

All this, you might imagine, was rather strong stuff for a young man from a good Church of Scotland family in sober Edinburgh. Did it overwhelm me and discomfort me? I have to say that it didn't, not at all. I settled into the life with great ease.

I never had a great deal of money, but I earned enough to get by. I always seemed to have about seventeen quid in hand. My father had lent me £25 to buy my officer's uniform, but apart from that I only once actually needed to borrow, when I was twenty-three. I went to one of my dear school friends called James Lockhart, who is a conductor of symphony orchestras now, and was then organist at a church near Brixton, and later became organist at All Souls, Langham Place. He was an accomplished organist, and I went to him to borrow money, because I really had nothing left at all, whereas James had a motorbike and everything, so he was obviously better off than me. I asked him if I could borrow some money, and he said, 'How much would you need?' I said, 'Well, if you could manage fifteen quid,' and he looked slightly shocked, and thought hard, and said, 'I can manage thirteen,' and I borrowed thirteen quid from him. Apart from that I got by, I never went into debt, and of course there was no such thing as a credit card.

After Mary Merrall's, I lived in two more bedsits in St John's Wood. It's a fashionable area, but my bedsits were the exception, and when I moved to Notting Hill Gate and had a fitted carpet, I felt really excited. It was my first-ever fitted carpet. It was pale beige. I had occasional work, summer concert parties and the odd pantomime in the provinces, but I was making no real headway. I had eight very lean years but I never doubted what I wanted to do, and there was never any question of my giving up. I worked as caretaker to a grand house in Hamilton Terrace, I looked after tennis court reservations in Regent's Park, I sold advertising space for the ABC Coach Guide, and of course I worked as a barman at the Buckstone Club.

I just about made ends meet, though I did have to move into a less salubrious bedsit, in King Henry's Road, in Swiss Cottage, with cold linoleum on the floor and a communal bathroom with a terrifying exploding geyser for hot water. And still I persisted.

The great musical comedy star Evelyn Laye hired a rehearsal room and coached me, taught me how to sing songs like 'Tiptoe Through the Tulips' and 'Have You Met Miss Jones?' Later, when I began to get bookings, she came to see me at the Stork Club in Streatham. Unfortunately people began throwing bread rolls at me. As a baker's son I naturally noticed what sort of bread rolls they were. They were a kind that you don't get these days, with a crispy, shiny outside and a lovely soft doughy interior. In Scotland they were known as Viennas, and they also used to be called 'dinner rolls'. I loved to eat them, but they were not the kind of rolls that you would wish to have thrown at you. With their hard exteriors they formed quite powerful ammunition.

Evelyn Laye stood up and tore into them (the audience, not the bread rolls). 'I've come here to see a young artist, in his early days, struggling,' she told them, 'and I have never come across such an ill-mannered lot as you.' What courage. What spirit. What concern for a fellow human being. The stereotype of the performer is as an egotist. Thank goodness it is not always so. Thank you, Evelyn, and thank you for the implication, in the words 'in his early days', that I might have a future.

It didn't feel very likely at the time. I was what she had

27

called me, a young artist, struggling. But life wasn't without its colourful and enjoyable moments. I used to go to a pub called the Star, in a mews in Belgravia. I have never been a very pubby person, but this was a pub and a half. It was run by a man called Paddy Kennedy, and there was an upstairs bar which was a kind of inner sanctum or upper sanctum. It would be frequented by cat burglars, jewel thieves, fraudsters and actors, including visiting American stars. Terry-Thomas would pop in after riding in Rotten Row. Here I became friendly with someone called Jimmy Hunt. He was a sweet man, though not above a bit of ducking and diving. He invited me to crew a motor cruiser across the English Channel and through the French canals to the South of France with him.

I once asked him if he would mind my using his name when I told stories about him.

'You can use Jimmy,' he said, 'but not Hunt. I'd rather you called me Jimmy La Chasse.'

Jimmy owned a lot of greyhounds, and I used to go around the bookies putting bets on for him, because he would be recognized. Terrific! I'd been years in the profession and I was getting a job because nobody would recognize me.

Jimmy died last year at the age of ninety-two. At his funeral the collection was for the Home for Retired Greyhounds. What a lovely footnote to a colourful life.

But I digress. Back to my career. At last I got a break, and it happened in that very lucky place for me, the Buckstone Club. One evening, I was polishing glasses and pretending not to listen to the conversation, and I heard a pretty good club comedian called Digby Wolfe telling Harry Fowler, the cockney actor, that he could get anybody on to television if they were clever enough. 'How about Ronnie?' asked Harry. I tried to look extremely clever, though there wasn't a lot of scope for that really behind the bar of the Buckstone. Anyway,

I succeeded. Digby took up the challenge, got me into a show he did on television, called, very reasonably, *The Digby Wolfe Show* and for good measure also got me on to *The Yana Show* on Saturday nights on the BBC. Even more importantly, as it turned out, he got me into the show at Winston's. Danny La Rue was the star there, but he was away for two months doing panto, and Digby, who was writing the new show, put me in it with Anne Hart – yes, the very same Anne Hart who would become my wife. I had a bit of financial security at last.

It was while I was at Winston's that I met Laurence Olivier. At the time I was playing Othello to Danny La Rue's Desdemona. That was about the nearest to Shakespeare that I ever

With all the gang at Danny La Rue's club. Danny cutting the cake with Toni Palmer on his right and Jenny Logan to his left, followed by Barry Cryer. I'm at the back next to Toni, who is sitting opposite Anne.

came. It was not a Shakespeare performance that Olivier would have recognized. But, during the run of our piece, an actor friend, Robert Lang, gave Anne and me tickets to see a production in which he was Iago to Olivier's Othello. After the play we went for supper to Chez Solange, a lovely French restaurant but perhaps too traditional to survive in today's world. We had a wonderful evening of sparkling conversation, and then Robert, to my horror, turned to Olivier and said, 'Shall we go on to the club?'

My blood ran cold at the thought of the man, fresh from his triumph, seeing my send-up of the role. Luckily Olivier said he was too tired. They drove us to the club and I was terrified that he would change his mind, but he didn't. As they dropped us off, he gave me a friendly smile. It wouldn't have been so friendly if he'd known what I was going to do to Othello a few minutes hence.

I did get occasional film parts, not all of them bad – I played a West Highland fisherman in *Whisky Galore* – but not all of them good either. In 1961 I thought my big break might have come. I was driving south along Tottenham Court Road – you could in those days – in my Austin Healey Sprite, and a taxi overtook me with the passenger gesticulating frantically at me. It was Terry-Thomas no less, and when I had stopped, and he had got out of his taxi, he said, 'I can't believe how lucky I am to bump into you,' and he said he had a part in a film for me. I was very excited. This could be my big break.

I telephoned Terry-Thomas that night as requested, and he said that the director of the film, Robert Day, wanted to see me. I began to get even more excited.

Robert Day told me that they were making a film called *Operation Snatch*, set in Gibraltar. It was said that as long as there were Barbary apes on the Rock, it would remain British.

In order to convince the Germans that the ape colony was thriving, they were going to dress up small British soldiers as apes. This was not the kind of star part I had anticipated.

I needed the money, so despite my bitter disappointment I took the job. It wasn't fun being an ape when actors like James Villiers and Dinsdale Landen were strolling around as officers, and I have to admit that the situation got to me and I felt my lack of dignity rather too keenly. The assistant director came to call us on to the set one day, with the cry of 'Apes'. I got on my high horse. 'Excuse me,' I said. 'I do not respond to "ape". I'd like to be called "artiste" at least, or perhaps you could use my name.' A bit pompous perhaps, but can you blame me?

In 1962 Anne was cast to play Dorothy in *Gentlemen Prefer Blondes* at the Shaftesbury Theatre, with Dora Bryan. She was married at the time, but it was quite a disastrous marriage. She had married quite young; he was in a vocal group and was away on tour the whole time, and when he came home she cried, and ironed his shirts, then he went away with his clean shirts, and came back again, and she cried again. She got fed up with being on her own all the time. She says that one day she came to work in the club and I said, 'You look terrible,' and she said, 'Thank you' – I can't believe I really said that, but if she says I did, who am I to argue? – and I discovered that she had about three hours between her theatre show and her night-club appearance. I asked her what she did to fill the gap, and she said she hung around at the theatre till they threw her out, so I suggested that she come down to the Buckstone to see me.

We'd known each other for about seven years, working together, admiring each other's work, but suddenly we began talking, and there was a relationship that hadn't existed before. At which moment, as a result of her brilliance in *Gentlemen*

Prefer Blondes, she was offered a six-month tour of New Zealand as Annie in *Annie Get Your Gun* (with a very young Kiri Te Kanawa in the chorus).

Just before setting off to New Zealand, Anne developed a bad dose of 'flu. On the night before she was due to go, I was really very concerned as to whether she would be fit to fly. I went round to her place at about three o'clock in the morning, peered in and saw her busy ironing and packing. I think it was probably at that moment that it fully dawned on us that we meant quite a bit to each other. There were some wonderful letters exchanged between London and New Zealand in those six months, and the romance not only survived but strengthened.

I suppose I'm not the right person to say how gifted Anne was. Let someone else say it, then. A book on Broadway musicals, discussing people like Ethel Merman and Howard Keel, described Marilyn Monroe as 'the world's most magnificent woman', rivalled only by 'the spectacular Anne Hart'. This of the woman who would soon give up her career for me, and who had also been, incidentally, a brilliant and spectacular fully trained ice skater.

Things were really looking up now. I was offered, after several auditions, the part of one of the Dromios in the London production of *The Boys from Syracuse* at the Drury Lane Theatre. The show was a Richard Rodgers musical based on Shakespeare's *Comedy of Errors*. On reflection I think I was wrong to suggest that my Othello at Winston's was the nearest I came to Shakespeare. This was nearer, but still not very near. There were two Dromios, twin servants to the twin Antipholus brothers. This was my first part in a real West End show. I was appearing at the time in a summer show in Yarmouth, and on the train I happened to share a compartment with Anthony Fell, the Member of Parliament

With my dear wife Anne.

for Yarmouth. He was very pleased to hear that I had got the part at Drury Lane, almost as pleased as I was, and we went to the buffet car to celebrate. And of course I was very pleased that he had been elected, almost as pleased as he was, so we had to celebrate that too.

After he had congratulated me a few more times on getting the part, and I had congratulated him a few more times on getting elected, it dawned on me that I had had a few congratulations too many. And I had two shows to do that night.

Fresh air was the only possible answer. I don't expect I looked a pretty sight, hanging my head out of the window near the loo in order to get as much fresh air on to it as I could, but it worked. Thank goodness trains still had windows that you could open. Here's a piece of advice that you may find valuable in life. If you ever find that you need fresh air rapidly, go to Great Yarmouth. They've got more air than they know what to do with.

On the strength of my part in *The Boys from Syracuse* at Drury Lane, where shows always ran for years, I felt secure enough to borrow £4,000 from the bank, and £500 from my father, to buy a large house in New Cross, with room to rent out three bedsits at £19 per week.

The show closed after six weeks. Never mind. My stock was rising, and I was soon in work again. This was in the aforementioned *Twang*, whose failure proved so important to my success. I had served my apprenticeship at last. *The Frost Report* beckoned.

4

Like me, Ronnie B. spent his childhood in a great university city. In his case it was Oxford. Like me, he never even considered the possibility of going to the university. Like me, he knew what he wanted to do and went for it.

He was actually born in Bedford, on 25 September 1929, so he was fifteen months older than me. I think you'll agree that his background was really very similar to mine. His maternal grandfather was a gas plumber. His father's father was a master . . . no, not baker, but butcher. His father was an oil clerk. Ronnie reckoned that this made his family upper working class, which had a better ring to it than lower middle class. I think mine would fit into the same category.

Like me, Ronnie was one of three, though in his case he came between two girls. His mother worked in munitions during the war but otherwise was happy to be a housewife. Most women were in those days.

His father was named Leonard, but everyone called him Tim. His mother was called Edith but was always known as Cis. His was a happy, relatively uneventful childhood.

Where did his talent come from? Well, there had never been an actor in the family, but his father loved to put on a straw boater and perform an old music-hall song entitled 'I'm Not All There'. Much later Ronnie discovered that this had been Eric Morecambe's party piece as a child.

Ronnie did exhibit, very early on, an interest in dressing up. He would creep into his father's wardrobe and don a pierrot costume which his father kept there, and he recalled that his elder sister, Vera, used to put on shows with some of her friends in local back gardens. They charged a farthing a time. Perhaps I should explain, for younger readers, that that amounts to about a tenth of a penny in today's money. Ronnie did feel that something of the acting bug may have got into him during these shows.

He began to go to theatres at a much younger age than me. His father would take the family to stand in long queues for tickets. There would be a queue for tickets at ninepence and another for tickets at one and threepence. If the nine-penny tickets ran out, they went home. People brought up in the last forty years can have no experience of how short money could be in Britain even in respectable working families in what are so often called the good old days.

The very first play that Ronnie saw was *Cottage to Let* by Geoffrey Kerr. It starred my mother's old classmate, Alastair Sim. A tiny coincidence, perhaps, but one of many. Later, the great man went to see a performance of Ron's, and afterwards called on him backstage to offer him a job – which, sadly, he was not free to take.

Ron's schooldays were scarcely more spectacular than mine, but he did at least manage to be naughty on one occasion. He actually played truant, though it was one of the most academically respectable truancies in the history of British education. He bunked off school to go and see Olivier in the film of *Henry V*. He only missed games, never his strong point, and in fact he had already seen the film on a school trip and been so excited by it that he felt he must see it again.

It was at school that he first discovered his talent for humour. A boy was reading a poem about a windmill, which included the lines 'The windmill cuts through the air, cuts through the air, cuts through the air.' Ronnie commented,

36

'He'll be bald in a minute with all that "air cutting".' The master didn't appreciate the joke, and Ron said that it was almost ten years before he made his next joke. Thank goodness they came rather more quickly in our time together.

He too found that he had a bit of musical talent. While I played the organ in my church, he sang in the choir in his. And while I was queuing outside the stage door in Edinburgh, he was doing the same thing in Oxford. We were both stage-door Johnnies, as such people were known in those days, though I suppose in our case it should be stage-door Ronnies. I actually find it rather moving, now, to think of the two of us, separated by so many hundreds of miles, oblivious of each other's existence, doing such similar things.

The very first autograph that Ron got was of that great actress Celia Johnson, star of *Brief Encounter* and much else besides. His brief encounter revealed a very human side to the star. There was a loud explosion near by, just as she signed his programme. He told her not to worry. It was Guy Fawkes night. 'Heavens!' she said, 'I must get home. I've got cats.' John Gielgud's was another distinguished signature to grace Ron's book.

We were both thoroughly starstruck and would have been astounded if anybody had told us that one day we would be stars, and that people would want *our* autographs.

Ron got into the sixth form at school a year earlier than was normal. He was good at languages and studied Spanish, then decided that the things he was learning were going to be no use to him in later life. He hurried out of school as soon as he could and studied to be an architect. In his class at the architecture school were two young men called Ian and Alastair Smith. They were the brothers of Maggie Smith. Ron soon realized that the architecture school was not the

Prime of Mr Ronald Barker and resigned, knowing that he would never be good enough.

Instead he went into a bank, inheriting the job of his elder sister, Vera, when she chose to move to nursing. He was no keener on banking than I was on helping to feed farrowing sows in Scotland. He was just treading water. In his case this was not because he was waiting for National Service. He failed his medical due to childhood nephritis and an operation for a tubercular gland.

While he was at the bank he joined a local amateur dramatic company, and made his debut in *A Murder Has Been Arranged* by Emlyn Williams. There was a play within the play, and Ronnie's role was as the musical director of this play. This meant that he had his back to the audience for much of the time, which is not generally regarded as a huge advantage to a performer, but it was a start, and might in fact have been quite welcome to him, as his main problem in his early acting days was what to do with his hands.

He was on his way, and before long he was auditioning for the Manchester Repertory Company, which was based in Aylesbury. Well, where else would the Manchester Repertory Company be based? Here he heard some very welcome words, thirteen of them, but they were not at all unlucky. 'I can offer you two pound ten a week – you can start tonight.' Characteristically, Ronnie wrote of this, 'The voice belonged to a middle-aged man with heavy eyebrows and a gammy leg called Horace Wentworth. Or rather, the man's name was Horace Wentworth. I don't know what the leg was called.'

His job was as an assistant to the assistant stage manager, but it wasn't long before he got his first part in the small role of Lieutenant Spicer in J. M. Barrie's *Quality Street*. He took to the life like an Aylesbury duck to orange sauce, but it was during his fourth appearance that he had his revelation, his equivalent of my *Babes in the Wood* moment. He was playing the part of Charles, the chauffeur, in *Miranda*, an everyday story of a mermaid brought to civilization by a man. In it Ronnie got his first proper laugh, a real belter.

'The sound of the audience on that Monday night all those years ago is as clear to me as if it were yesterday,' he wrote much later. 'The thrill that I experienced on hearing that most wonderful of sounds! I get goose-pimples even now, just thinking of it. This is what I want to do, I thought. I want to make people laugh. Never mind Hamlet. Forget Richard the Second. Give me Charley's Aunt. My mission in life is now crystal-clear.'

Of course Ronnie had the talent to be a great straight actor, and I know that there are people who thought that he was selling out in doing things like *The Two Ronnies*. Not at all. He was fulfilling himself, just as much as I was.

Evelyn Laye had described me as a young artist, struggling. And that was what Ronnie was too, in his very different environment. In weekly rep you did a different play every week, and rehearsed next week's play in the set of that week's play. It was tiring, ill-paid work, but Ronnie enjoyed it very much. With the number and variety of the plays that he learnt and performed, it seemed to me to be like a degree in English, and a lot better perhaps. He estimated that he had appeared in 350 plays before he made it to the West End. And most of those had to be learnt in less than a week. I'm sure that the experience contributed greatly to Ronnie's love for, and mastery of, the English language.

A company called the Manchester Repertory Company could hardly stay in Aylesbury for ever, and they didn't. They moved to Rhyl, in North Wales. Ronnie's last performance at Aylesbury was his first starring role, playing a fourteen-year-old schoolboy in *The Guinea Pig*, by W. Chetham Strode. It was a good part, played in the film by Richard Attenborough, and Ronnie went to Rhyl to reprise it there.

The theatre company didn't last long in Rhyl (the setting for Les Dawson's inspired night club, 'The Talk of the Groyne'). In 1949 Ronnie went back home to Oxford for his first spell of unemployment, or rather, of 'resting'. He worked as a hospital porter at the Wingfield Hospital. There he came into contact with polio victims and found himself so disturbed that he couldn't eat – an unusual circumstance. He was, of course, barely twenty. What's particularly interesting to me about this experience is that he found, in his stress and distress, that he needed a character for himself as the hospital porter. Suddenly, and without any premeditation, he announced that his name was Charlie, and he never told anybody at the hospital that he was an out-of-work actor. Being himself would be a problem for him much later, in our shows together.

Ronnie used humour to bring a laugh to those sad polio sufferers. With a male nurse, he did routines with bedpans, empty and full. The mind, I have to say, boggles. But if Ronnie ever had doubts about the value of comedy, I'm sure that the memory of his work at Wingfield Hospital would have reassured him.

After about six months he did get another job – with the Mime Theatre Company. I don't know whether to laugh or cry at the thought of this mildly overweight young actor, who admitted that he hadn't yet learnt what to do with his hands on stage, and who would become such a master of verbal dexterity, trapped in a mime company. Maybe it would all have gone better if this mime company's repertoire hadn't consisted largely of folk songs and dances. *Mimed* folk songs? Maybe these folk songs and dances would have gone better if they hadn't been performed largely in schools. And maybe these schools would have been more fun to perform mime to if they hadn't been in the wilds of Wales and then in the poorer parts of the north-east, where mime was not hot on the agenda. 'It's not a bad cold, Mam. I just can't miss school today. We've got mime.' Anyway, not surprisingly, the company began to fail. Bookings fell away. Payments dwindled. Finally, the company folded.

Maybe it would have been easier if it had folded in London, not between Penzance and Land's End. Even then, things would have been more comfortable for Ronnie if the company could have afforded six rail tickets home, not five, and if he hadn't drawn the short straw. It's a long walk, Land's End to London. It beats hard bread rolls hands down in the Struggling Artists' Humiliation Stakes. True, he did manage to hitch the occasional lift, but it still took him three days to get home.

After that, Ronnie never looked back – certainly not towards Land's End. He got a job at the Playhouse in his beloved Oxford, 'city of dreaming spires and lost bicycles' (his words). Here he did excellent work in a variety of roles, came to the attention of Peter Hall, later of course to become *Sir* Peter Hall, and through Peter Hall he got his first parts in the West End.

But before I leave the subject of weekly rep, in trying to give a complete picture of the man who was to become my dear friend, I have to emphasize that he really was good-looking and dashing then. In fact he was frequently dashing from the theatre into the arms of a willing young woman. If I tell you that he was engaged twice, that a young lady from a very respectable upper-class family took all her clothes off to dance for him in a cornfield, and that on two occasions, due entirely to the persistence and eagerness of the young women concerned, he found himself having affairs with two

Ronnie performing for the Mime Theatre Company, 1950.

Ronnie as Poirot, Oxford Playhouse.

Ronnie as Danny in Night Must Fall.

Ronnie as Lieutenant Trotter in Journey's End.

Ronnie in The Private Secretary, *Oxford Playhouse.*

at the same time, you will begin to see that Ron sowed his wild oats rather more thoroughly than me.

None of this interfered with his great professionalism on stage, although this did lapse once. Just like me, he once had too much to drink before a performance. Unlike me, he didn't have a train window out of which to lean. His indiscretion involved a very famous actress, Jessie Matthews, in the later years of her career. There was a pub, the Gloucester Arms, just across from the stage door of the Oxford Playhouse, and a theatre electrician who liked his pint had fixed a buzzer in the saloon bar, warning of the rise of the curtain at the beginning of each act. Ronnie only had a two-minute scene in the play, five minutes after the curtain-up in act three, but he had discovered a new drink, iced red wine with water – very refreshing on a warm summer's night – and on this warm summer's night he had refreshed himself a bit too much. When the buzzer for act three came, he realized that he had drunk too much. Being a little unsteady on his feet, he pulled a chair over next to the door to the set, forgetting that Miss Matthews was due out of that door to make a quick costume change. In Ronnie's own words, 'She flew out and ran slap-bang into me. She pitched forward and sort of rolled head over heels, her legs going places that they hadn't been for years, helped by the fact that her evening dress split from top to bottom or rather from hem to bottom, revealing underwear very similar to that which we all know and love from her early films.' It was no surprise to find, later that year, that he was not on Miss Matthews's Christmas card list.

Most actors would be grateful for one job in the West End. Very early in his career there, Ronnie had two in one evening. He played a gipsy in the first act of *Listen to the Wind* at the Arts Theatre and an Italian peasant in the third act of *Summertime* at the Apollo in Shaftesbury Avenue. He took only four minutes to walk from one to the other, in his composite gipsy/peasant make-up, getting a few odd stares as he went. One can imagine the surprise of an observant newspaper vendor. Why does this gipsy/peasant walk down Shaftesbury Avenue at 8.47 every evening?

It is not perhaps a startling coincidence that Ron and I should both have come across Laurence Olivier. Ron actually found himself in a play presented by the great man – *Double Image* at the Savoy. He even found himself talking to Olivier at a party given on the stage to celebrate the seventieth birthday of the actress Zena Dare. Ronnie had to inform

Olivier that he was leaving the cast to appear in the Tennessee Williams play *Camino Real*, directed by his old friend Peter Hall. Olivier used only five words in reply, but they were words which showed his style, friendliness and charm. 'Swine – have some more champagne,' he said. Many years later Ronnie met Lord Olivier at a BAFTA awards ceremony, and Olivier told him how much he admired him.

No, that wasn't an extraordinary coincidence, but the next one was. Entirely unknown to each other, Ron and I both went up for the same part of one of the Dromios in *The Boys from Syracuse*. And I, as you know, got it. This was actually because they had to find two Dromios who could look identical, and they found a match for me but not for Ron. I pretended, however, that the decision was down to a little thing called talent.

I've found all these parallels in our lives, great and small, important and trivial, but I haven't yet mentioned what is perhaps, in the world of show business, the most extraordinary parallel of all.

We both met wonderful ladies, we both worked with these wonderful ladies, we both fell in love with these wonderful ladies, we both had long and happy marriages, both the wonderful ladies gave up their careers for us, and we lived happily ever after with them. It almost defies belief.

Yet it happened.

Funnily enough, as I mentioned, I met the aptly named Joy before Ron, when she was stage manager of a pantomime in Bromley. Ron met her in Cambridge when he was cast to do two one-act plays, Somerset Maugham's *The Letter* and *The Bespoke Overcoat* by Wolf Mankowitz. Another actor had dropped out, Ronnie replaced him, and something that he did at the very first reading, a little bit of comic business over smoking a hookah, made Joy laugh, and she realized immediately that she was attracted to him. The feeling was mutual. All the apparent intensity of those entanglements of Ron's in the rep days faded. This was the real thing.

Even the real thing doesn't always run entirely smoothly, though. A large amount of chopped liver had to be consumed by Ronnie in *The Bespoke Overcoat*. He loathed the stuff. He could barely get it down. Joy thought long and hard about ways to ease the misery of this man to whom she had become instantly attracted. She worked out that stiff chocolate blanc-mange would look like chopped liver at a distance. Every day, she made one for Ronnie to eat on stage. When they were married Joy promised to make him a chocolate blanc-mange, and Ronnie had to confess that it was the only other dish that he detested. He hadn't dared to admit it before, because she was going to such trouble.

It wasn't long before they were married – just about nine months, in fact, although there is absolutely no significance in that figure. Ron proposed to her over drinks in the club at the Royal Court Upstairs, in Sloane Square, and in the morning, when she realized that he remembered doing so, she accepted. They were married in July 1957. It was a very quiet wedding. In Joy's witty words – she is a very witty woman – 'We had it on a Monday so that nobody could come. There were eleven people there. There's always one person who will take the day off when you didn't really want them there.' They went to Shipston-on-Stour for their honeymoon, because Ron was working at the weekend, and because they had very little money. They began married life in Ron's tiny flat in Hampstead. Actors do not get rich from stage work. I think the public would be astounded and shocked if they knew how low salaries are in the theatre for all but the greatest stars.

With women like Joy and Anne behind us, and with all

the similarities that I have listed between us, how could Ronnie and I have failed to get on well? How could we have failed to succeed, if you see what I mean?

5

In 1966 Britain announced that it would adopt decimal currency within five years. Neil Armstrong and David Scott completed the first successful docking operation in space, and the Russians sent two dogs into orbit. Harold Wilson's Labour government was re-elected with a 97-seat majority, Britain and France agreed a compromise plan for building a Channel tunnel, in South Africa Prime Minister Verwoerd was stabbed to death on the front bench of parliament by a messenger who said he was doing too much for non-whites, and *The Frost Report* began.

I was by now a married man, and Ron was a father with two children. Larry had been born in 1959 and Charlotte in 1962. Their third child, Adam, would be born soon after the programme had run its two-year course. We were starting a family too. Anne had actually got pregnant before we were married. I think we both worried that our parents would be upset, but not a bit of it, they were delighted for us. This was 1965, after all, and attitudes were changing. In fact I never actually proposed to Anne. I didn't need to. It was an assumption. As she put it, 'If he hadn't married me, my dad would have been around with a shotgun.' We married very quietly, in the unglamorous surroundings of Brixton Register Office, with just our mums and dads and two witnesses present.

We worked hard. Anne used to double, doing the Crazy Gang show in the evening and the club at night. At one glorious period I was doing three jobs in a day. I did the afternoon show of the Enid Blyton *Noddy in Toyland*, the evening show, also of Enid Blyton, of *The Famous Five*, both at the Shaftesbury Theatre, and then cabaret at the Côte d'Azur in Soho at night.

I sold my house in New Cross in 1965 for £13,000, and we bought a huge, red-brick Victorian house in Upper Norwood for £7,300. It was not exactly cosy or bijou. In fact I kept thinking I saw bits of it in Alfred Hitchcock's films. Anne continued working at Winston's well into her pregnancy. 'More feathers, darling,' Danny La Rue would say. Steadily, until it was time to give up, more and more feathers were needed to hide the growing bulge.

Nobody's life is a fairy tale, and our happiness was cut short. Andrew was born in April 1966, the year of the beginning of *The Frost Report*. It was obvious from the first moment that something was very wrong. His heart was on the wrong side and he had several holes in it. He was allowed home for a while, but it was clear to us that he wasn't going to make it. Maybe today something could be done, but not then. I continued in the show at the club, but it was strange and emotionally very difficult to make one's living from laughter at that time. I kept thinking of Anne at home with the poor little thing. He was taken back into hospital, and operated on, but it was not a success. He lived just six weeks. We still think of him, and of the life that he might have led. He would have been forty this year.

Anne went back to work, but not for long. She was soon pregnant again. Our first daughter, Emma, was born in the following April and our second, Sophie, in the April after that. Thank goodness they were healthy.

The loss of a child puts everything in proportion, and it makes you all the more careful about protecting your other children. Anne had a glittering career ahead of her, but she had no hesitation in giving up for a while to look after the girls. She never intended to give it up for ever, but she remembered, when she was growing up, how her mother was always there for her, and she wanted our girls to come home to a house with life in it, a house where the kettle was always on, and where there were animals. We've always had dogs and usually a cat. We've had springer spaniels, golden retrievers, cairn terriers. We love them.

There was always so much for Anne to do. Parent/teacher evenings were almost impossible for me: everyone knew me and everyone felt they had a right to speak to me. By appearing in public I had been deemed to be public property, and so I stopped going. This made things difficult for Anne, who had spent much of her school life at Conti's learning drama and at Queens training to be an ice skater; she really was a class ice skater, and had not had any normal education at all, so she felt out of her depth when teachers asked awkward questions.

The children needed Anne, and the years passed, and when she was offered work it never seemed to be the right time. In the end, people gave up offering, and suddenly she found that she hadn't worked for thirty-eight years.

It wasn't easy for her. For many years she would burst into tears if she heard anyone singing a song that she had sung. She couldn't listen to Barbra Streisand or Judy Garland, whom she had mimicked in the clubs. She started to listen to pro-grammes like *Gardeners' Question Time* instead, because they didn't remind her of her lost career.

The only plus points for her were that she had always been a nervous performer, so there was some element of relief, and that my career regularly brought her into contact with show business and gave her some of the atmosphere. I would always ask her opinion, and so she felt that she was a part of it. She says that she would have gone mad if she'd married a bank manager.

Ron and I had had our moments, Ron particularly, but the fact remained that he had been a jobbing actor for nineteen years and I for only a few years less. Now, with families to provide for, we were both hugely grateful for *The Frost Report*, and there was a real aura of success around it. Much of this was due to the quality of the writing and, dare I say it, the performances, but there was an extra element – David. He behaved as if it was a huge success, and it became so. It was a self-fulfilling prophecy. In fact, looking back on it, David himself was a self-fulfilling prophecy.

The show went out live on Thursday evenings, immediately after the *Nine O'Clock News*. We would begin putting the programme together in the studio in the morning, and David would arrive after lunch with a great armful of papers, covered in jokes written with a thick, felt-tipped pen. Out of this chaos would emerge his CDM. That stood for Continuous Developing Monologue, which was based on Tony Jay's essay on the subject of the week, liberally studded with jokes.

Not all of these jokes were sophisticated. When the subject was 'law', there was a quickie in which two policemen greeted each other. 'Morning, super,' said the sergeant to the superintendant. 'Morning, gorgeous,' came the reply. No, not all of them were sophisticated, but most of them were very funny.

The final hurried rehearsals and the live transmissions were fairly hair-raising. I think John Cleese found it all quite difficult. He would go very white before his performance. Ron was helped so much by his time in rep, and I by my long spells performing in night clubs.

The fact that the shows were live helped to give them a real sense of occasion. We were slightly hampered at first by an imminent General Election. We couldn't use overtly political material. The first show went out on Thursday,

10 March 1966. The election was on Thursday, 31 March. In those days, polling stations closed at nine o'clock, so our fourth programme – on 'politics', naturally – was the very first programme to be free from restriction. This helped to give the series an even greater impact.

At the end of the series, David Frost gave a party. A little affair for a few friends? Not quite. He hired the whole of the Battersea Funfair. I shall never forget the slightly frightened look of some of our writers as they were plunged up and down on the Big Dipper, some of them still clutching their glasses of red wine.

After the first series we recorded a one-off special, called *Frost Over England*. The aim was to win the prestigious Golden Rose award at the Montreux Television Festival, and it duly did win it. I recall David bursting into our rehearsals in great excitement and saying, 'We're on the cover of the *Radio Times*.' Ron and I were pretty excited too. It really was a great achievement to make the cover, and on our way home we both stopped to buy copies, only to find that it was just David who was on the cover. By 'we' he had meant the programme. Oh well. We got our own cover in the end, much later.

Ron and I weren't yet important enough members of the team to be invited to Montreux, but the BBC threw a celebration party – well, perhaps 'threw' is an exaggerated word to describe a BBC party – they gently tossed a celebration party. Performers and writers were invited with their wives. Graham Chapman, that sublimely funny man, had recently 'come out' as gay, not as easy then as it would be today. He took his somewhat weirdly dressed boyfriend, complete with a name tag saying 'Mrs Chapman'.

A second series of *The Frost Report* was commissioned, but the BBC had not thought yet of Ronnie and me doing

Winning the Golden Rose. Back row – from left to right: Ray Millichope (film editor), Barry Cryer, Terry Jones, Michael Palin, Dick Vosburgh. Second row – from left to right: Fiona Gilbert, Joy Barker, David McKellar, Graham Chapman, John Cleese, Bernard Thompson, Anthony Jay, Michael Wale, Eric Idle, Sally (Jimmy Gilbert's secretary), Neil Shand, Bill Wilson and his wife. Front row – from left to right: Marty Feldman, Sheila Steafel, David Frost, Jimmy Gilbert, Julie Felix and Ronnie Barker. For some reason I was not there that day!

anything together as a pair. David Frost was a little more far-sighted. He signed us both up under contract to his company, David Paradine (Paradine is his middle name) Productions.

The rehearsals for *The Frost Report* took place in a dusty church hall in Crawford Street. Sometimes David put in an appearance, and whenever he did, they would end in a frenzied three-a-side football match. David and John Cleese were both mad on football, while Ronnie B. definitely wasn't. I loved the game, and often played for the Television All Stars, but I think I did prefer it on the football field. I must say, though, that the sight of David, sometimes criticized for being interested only in money, power and fame, hurling himself across the rehearsal-room floor in goal in a natty suit, was rather endearing. And then he would go off, covered in dust, to have lunch with Tony Snowdon or Norman St John Stevas or Princess Margaret.

But of course those were the days when David was becoming all-powerful. Soon he would be interviewing American presidents. There was a joke about him that he was driving his drop-head Mercedes with the roof down, and it began to rain. No problem. He just pressed a button, and the rain stopped. You may laugh – please – but round about this time David went to a Test Match at Lord's, and had to leave at twenty to one for a lunch engagement. At quarter to one the heavens opened, and play was abandoned for the day.

While we were signing up with David, he in his turn had signed on with Rediffusion, the company that provided ITV's weekday shows for the London region, and now he sold a Ronnie B. series and a Ronnie C. series to Rediffusion.

My series was a situation comedy called *No, That's Me Over Here*, with Rosemary Leach. I played a bank clerk, bowler-hatted and bespectacled. It was quite a conventional subject, but imaginatively treated, as one would expect from something written by the aforementioned Graham Chapman, with Eric Idle and Barry Cryer. Graham was a wild young man. He drank heavily. When he was offered a drink, he would sometimes say, 'Oh, thank you. Three pints, please. Well, I drink faster than you.' He was easily the wildest and silliest of all the Pythons, so it was genius on their part to cast him as the officer type who tried to keep the programme from getting too silly. Even at his most impossible, Graham retained great charm and warmth. He died tragically young, having abused his body too much for too long, but lives on triumphantly as the man mistaken for the Messiah in *The Life of Brian*.

Eric brought a different, individual, Pythonesque tone to the comedy, and, after all the hilarious shows he had written for the night clubs where I worked, Barry probably understood better than any man alive what I could and couldn't do. Add that comic genius Marty Feldman as the executive producer, and I couldn't complain that I wasn't well served.

Ronnie B.'s series was called *The Ronnie Barker Playhouse* and it illustrated one of his greatest talents, his immense versatility. Just to give you a flavour, the six shows presented him as a loud-mouthed Welsh poet, an English lord not over-endowed with intelligence, the chairman of the Hendon Cowpokes' Association, an escapologist with ambitions to become the new Houdini, a silent monk caught between a married couple, and a shy Scotsman persecuted by a group of possessive women and a domineering mother.

The aim, of course, was to find a winning formula for a situation comedy. In the event the poet was too foul-mouthed, there wasn't thought to be enough mileage in gun duels in Hendon, the Houdini character disappeared, the monk was destined to remain silent for ever, and he very kindly but unknowingly left the subject of a domineering mother for me to exploit later – much later. So I don't need to tell you that the character who was eventually chosen for his situation comedy was the English lord not over-endowed with intelligence.

In addition to *The Ronnie Barker Playhouse*, he played guest roles in two hugely popular TV series, *The Saint* and *The*

Avengers. His role in the latter could almost have come straight out of *The Two Ronnies.* He played a mysterious cat fancier called Cheshire, who was head of an organization whose acronym was PURRR – the Philanthropic Union for the Rescue, Relief and Recuperation of Cats.

He also played the role of the Russian ambassador in a situation comedy entitled *Foreign Affairs,* written by Johnnie Mortimer and Brian Cooke, and starring Leslie Phillips, who had of course been with him in *The Navy Lark,* and he landed a part in a film, *The Man Outside,* starring Van Heflin. It wasn't a huge part, but there were a couple of good two-handers with Van Heflin right at the beginning, and the film had a full American release.

The second series of *The Frost Report* was, if anything, even more successful than the first. The party at the end of it was bigger too, though not, I felt, more successful.

David held it at the White City, where we ate overlooking the athletics track. It's all gone now, of course, built over and handed to the massed ranks of the BBC's accountants.

It was a strange evening. There was a three-course sit-down meal, but it was interrupted by athletic events in which we all had to take part or risk being labelled bad sports. Some of the writers had to run the Olympic steeplechase course and eat a plate of cornflakes on top of the water jump. Personally I didn't think the scripts were that bad. But at least, after their four-course meal – starter, steeplechase, main and dessert – they could relax and watch other people being humiliated.

I don't want to boast, but I think the talents of the Corbetts shone that night. In the egg and spoon race, Anne carried all before her, including her egg and spoon. Tommy Docherty, the legendary football manager, had suggested that she stick a piece of chewing gum on the spoon to keep the egg in place, but I like to feel that she ignored his advice and won through natural talent – and the superb balance of an ice skater. I had a chance to show off my natural talent in the all-star football match which brought the event to its conclusion at, I think, about 2 a.m. I positively sparkled on the wing. I have been to many Frost parties, all the others thoroughly enjoyable, but I wasn't quite sure about that one. I decided that on the whole I didn't want to run relay races when I went to parties.

I never asked Ronnie for his opinion on that party, but since he was less of a partygoer than me, and less athletic, I can't imagine it was one of the great highlights of his life.

No matter. We owed a great deal to David Frost, especially me. By the end of the two series of *The Frost Report*, my life had been transformed and my career had been turned round. I felt a new confidence about the future, which I never quite lost. It seemed that David had waved a wand over my life. He was the founder of the feast in my life.

Where would his wand take me next?

6

It took me to *Frost on Sunday*. David had also had the idea of forming a consortium to bid for the ITV London weekend franchise, held at the time by ATV. A formidable team emerged, including many of the most senior and experienced men in television, but the driving force was this great bundle of energy and ambition, David Frost, who had still not reached the age of thirty. They won the franchise. London Weekend Television was born.

I don't imagine that the first part of the new company's autumn schedule took long to create. There would be three Frost programmes, one for each night. The Sunday one would be an entertainment show, and it would star . . . us, Ronnie and me.

John Cleese had gone to pastures new and extraordinary. Sheila Steafel was replaced by Josephine Tewson, a very accomplished comic actress. In two series of *The Frost Report* we had done twenty-six half-hour shows. Now we would do twenty-six shows that were fifty minutes long, and they would be live, and in each show we would do four or five sketches, so that would be more than 150 sketches in all. It was daunting, but we were too excited to be daunted.

In 1968, the House of Commons approved Harold Wilson's programme to reduce Britain's role as a world power, under which we would withdraw from east of Suez by 1971. There was a succession of peace plans to end the Vietnam War, but despite them all it continued escalating. Martin Luther King was shot to death in Memphis, Senator

Ron and me with Josephine Tewson.

Robert Kennedy was assassinated in Los Angeles, and 400,000 cows were slaughtered because of foot and mouth. Such events make the need for some humour and comedy in life all the greater, and it was with eager anticipation that we prepared our first show, to go out live on Sunday, 4 August 1968, at 9.10. It didn't. There was a strike. Some aspects of the formation of the new franchises had upset the unions. The very first London Weekend Television show, at seven o'clock on Friday, 2 August, would have been Frank Muir in a programme called *We Have Ways of Making You Laugh*. In the event he had no ways of making you laugh at all. The programme was blacked out completely. We were luckier than that, but it was clear early in the day that our studio would not be ready. We moved to the much smaller *World of Sport* studio, and a programme was cobbled together by the management. The show was taped from 9.30 and finally got on the air at 10.40. What an anti-climax, albeit a heroic one.

Worse was to follow. The unions were upset at the management's heroics, and for the next two Sundays there was no show at all.

So it became a series of twenty-three shows. I said that it would star us, but as we got into the series it didn't feel like that. Being a show of David's, it attracted hugely famous and talented guests, and they were the stars. We were an enormously important part of a very successful show, but in no way were we stars. If I tell you that in the first week of September the guests were Peter Sellers, Sammy Davis Junior,

From left to right: Josephine Tewson, me, David Frost and Ronnie,
Frost on Sunday, *1968.*

Danny La Rue and Ted Ray, and the next week's show was topped by the Beatles singing 'Hey Jude', you will get some sense of the scale of it. 'We knew our place', to quote John Law again.

David Paradine Productions had also signed both of us up to do a show of our own, without the other Ronnie. Mine was a series called *The Corbett Follies*. I hosted the show, looking, if I may say so, extremely natty (lovely period word) in a fancy dinner jacket or a white silk jacket piped in black, and I would be fronting a lot of very glamorous girls, who all seemed to be about six foot tall. There was quite a lot of fronting going on. These were the sort of girls that you would find in those shows I mentioned in glittering night clubs like the Talk of the Town, and the idea was to give my show some of the feel of the night-club world that I knew. We did sketches and we had famous visiting American artists like Henny Youngman and Peter Nero. It was quite an achievement for me, I felt, at this relatively early stage in my career, to have visiting artists of the calibre of Engelbert Humperdinck, Tom Jones and Sergio Mendes. The new element was the patter, my patter. The most significant thing about the show, I suppose, was that I was beginning to find the style that I would use in the chair in *The Two Ronnies*. In this I was enormously helped by the arrival on the scene of a writer called Spike Mullins.

Many of the team of writers from *Frost on Sunday* were working with me again on *The Corbett Follies*. Particularly valuable was Barry Cryer, who knew my work so well from my night-club days. There were also Ian Davidson, a very clever writer who had worked a great deal with David; Dick Vosburgh, of whom more anon; and a team of three, David McKellar, Peter Vincent and David Nobbs, who were referred to, corporately, as McVinnob. When David McKellar left for a new career in the expanding world of corporate videos, the name died. McVinnob had a certain ring. Vinnob would have sounded like a rather disgusting medical product.

But the great new mystery ingredient was Spike. He telephoned me and he said, in his dry, rather whiny north Slough voice, 'I've noticed that when you do your introductions, you waffle a bit. I think I could waffle a bit better for you.' He said it without fear, but also without conceit. It sounded like a fact, and it was a fact. He waffled a great deal better for me. He raised waffling to an art form. He would deliver a vital element of *The Two Ronnies*, though of course we didn't know that at the time.

The shows ran for half an hour weekly at 6.30 on a Saturday night, setting the tone for the ITV evening, and in all I think there were three series, each consisting of eight programmes. It was definitely a success, albeit not to the extent that would come with *The Two Ronnies*, and I thoroughly enjoyed doing it, but I think that the most significant thing about it was that I got well on the way to establishing my style as a stand-up comedian.

Ronnie's series was called *Hark at Barker*. It was the one about the English lord not over-endowed with intelligence, which was chosen from *The Ronnie Barker Playhouse*. He was given the name of Lord Rustless. Supporting Ronnie was Josephine Tewson, and it was also notable as the very first time that he worked with a promising young character actor named David Jason.

And then it was back to *Frost on Sunday* for a second series. How good it felt to be so busy and have so much continuity in our work, after all our years of struggle in this most precarious of professions.

Ron and I, along with David, were now the main regulars on the programme. There were twenty-six shows in a series, and we did our sketches live. It was exciting, but it was also demanding. In fact I would say that it was a great bonding experience. We had got on well on *The Frost Report*, but now we were more reliant on each other, and our respect for each other, and our trust, deepened. David had always been the boss on *The Frost Report*, but for the first time, at London Weekend, we would sometimes knock on his door and say, 'Look, David, we're not saying this. This isn't right.' We were starting to be more aware of what we were doing. It was a major coming together for the two of us.

Nevertheless, it was during the run of *Frost on Sunday* that Ronnie and I had the one serious argument that I mentioned in the first chapter. We came nearer to falling out with each other than at any other time during our long, happy relationship. It was all about the casting of a sketch. Usually we had no problems about which of us should play which part. Sometimes writers would put RC and RB in front of their dialogue, but even if they gave the characters fictitious names, it was obvious which of us should play which role. There was a kind of fictional reality to our relationship. Stray too far from it, and our comedy would be less effective. For instance – and I'm not a bitter man, it didn't worry me – if there was a girl to be got, guess which Ronnie got her. It got so bad – not, as I say, that I'm bitter about it – that even when we did a wedding sketch, in which Ron was the vicar and I was the groom, it was the vicar who walked off with the girl.

On this one occasion, however, Ronnie and the director, Phil Casson, suddenly wanted us to swap roles in a particular sketch. I was dead against it. I couldn't see a valid reason for it. There was something unusual in the atmosphere, a feeling that Ron and Phil were colluding, that I was being manipulated. I strode off to the loo to cool down, but I was still very

With Josephine Tewson and Ron, Frost on Sunday, *1968.*

annoyed when I walked back. The whole atmosphere was uneasy. Our goodbyes at the end of the rehearsal were brusque and strained. It was not at all a pleasant feeling.

When I got home I complained to Anne. 'I'm being got at and I don't like it.'

Anne said I should forget it, it wasn't worth falling out over. I tried to forget it but I was still in a curmudgeonly mood the next morning at rehearsals. This was very unusual. I was the placid one. If anybody was at all pernickety, it would be Ronnie, but his pernicketiness wouldn't be directed at me, it would be directed at somebody who wasn't getting something right on the show. Ronnie wanted everything to be of a very high standard, so he could be demanding, but only for rational reasons. Here I felt that something irrational was going on, and that it was directed at *me*.

Another of our sketches in the show that week was on the subject of *This Is Your Life*. It was about a man who was paranoid about appearing on the programme. If the milkman or the postman came to the door, he was convinced that it was Eamonn Andrews with his big red book. In the end Eamonn turned up, and he didn't recognize him. Now there was a problem with this sketch. The tag wouldn't work unless it was actually played by Eamonn Andrews, and he was a very busy man, not likely to be too eager to come in just to play the tag line in a sketch.

The sketch had been hanging around for some time, but suddenly they announced that Eamonn was available. Now what I didn't know was that I had been chosen as the secret subject of that week's *This Is Your Life*, so I had to play the lead part in that sketch. This meant that Ronnie had to play the lead part in the other sketch, in order that the show should not seem too unbalanced, since it was an absolute principle of our shows that we had, overall, a roughly equal amount of the comedy. I was right. I *was* being manipulated. My dear friend Ron, my estimable producer Phil and my beloved wife Anne were indeed in collusion, and for the very best of reasons, and there was I being temperamental and suspicious about the whole thing. It must have been very annoying for them.

Even so, it was touch and go. I saw Thames Television vans everywhere when I went to the canteen.

'I wonder if they're doing *This Is Your Life*,' I said. 'I wonder if that's why Eamonn has agreed to do the sketch.'

Ronnie didn't turn a hair.

'I bet it's David Frost,' he said. 'I'll go and find out.'

He went, came back and said, 'I was right. The rumour is that it *is* David.'

'Of course, it could be one of us,' I said.

'No, it couldn't be one of us,' said Ronnie.

'Why not?'

'Because the other one would know.'

This was devious, not to say wily. It was quick thinking of a very high order. It was nonsense, of course. He did know. But I didn't have time to work that out, and he said it so convincingly that he saved the situation. So it was a complete shock to me when, at the end of the sketch, Eamonn said, 'Ronnie Corbett, this really *is* your life.'

I mouthed, 'You bastard' at Ronnie. Quite a lot of people seem to mouth that when caught by the man with the big red book.

The sets for *This Is Your Life* were actually hanging there, in the flies, above the sets for *Frost on Sunday*. If I'd looked up, I'd have seen them. But we weren't doing a class sketch that day, and, since I do have to look up at people quite a bit, I tend not to look up when I don't have to.

The audience for *Frost on Sunday* got a completely un-expected bonus, an edition of *This Is Your Life*. They were asked if they were prepared to stay on, and they all did, and loved it. I enjoyed doing it too. The show, of course, was very sweet and moving. My mother and father were there, my mother forgetting what she was supposed to say and being prompted off camera by my father, putting words into her mouth much as he always did. My dear brother, Allan, the tall one, was also present, pretending that he spent most of our childhood beating me up. My sister, Margaret, had been flown in from Florida, very pregnant with her second child. My old Sunday school teacher made an appearance, as did Danny La Rue, wearing an identical kipper tie to mine.

About three years ago they approached Anne with the idea of my doing it again. She said 'no', quite rightly.

Ronnie never did the show. He had made Joy swear that,

if ever they approached her for him to do it, she must tell him. He just didn't want it done. He was intensely protective of his private life.

I've said already that Ronnie and I didn't consider ourselves to be stars. In fact he was so starstruck that even at the height of our success in *Frost on Sunday* he was still approaching all the famous acts that appeared on the show and getting their autographs. One of the reasons that I didn't twig what was going on that day was that I really didn't consider myself a big enough star, certainly not at that stage in my career, to be the subject of *This Is Your Life*. I was flattered as well as moved.

We had a very good team of writers, and they wrote some very good material, but at times we did feel the strain of having to do more than 150 sketches. A few well-known writers were occasionally drafted in to supplement our regular team, but sometimes their difficulties showed just how good our team was, and proved how hard it was to get our material exactly right.

In fact at one stage the writers were summoned to David's house for what was described as a crisis meeting. David dealt with the crisis in his own way. 'I've called you here to congratulate you on an absolutely super series and to work out how we can make it even more super still.'

Then one day Ronnie came in with two sketches that he said had been given to him by Peter Eade, his agent, written by a client of his who had his reasons for not wanting his name to be revealed, so he had sent them under a pseudonym, Gerald Wiley. They were very good, and we did them. Ronnie said he thought they might be from some short-story writer or possibly even a playwright who wanted to try his hand at something different.

One of the sketches was a particularly good vehicle for me. It was set in the waiting room of a rather posh doctor's surgery. Seven or eight people were sitting around, looking tense, wondering what the other patients were there for and not sitting too close to them in case it was infectious. They were all reading magazines like the *Tatler* and the *Field*.

Then I breezed in, carrying a copy of the *Telegraph*. My whole manner was altogether too cheery for the setting.

'Good morning,' I said.

No response.

'I said, "Good morning".'

Still no response.

I plonked myself down next to Ronnie Barker, who was playing a very military moustachioed type, aged about sixty.

'Isn't it extraordinary how nobody ever talks to each other in a doctor's waiting room?' I commented.

Again, there was no reply.

'I see they are stopping all the tube trains tomorrow,' I said.

There was some surprise at this, but no eye contact from anybody. Nobody wanted to get involved with this strange new man.

'To let the people get on and off!'

I smiled at my wit. The patients showed no amusement, burying themselves in their magazines.

Next I recited 'Simple Simon met a pieman', and when this failed to elicit a response, I sang 'Night and day, you are the one', ending with a soft-shoe shuffle and a tap dance.

'Well, I've done my best,' I said. 'I can't think of anything else.'

Suddenly Ronnie B. was shamed into standing up and reciting A. A. Milne's poem 'John had great big waterproof boots on'.

One or two patients clapped. The ice had been broken.

A very sweet maiden lady now stood up and sang, very

sweetly, 'If you were the only boy in the world, and I was the only girl . . .'

We were off. We were at the races. Everybody joined in. All the patients were on their feet.

'Wonderful, wonderful,' I exclaimed. 'Right. Everybody conga.'

I led them round and round the waiting room, doing the conga.

'Come on, everybody,' I shouted. 'Back to my place.'

I led the conga out of the waiting room into the street.

There was a short pause, and then the door to the doctor's room opened and a nurse came out.

'Doctor!' she cried. 'There's nobody here.'

The doctor emerged and said, 'Ah, I thought as much. That bloody little Doctor Corbett has been here again and pinched all my private patients.'

It was a very good sketch, with a very strong tag, and it played beautifully in the show. (It also demonstrates that we weren't averse to another actor getting the tag line, if the situation demanded it.)

During the rehearsals for the next show, Ronnie said to me, 'I don't know why you don't try to buy the rights for the waiting-room sketch, because it would be excellent for you when you do your summer seasons,' and indeed I did do it in a summer season in Brighton, with Anne playing the lady who stood up and sang.

He suggested that I got my agent, Sonny Zahl, to ask Peter Eade if he could get in touch with the author and make an offer for the rights. The message came back a couple of days later from Peter Eade that the author would like £3,000 for theatre rights. Ronnie asked me if I'd followed up his suggestion, and I told him I had and I told him that the author was asking for £3,000.

69

'Three thousand!' said Ronnie. 'That's a bloody cheek. I should offer one thousand for the rights for everything, and see what happens.'

So I told Sonny that Ronnie thought £3,000 was ludicrously steep. Sonny rang Peter and came back to me and said, 'I've been on to Peter, and the author has very kindly said that, because of the joyous way you did it, he's going to give you the rights for nothing in perpetuity.'

So next day I said to Ronnie, 'Well! Gerald Wiley has given me the rights to this sketch for nothing. What a darling person he is.'

So I went to Aspreys and had some goblets, half a dozen cut-glass goblets, made, and had them engraved with the initials GW, and send them to Peter Eade to give to this darling person.

The sketches kept coming in. Most of them did very well, but one, a ventriloquist sketch, didn't work, and Ronnie said, 'Well, Gerald Wiley let us down there.' I said, 'Give him a chance. He's given us seven or eight belters. He's bound to fail occasionally.'

And of course all the time speculation grew as to who this mystery writer could be. All sorts of names were mooted, including Tom Stoppard, Alan Bennett, even Noël Coward.

In fact Tom Stoppard – speaking on tape in an awards show many, many years later, by which time he was *Sir* Tom Stoppard – said, 'One of the sort of bitter-sweet memories of my life was when the rumour got around that I was actually the famous Gerald Wiley, the mystery man contributing brilliant sketches. I had to admit to myself that I hadn't written them, and somebody else must have.'

By this time we were rehearsing the very last of the twenty-three shows. All the others had been done live on a Sunday night, but for some reason this last one was taped on the

Thursday before transmission, and it was arranged that, afterwards, there would be an end-of-series dinner at a Chinese restaurant over the road from the studios, and Ronnie told us that Gerald Wiley had accepted an invitation to come and reveal himself. Well, reveal who he was, not reveal himself. It wasn't that sort of restaurant.

By this time speculation was even more rife. I had rarely known things to be rifer. And then, halfway through the studio rehearsals, there came a knock on the door of my dressing room. It was Ronnie.

'I just want to tell you,' he said, 'before I tell everyone else. I am Gerald Wiley.'

I was stunned. And thrilled.

And so we all met in the restaurant that night, production team, actors, writers. I appreciated Ronnie having told me in advance. Not only was it much less embarrassing for me, but I was able to relish the drama of the situation all the more.

There was an empty chair, and it was past the time for the meal and there was still no sign of Gerald Wiley. Perhaps there was a party at the Pinters' and he couldn't drag himself away. Or perhaps his flight from the Caribbean had been delayed.

Then Frank Muir, our boss at London Weekend, came in and there were cries of 'It's you!'

'No,' he said. 'I can't stay. I just popped in.'

So then Ronnie stood up and said, 'It's me. I'm Gerald Wiley.'

There were cries of 'Sit down' and 'Shut up', and there was laughter, but then he spoke again, very seriously, and said, 'No. It really is me.'

There was a stunned silence. Michael Palin later described the moment as 'a wonderful sort of Agatha Christie revelation'.

The silence was eventually broken by Barry Cryer, that great breaker of silences, with 'Nobody likes a smartarse.'

I think that to an extent Ronnie regretted that he had revealed the secret so early in our working lives. The reason for the deception was that he wanted his material to be judged strictly on its merits, and not because of who he was. He didn't want us to do sketches that weren't good enough just because he'd written them. Now, of course, with the cat out of the bag, he was in the position he had tried to avoid. I think there was a tinge of feeling among the writers, as *The Two Ronnies* progressed, that some stuff that he wrote *did* get on because of who he was.

But, of course, when he revealed that it was him, neither of us had any idea that it *was* so early in our working lives. *The Two Ronnies* had not yet even been considered as a possibility.

Also, I think he enjoyed the deception too much to have carried it on successfully much longer. Joy did all Ronnie's typing, and they must have invested in a second machine, with a very different typeface, for the Wiley stuff, because it didn't look at all like the letters and rewrites and other little things that were typed for Ronnie by Joy. And then there were all the remarks that he made. 'He's really let us down this time.' Even, on one occasion, 'I don't understand this line. What's he getting at?' Wily, indeed.

If he had revealed it after about twenty years, I might have felt a little bit irritated at being duped for so long, and Ronnie might have got more goblets than he'd have known what to do with. I can imagine him saying, 'Joy! Ronnie's coming to dinner tonight! For God's sake hide all those goblets.'

The following Sunday, David Frost gave a vast party for what the newspapers described as 2,000 of his closest friends. It wasn't just for our show, it was to celebrate the success of

London Weekend Television. The Alexandra Palace, high on its hill above the North Circular Road and the unexciting suburbs of North London, had been transformed into a huge fairground. As we wandered among the celebrities thronging the helter-skelter, dodgems and all the side shows, Ron and I felt confident that we now belonged in such a world, and that the ending of *Frost on Sunday* was not the end of the road, but merely a staging post.

Now, however, quite unexpectedly, a problem arose. A rift had developed between London Weekend Television and David Paradine Productions. Stella Richman, the relatively new programme controller at London Weekend, made it clear to us that, while she admired us, she was no longer prepared to work with David's organization, to whom we were still under contract. It was never suggested that, if we broke with Paradine, we could continue to be employed by London Weekend, but we couldn't help wondering if there was an implication there. Creative artists almost invariably leave the politics to others. The very qualities that make them good at what they do render them highly unsuitable for political in-fighting. Was there an implication? We'll never know, because we had no doubt what to do. Our association with David had done us nothing but good. I described him as waving a wand. I wanted him to continue to do so. We would see out our contract with Paradine.

In effect, though, we had been sacked. In effect, for the time being, we were unemployed. It was a shock.

But the *Frost on Sunday* team had one last role to play. David, Ronnie, Jo Tewson and I were asked to provide the entertainment for the BAFTA (British Academy of Film and Television Arts) awards, which were being broadcast from the London Palladium.

We did a sketch in which Ronnie was Henry VIII, I was

a camp, Jewish Cardinal Wolsey, with a large cigar and a costume with a twenty-yard train, and Jo was all six wives. It doesn't sound like our kind of thing, more Morecambe and Wise, but it went down very well.

During the evening there was a technical breakdown, and we had to hold the fort while they sorted it out. Apparently it lasted eight or nine minutes. It is a myth to think that time goes at a constant pace. Eight or nine minutes with a beautiful woman passes in a flash, if you'll excuse the phrase. Eight or nine minutes chatting up a celebrity audience off the cuff is an age. And it wasn't the kind of thing we were good at, especially Ronnie.

We both must have been pretty good that night, though. Obviously there is no record of what we said, because of the breakdown, and we couldn't remember a word of it because we were panicking throughout, but it must have been all right, because it impressed Bill Cotton, Head of Light Entertainment at the BBC, and Paul Fox, Controller of BBC1, who was sitting next to him in the Palladium audience.

On one of our award shows, Bill Cotton told what these two powerful BBC men whispered to each other than night.

'How would you like to have Corbett and Barker on your network for the next three years?' whispered Bill.

'But they're tied to London Weekend Television, to David Frost,' whispered Paul.

'I didn't ask you what the problem was,' whispered Bill. 'I just asked whether you'd like to have them.'

'If you say so, that's fine by me,' whispered Paul.

The next day Bill Cotton turned up at David Frost's office and made an offer of a contract for six shows with Ronnie B., six shows with me, and thirteen episodes of a show featuring the two of us. He didn't know that, in effect, we had been sacked from London Weekend Television.

We had a meeting with Bill Cotton, and he asked us if we would come over and do a show together for the BBC. Just the two of us, not David Frost. Could they entice us?

Ronnie and I looked at each other and were glad, at that moment, that we were actors. There we were, unemployed, but we nodded in an 'I suppose we could possibly, just possibly, consider it *if* the fee and the whole package was right, but of course I can only speak for myself and not for Ronnie' kind of way.

A deal was struck. Bill Cotton later commented that, when he heard that we had been sacked, 'I thought I must have offered them too much money.' But I don't think in fact that he ever had cause to regret it.

So, although we were still with David Paradine Productions, we joined the BBC. We would do a primetime comedy series together. Everything was settled. Well, almost everything. What could we call the series? We just couldn't think of a title.

7

Hindsight is an amazing thing. In hindsight it seems as if the whole of our two careers were building to this moment, the creation of our show as a double act. There we were, one of us little, the other large, having done lots of sketches together in very successful programmes, and both called Ronnie. It seems absolutely obvious that the two of us should do a variety show together. All I can say is that it didn't seem so obvious to me at the time, or to Ronnie B., or to either of our very good, experienced and perceptive agents, or even to David Frost, who was almost as shrewd about other people's lives as he was about his own. As we have seen, it took David's production company having problems with London Weekend Television and a BAFTA breakdown to get us to the starting post. There is so much luck in our business. We might have got there eventually, but who knows?

It seems incredible, in hindsight, that there was any problem in finding a title for our new show. Perhaps *The Two Ronnies* was just too obvious. We often miss what's staring us in the face. Time and again, throughout *Frost on Sunday*, people had referred to us as the two Ronnies. 'Have we got the scripts for the two Ronnies' sketches?' etc. Yet still the penny didn't drop. There were discussions and debates about the title. Eventually somebody in the office at David Paradine Productions said, 'Why not call it *The Two Ronnies?*'

There is something particularly daunting about being named in the title of a show. Nobody would ever have said, of *Frost on Sunday*, 'Did you see it last night? The two Ronnies weren't very good, were they?' But now that was exactly what they would say, and we couldn't assume that we would be successful in the future, just because we had been successful in the past. We were there to be shot at, and we knew it, so we knew that we had to work very, very hard on the format and content of the show. We had to have it very carefully planned. Luckily, nobody was better than Ronnie B. at that.

We were both determined to continue our policy of ensuring that we had separate careers outside *The Two Ronnies*, and the BBC were just as keen on this as we were. It was in nobody's interests that we should get typecast, either singly or together. In fact we both began our return to the BBC by recording a variety special, an hour-long one-off programme, before we started on *The Two Ronnies*, and we both made a guest appearance in each other's show. This was actually extremely convenient, as during our rehearsals together for these specials, we were able to sit down with our director, Terry Hughes, and our executive producer, Jimmy Gilbert, and work out what the elements of the show should be. These discussions took place round a big table at the BBC rehearsal rooms in Acton, a charmless modern block on the A40, sarcastically known to everyone as the Acton Hilton. If the Hilton ever saw it, they'd sue.

Because we were both well prepared, theatrically experienced and thoughtful, and because attention to detail was our watchword, and because we had worked together so much – twenty-six editions of *The Frost Report*, forty-nine of *Frost on Sunday* – we knew what we could be and what we couldn't be. Above all, we knew that we could never be a double act in the way that Morecambe and Wise were. Morecambe and Wise were brilliant, and to court any kind of comparison with them would have been disastrous. But it went deeper

77

than that. Neither of us would have been happy in a traditional double act, though for very different reasons.

Ronnie was not, and never could be, a stand-up comedian. He was a very private man, a quiet man, who loved his family and his home and had the sort of hobbies that you might expect a bank manager or a schoolmaster to have. More of that later. Above all, he was an actor. He found it almost impossible to talk directly, as himself, to an audience. He had to be in character. If he was asked to open a village fête, he would be unable to do it unless he could do it in character as Arkwright or Fletcher or Lord Rustless or some other of his characters. And that, of course, was not what people wanted – they wanted a glimpse of the real man. So he didn't do these things in order not to disappoint them.

All this meant that it would have been very difficult for Ronnie to talk to the audience directly, as himself, and it also meant that he would have found it hard to talk to me, as himself, in front of the audience. I can't emphasize this too strongly. We would have found it very difficult to talk naturally to each other as ourselves and to the audience at the same time, even in the tiniest way, like saying goodnight at the end of the show. It would have sounded stilted. That was why we ended the show on a little joke. 'It's goodnight from me.' 'And it's goodnight from him.' That little ruse enabled Ronnie to say goodnight, and it gave us a much-loved little catchphrase.

I'm very different. I had an act. I did a spot. I was used to talking directly to an audience. In fact, I loved it. But I didn't want to be a double act any more than Ronnie did. My reason was my height. I've shown, I hope, how I have not been deeply sensitive about my height since my RAF days. I wouldn't go so far as to say that I was completely at ease with it, but it wasn't important enough to stop me leading a very happy life. It didn't stop me courting a woman who was more than six inches taller than me. Thank goodness it didn't.

But learning to use it as an advantage was a different matter. During our tea at the Ritz, David Frost said that he thought it could be an enormous plus, and it has been. I've grown into it, to use a very unsuitable phrase. I will come on and say to an audience, 'Oh my goodness, he's even smaller than I realized,' and feel perfectly happy about it. But I was always careful not to over-use it, and I think that if I was in a double act I would inevitably end up on the receiving end, the relationship would be defined by height. I certainly didn't intend to go through life being persecuted with flour and water and hit with rubber hammers and that kind of thing. Of course an act with Ronnie B. would never have been that physical, but there would have been a real danger that I would have ended up playing for sympathy.

Just about the first decision we made about the show was that, in the cause of preserving our separate identities, it would contain a solo item for both of us. It was clear, from the differing nature of our skills, that the two spots would be very different in character. Ronnie was very much more of a character actor, with numerous and varied voices at his fingertips, and I realized through *Frost on Sunday* and *The Corbett Follies* that I had a sort of ability to talk as myself, or at least as people imagined me to be, so the two solo spots would be quite different. I would be me being me as me, if you see what I mean, and Ronnie would do the character part. I would sit in a chair, as myself, and talk to the audience, and Ronnie would be playing a part, a spokesman or a mad scientist or a man who pispronounced his worms or whatever. Ronnie's monologue would always come before mine in the show. We knew instinctively that that was right, although to this day I couldn't say why.

But how should we front the show, how should we begin it and how should we end it? With *Frost on Sunday* we hadn't faced this problem. David had done all that. Ah! Supposing we did phoney news items, like David. He, of course, had always been himself, barking out his bofferoonies, as he sometimes called them. We couldn't, as I have shown, be ourselves. What part could we play, to read out these news items? It didn't require a genius to suggest that we became newsreaders. As Jimmy Gilbert pointed out, the news bulletins regularly used two newsreaders sitting side by side. So there we would sit, at the beginning and the end of the show, side by side, together but separate, like our careers.

In the early shows we remained po-faced throughout the news item sequence, but in the end there were jokes that one or other of us couldn't resist, and we began to smile and titter and giggle and be human, and perhaps, in those moments, the audience came to see glimpses of the real Ronnie B. It can look awfully smug when comedians laugh at their own jokes, but we weren't doing that, we were laughing at each other's jokes. I know some people found this a bit cosy, but my answer to that would be that in this harsh world of ours there are worse things to be than cosy.

At first we relied on our regular writers to provide news items. No one was better at it than Gary Chambers, who was

At the desk.

a master of the mordant one-liner. Gary's humour, like that of Spike Mullins, was dry, as dry as a desert, but Gary's gags were concise and miniaturist, while the essence of Spike's humour was its rambling nature. I will return to the subject of Spike's writing later.

The following exchange occurred between Gary and another of our regular writers, David Nobbs. It illustrates Gary's sense of humour perfectly.

GARY: Is it true you're moving to Barnet?
DAVID: Yes.
GARY: I'm really upset about that.
DAVID: Why?
GARY: I'm going to have to remove the board I have up in my garden.
DAVID: Why? What does it say?
GARY: Last comedy writer before the M1.

As soon as the show started to hit the screens, would-be writers from all over the country began to bombard the BBC with jokes. It was a way of beginning on the long road to a career as a writer. Many of them failed, of course, but not all. One of our hopefuls was a young man named David Renwick, from Luton. I'll come back to him later too.

The process for selecting the jokes was unvaried, and logical. Our script editors, Ian Davidson and Peter Vincent, would come to our unlovely 'Hilton' in unlovely Acton armed with great piles of gags. They would have sorted through about 400 and whittled them down to about 397, and typed them all up and numbered them, and we would solemnly read them all out alternately. Ron would read the first one one week, and I would start the next week, and we would mark the gags as we read them. The gags were all anonymous, and we would never permit ourselves even the hint of a smile, for fear it would influence the final judgement.

'A man who swallowed a barometer was admitted to Cheadle Cottage Hospital today. His condition was described as "set fair – stormy later".'

'Bognor Regis District Council announced a revolutionary new plan for treating its sewage today. They'll take it to London to see a show and then for a little dinner in an Italian restaurant.'

'An unemployed labourer appeared in court today charged with running up Downing Street shouting, "All the government is barmy." He was fined two pounds for being drunk and disorderly, and sent to prison for ten years for revealing a state secret.'

The world was at work, sober and serious. Car makers were making cars, dentists were filling teeth, merchant bankers were banking merchants, and here were we sitting at a table reading jokes with utter solemnity. If you stopped to think about it, it was bizarre, which was probably why we never stopped to think about it.

You may have noticed that our jokes were not what you would call hotly topical. In the world of the BBC it's a foolish man who forgets repeats. You can see our routine at the desk twenty years later, and hardly anything seems anachronistic. We tried to avoid proper names as much as possible, again in the interests of repeats, but it just wasn't always possible. On the whole, though, we liked 'Are there too many government ministries? We'll be talking later to the Minister for Steak and Kidney Pudding' more than we liked 'In the House of Commons last night, when the heating failed, MPs had to don spare overalls to keep warm. Mr Callaghan wore four pairs while Mrs Thatcher wore three, an overall majority of one.'

Some of our gags, if told now, might fall foul of the intense sensibilities of our guardians of political correctness. 'The West Ham Short-sighted Society held a picnic today on Clapham Common, and the East Ham Short-sighted Society held a picnic on the West Ham Short-sighted Society.' Oh dear. Imagine the letters in 2006. If that was cruel, it was about as cruel as we ever got.

Not all our jokes at the desk were news items. We would issue the occasional warning – 'Here is a message for seven honeymoon couples in a hotel in Peebles. Breakfast was served three days ago' – and we would announce forthcoming events in the show under the heading 'In a packed show tonight . . .' For example: 'In a packed show tonight we'll interview the Romford girl who took the pill washed down with pond water and was today diagnosed as being three months stagnant.'

Another regular feature of the show was the big musical finish. The inspiration for this came from an item in my one-off special, which was called *Ronnie Corbett in Bed*.

Ronnie's show was called *The Ronnie Barker Yearbook*, and it wasn't a very happy experience for him. I think that, unlike me, he was actually not very keen on doing a variety special on his own. It wasn't really his bag. Since he couldn't present it as himself, there was a bit of a hole in the middle. The idea was to do twelve items, one for each month of the year, items suited to the nature of the month. In the end, the producer, Jimmy Gilbert, said there wasn't room to film the first two items. The January item would have consisted of very fast shots of professional skaters falling all over the ice. Ronnie suspected that it was dropped because of the time and expense that would be involved in the filming. He protested strongly, only to be told by Jimmy, very firmly, 'Excuse me. I am making here an executive decision.' We worked a lot with

Jimmy, and owe a lot to him, and this was the only time either of us ever had what could be described as a row with him.

Frank Muir, former Head of Comedy at the BBC and London Weekend, once said, 'God preserve me from good ideas.' It sounds strange, but I know what he meant. A good idea can become a straitjacket for comedy, and I suspect that might have been the case with the yearbook idea. But I must say that I agree with Ron that, if you're going to do it, you have to do it properly. I would have been a bit upset to have a yearbook without January or February, but Ron, with his fastidious nature and his almost compulsive attention to detail, must have been mortified. Anyway, it was only a one-off and it was soon forgotten.

We didn't have these problems with *Ronnie Corbett in Bed*, in which I introduced the show from my bed. This may sound like an idea for an offbeat little show, but this was mainstream television. The guests included Howard Keel and Blossom Dearie. What a privilege to be able to sing and play the piano in the company of someone as accomplished as Blossom Dearie.

At one stage in the show, I was in bed doing my stand-up routine, known for this one show only as my lie-down routine, and it was time to introduce a guest. 'Once in a while,' I began, 'you get the chance to welcome on to your show somebody who's a particular favourite of your own, and tonight I'm very fortunate to be able to introduce to you . . .'

At which point an actress playing my mother came in with a cup and saucer.

'Beef tea,' she announced.

'Thank you, it's very kind of you, Mother, very kind of you to think of that,' I said, 'but I'm just doing a television show at the moment and . . .'

'I'm sure Robin Day doesn't say no to a nice cup of beef tea when he's got a TV show to do.'

'Mother, I'm introducing the next item, now just . . .'

'You can't introduce the next item with your sheets all crooked.'

'Mother!'

She busied herself, tidying my sheets, saying, 'I don't expect Ronnie Barker introduced his next item with his sheets all crooked.'

'Yes, but he wasn't in bed.'

The show was written by Barry Cryer and Graham Chapman, and many, many years later, a similar idea would inspire a sitcom that gave me a starring role for five years.

The big musical number that finished the show was written by Dick Vosburgh. Dick is a tall, bearded, caustic but warm American from Elizabeth, New Jersey, with an encyclopedic knowledge of show business on both sides of the Atlantic, a sharp sense of humour, a love of complicated ideas and clever lyrics and the understanding that you can only satirize successfully what you love. He came up with the brilliant idea of *Romeo and Juliet* set to Sousa marches. It was a sheer delight, and it became the model for the big musical number which regularly formed the climax of *The Two Ronnies*.

So we had our opening routine at the desk, our Ronnie B. monologue, our Ronnie C. monologue and our big musical finish. There would be guest spots each week, and of course there would be sketches. A genre that we would make our own was the party sketch, with the two of us meeting for the first time as guests at a party. This was very often the first sketch in the show, and it helped set the tone for our comedy mood.

The format felt good, but it also felt as though something was missing. Most of the items would run for between three

A typical big musical number.

and five minutes. We needed to vary the pace. A few quickies
would help, but there was a sense that we needed something
more solid, something weightier, something to anchor the
show, something to give it more variety, if we were to achieve
the response that we wanted for a fifty-minute show at peak
viewing time on a Saturday night. Yes, the BBC pitched us
straight in to that prestigious slot. No experiments on the
edge of the schedules. Straight in, the main event for all the
family. No wonder we were being so punctilious in our
approach.

We decided that the missing ingredient must be on film,
to vary the visual effect of the show, and it must be quite
long, to vary the feel of the show. The filmed serial was the
obvious answer, and we included one in every series.

We had our format. We decided to change that format just
once, nothing very startling, just a change of order. In fact I
can't even remember now what exactly we did, but whatever

A classic party sketch.

it was, it didn't work. Never again. We had created our template, and we had to stick with it.

Of course we had our critics. We were not at the cutting edge, and we didn't pretend to be. We were trying to create more than a show. We were trying to create an event, and that event was a moment for the whole family, to sit and relax together, to laugh and smile together, without embarrassment. The viewing figures suggest that we succeeded, and I venture to suggest that the families that our show was aimed at were intelligent, quite well informed, literate, musical and nice.

I don't think we were ever what you would call violent. I don't think we were ever wilfully cruel. If we were rude, we were rude in a very British way, in the manner of the seaside postcards that dear Ron loved so much. We had double entendres. Nowadays they have single entendres. I remember a double entendre of Ken Dodd's. 'My uncle was a farmer. Not in a big way. He had a smallholding and two acres.' Maybe you have to spell it 'achers' in print. Anyway, the audience didn't get it straight away, so he looked at them till they did. It's nice to make the audience work just a bit.

It was a good format because, although it was the same every week, it allowed scope for enormous variety in the jokes within that format. It combined familiarity with freshness.

8

On 10 April 1971, it was announced that Britain would supply Libya's revolutionary regime with £60 million worth of arms, Glasgow was six degrees warmer than London, teachers voted for action in pursuit of their 15 per cent pay claim, Prime Minister Edward Heath's new 41-foot yacht *Morning Cloud* was launched in the Solent with champagne, and the very first edition of *The Two Ronnies* was launched on BBC1 at eight o'clock, right in the middle of the peak viewing period. I don't think either of us felt, in retrospect, that this first show was particularly good. We felt that we began to hit our stride with the second, and were in full form by the middle of the series. Nevertheless, I think it would be interesting to take a look at the contents of that very first programme.

Our beginning at the news desk wasn't typical: we were introducing ourselves and we didn't actually do one single news item.

'Good evening, and welcome to the show,' I began. 'I must say it's very nice to be with you all, isn't it?'

Ronnie's very first line in the series did not exercise his verbal dexterity to the full.

'It is,' he said.

'And to be with you,' I continued.

'Thank you, Ron,' said Ron.

'We decided, actually, to call the series *The Two Arthurs*,' I went on, 'but then we thought that wouldn't work, because Ronnie Barker isn't called Arthur, so we decided to call it *A Ronnie and an Arthur*. So then someone pointed out that I'm not called Arthur either, so we rather smartly thought up the title *The Two Ronnies*.'

'Thank you, Arthur,' said Ron.

Then we moved into our very first sketch, and our very first party sketch. I would say that this was probably the most important sketch we ever did, because it set the tone for ninety-eight shows. It was written by Michael Palin and Terry Jones, and it was very funny, as you would expect from those two clever men.

Ronnie B. stood in a dinner jacket, sipping wine, and I approached him, and he slapped me quite hard across the cheek. In fact he kept doing this. One time when I thought he would he didn't, and I relaxed, only to fall straight into the next stinging slap. He apologized profusely, said he couldn't help it, suggested I duck. So I ducked, and he kicked me somewhere very close to the Trossachs. He poured all sorts of things on me, including a large amount of icing and a couple of meringues which were supposed to attach themselves to my ears, but didn't, so that in the tension of those early days I couldn't avoid a degree of suppressed corps-ing that wasn't quite suppressed enough. But that all seemed to add to the fun.

What was so great about the sketch was that neither of us ever deviated from polite party attitudes. He was almost in tears as he explained that he just wanted to be loved and nobody loved him, and I would have bent over backwards to help him if I hadn't thought that if I did he would kick me up the backside, which indeed he did when I'd finally had enough and was walking away.

The written tag was said to another guest on his approach to Ronnie B. – 'I thought I'd never get rid of him' – but, as Gerald Wiley, Ron added a tag upon a tag and began slapping this man too.

Next came our first musical guest, Tina Charles, just sixteen years old and making her first appearance on television, singing 'River Deep, Mountain High'.

This was followed by Ronnie B.'s monologue, in which he played a doctor who couldn't help saying everything twice. He had been to Baden-Baden Baden-Baden and had been to see *Chitty Chitty Chitty Chitty Bang Bang Bang Bang*.

Our first-ever classic serial was called 'Hampton Wick' and featured the delightful Madeline Smith, well endowed with talent and two other things that Ron greatly admired. It was a period piece about a naive young girl in a world of hungry men. Ron and I each played about twelve hungry men. The first episode looked stylish and beautiful, as Madeline arrived at the home of a sex-starved aristocrat (Ronnie B.) as governess for his 36-year-old son (me).

Then there was a quickie, quite a long quickie, in which I took a long while to get through on the phone to Interpol, and then asked them to send some flowers to my mother. This was followed by our resident male group, New World, singing 'Rose Garden', and my very first monologue from the chair. The next item was a sketch about a man asking for a hearing aid from a deaf provider of hearing aids, both saying 'Pardon?' to each other quite a lot – once again I can just imagine the letters of protest these days – and so we reached our third guest, a speciality act, a man called Alfredo.

What can I say of Alfredo? He was, quite simply, the very best act involving doing a silent impression of Sammy Davis Junior, gurning frantically to give an impression of a military parade of old soldiers while playing a one-man band, running in circles round his musical instruments with a pint of beer on his head, saying 'cheers' in eight languages, drinking the pint of beer to the accompaniment of loud plumbing noises, producing large numbers of ping pong balls from his mouth, and spitting some of them on to a music stand from which they bounced back to be caught in his mouth that I have ever seen. Anne actually recommended him to Terry Hughes, and I think she has always had slightly mixed feelings about having done so.

The show ended with three songs from our post-Woodstock, long-haired Country and Western duo, Jehosaphat and Jones. This was an act that we returned to from time to time. The lyrics for the hairy duo were written by Gerald Wiley, often unashamedly influenced by the McGill postcards that he loved so much. A brief extract from a typical Jehosaphat and Jones song will give the flavour and bring it all back.

VERSE: One day she went into a department store
               And she said to the guy who stood by the door

I need some material to make a new belt

Perhaps you can tell me where I can get felt.

CHORUS: We knew what she meant

We knew what she meant

We heard what she said

But we knew what she meant.

And then, for the very first time, it was goodnight from me, and it was goodnight from him.

The format for that very first show was almost exactly the one that kept us going throughout the next ninety-seven shows. The only variant was that, over the years, we began to do more sketches and had fewer guest stars. We dropped the speciality acts fairly early on (well, where would we have found ninety-eight acts as eccentric as Alfredo's?) and in the end we had just the one musical guest. We were beginning to realize, to our joy, that it was us above all that people were tuning in to see.

Ron and family had moved into a very nice, comfortable, roomy house in Church Lane in Pinner, in north-west London, near Harrow. It was called New House but in fact had quite a history. Lord Nelson's illegitimate daughter Horatia had lived there in her old age, and George Black, a well-known impresario, had owned it with his brother Alfred. In fact Ron and Joy weren't even the first Barkers to live there. It was once occupied by Sir Herbert Barker, a celebrated bone-setter, and no relation. Ron also recalled that Elton John used to deliver the papers there when he was still Reg Dwight. I can't help wondering how far his career would have gone if he'd remained Reg Dwight.

Anne and I also fell in love with a house, and during this year of the first series of *The Two Ronnies* I felt secure enough to buy it. It backed on to the golf course, in Addington, in lovely country within a stone's throw of unlovely Croydon. It wasn't an old house, it was built between the wars, but it was rambling and rather spectacular. It had turrets at either side of the front door, and gables at each end. There were eight bedrooms, and one and a half acres of garden. It cost £31,000. In front of the house there were handsome woods. We were in, yet not in, London. It was a dream.

Our life was a bit of a dream now, really. From 1971 until 1986 it was dominated by *The Two Ronnies*. Ronnie and I both did shows on our own, but every year, except the one we spent in Australia, we spent four months making *The Two Ronnies*. You've seen the shows. Now's the time to give you a bit of an insight into how we put them together.

9

Before we went into the studio to record the weekly episodes of *The Two Ronnies*, we would go on location to do all the items for them that needed to be filmed. The main one was the weekly serial, and since this would last for not much short of ten minutes each week, we would really be doing at least two-thirds of a feature film in the course of the series, and incidentally at a fraction of the time and cost.

We would be away for several weeks, sometimes staying in the same hotel. Anne never came to the filming, and Joy only very, very rarely. They both had families to run, children to get to school. Besides which, although filming can be very stimulating for those involved, the hours are very, very long, and the process can be extremely laborious, with a scene being shot over and over again from different angles. It is not a spectator sport, as any of you who have ever stood and watched the process will know.

So, during the filming, Ron and I reverted to a kind of bachelor life. Not that we were burning the candle at both ends. The work was far too hard and tiring to leave us with the time or the energy to do that. It's important on location to stay somewhere where one is comfortable. Ron and I usually stayed in the same hotel, and we would almost always eat together in the evening, often with the director.

I was always happy if we could find somewhere that was near a golf course, or even had a golf course of its own, so that I could nip off there when there was a break in my schedule. I didn't necessarily need to have time to play a round. A short walk on a golf course in the evening sunshine, enjoying the smells that came from the cutting of the grass and the watering of the greens, was a very special way of unwinding for me.

I have particularly happy memories of the Green Man, at Shurdington, near Cheltenham, of leaving my shoes outside the door to be cleaned, of luxuriating in the bath – they can't touch you for it – changing into crisp, clean clothes and sitting outside on the lawn with a tincture and settling down to a serious study of – no, not the next day's script – the menu. The script could wait, because I was a very quick study, we both were.

On another occasion we filmed around Chagford, in the beautiful Devon countryside on the edge of Dartmoor, a land of deep valleys, rolling woods and thatched cottages. On this occasion, unusually, we didn't stay in the same hotel. I went to the Manor in Moretonhampstead, because it had its own nine-hole golf course, while Ron chose to stay in Chagford. The Manor was a rather handsome house which had once been the home of W. H. Smith, the famous stationer, who later became Lord . . . er . . . Lord something or other. I think the fact that we could stay equally happily in the same hotel or in separate hotels shows the stability of our friendship.

The days were long. We would usually start work at about seven. But the unions were still quite strong in those days, and we would usually 'wrap' at about five or half past. Nowadays money is the god, and filming can go on from six in the morning till eight or nine at night, seven days a week, which is terrible. Nobody can do first-class work under that pressure.

Ron would unwind, when he had time, by wandering round antique shops and bric-à-brac shops, looking for items to add to his collections. And actually I think he had a lot more unwinding to do, because he involved himself in every aspect of the filming. In fact these moments on location were his favourite part of the whole process of making the show.

The serials were the part of the show that Ronnie involved himself in most closely. He wrote many of them. For one of them, 'The Phantom Raspberry-blower of Old London Town', the writing credits were 'By Spike Milligan and a Gentleman'. This was based on a script that Spike had written for an earlier one-off show of Ronnie's. I'm afraid we can offer no prizes for the first three correct answers as to the identity of the Gentleman. Gerald Wiley brought his sense of structure and discipline to the wilder creations of Milligan's comic genius. There were shades of Jack the Ripper and the Keystone Cops in this piece. It was full of thunder and lightning and loud music and over-acting. There were some very rewarding roles for Ron and me. My main role was as the splendidly named Scotland Yard detective Corner of the Yard, with his mutton-chop whiskers and bemused expression, as he failed like all Scotland Yard detectives in period fiction to make any headway whatsoever with the case, which reminds me of an ad-lib by John Cleese that I was told about during *The Frost Report*. All the writers were gathered round a table, thinking up ideas, when somebody said, 'The police are working on the theory . . .' and John butted in with '. . . that they have been completely outwitted by the criminals.' The police get a hard time in comedy, almost as much as accountants.

This was one of the very few serials that we filmed around London and it was also one of the very few to involve shooting at night. I remember one very creepy night shoot in Highgate Cemetery, which is full of ornate graves and the graves of many famous people, notably Karl Marx. It felt like a bit of a desecration to be filming there, and I think we were all glad when morning came.

Rumour had it that Spike Milligan had given us the rights to the serial free on condition that he be allowed to blow all the raspberries. I have to say that they were magnificent, loud, ripe and squelchy, the work of a master. But nobody seems to have seen Spike around the studios in his raspberry-recording gear, and Corner of the Yard was convinced that we could add raspberry blowing to the list of Ron's talents.

Ronnie would get up in the morning earlier than me. He would sniff out the weather, consider the possibility of changing the order of the filming because of the weather, or how he could alter a line because of the weather, or how he might be able to use the weather for an extra sight gag. All this while I was still enjoying my beauty sleep.

He knew what he wanted, and he wasn't shy of saying so. I don't think this was arrogance, and I don't think our directors ever felt it to be so. As he wrote it Ronnie knew how he wanted every shot to look, and even after it had been shot, he would go to the editing suites in the bowels of the Television Centre, where unsung, dedicated men who rarely see the sun work long and hard with electronic equipment to cut the film rushes into their final shape. Ronnie was a perfectionist. These serials were his babies, and he would never leave them at home alone. In this context I must give credit to a marvellous technician named Jim Franklin. He was far more than an editor. He was creative and constructive and inventive and could transform a script in post-production. We were so fortunate to have such people helping us.

I left Ron to get on with all this sort of thing. I trusted him utterly, and he knew that I trusted him utterly, which in a way was a kind of trust in me. Trust was the cornerstone of our relationship. It's an underrated quality. There are lots of songs about love, not many about trust. There was also, incidentally, complete trust between me and Anne and between Ron and Joy. If any of this trust had ever been eroded, I don't think we could have done fifteen happy years of intense work together.

The two of us always shared a caravan on location. We'd have our breakfast there and our lunch there and we'd blether away about anything and everybody; we were quite gossipy and chatty.

That reminds me of something which I always used to say: 'When we were filming, the principle would be that Ronnie would write a sketch, and I would queue for his lunch . . . simple really . . . a very simple formula.' That was me being British, avoiding being sentimental and seeking refuge in a joke.

In fact I didn't queue for Ronnie's lunch at all. We were very lucky. We had our individual dressers and they would very kindly queue for our lunch. Ronnie's used to come in relays: anything with sauté potatoes, or pilaff, or rice with sauté potatoes, and sponge with custard on it, all the really fattening stuff, he used to eat. And I'd have a little delicate salad, with a bit of Emmenthal cheese on the side, and a water biscuit. Mine looked like a David Hockney painting on the plate, while he, to steal a phrase from an old jockey friend of mine, had a pile of food on his plate that Arkle couldn't jump. And we would sit over our lunch and blether away about this one and that one and enjoy each other's company in that way. These were very nice, relaxing moments in the middle of all the hard work. We were quite disciplined, however: we would never have a glass of anything at lunch on location.

These filmed serials were wonderful for me, because in the context of the comedy I could play all sorts of roles that I would never have got otherwise. Let's face it, if I did a film like *The Shooting Party*, I would never be one of the guns, shooting alongside Edward Fox and being told, 'Damned fine shot, Carruthers.' I'd be the gamekeeper's assistant. Not so in our serials. I could be the Earl of Mortlake, and Ronnie could be my butler. It really all was enormous fun. Never mind if the hours were long and the starts early, we were so lucky.

In fact Ronnie was butler to my Lord Loam in our spoof of J. M. Barrie's play *The Admirable Crichton*, in which a great London family are shipwrecked and, having never had to lift a finger to help themselves, prove utterly incapable of surviving but are rescued only by the resourcefulness of their butler. Of course, when they have been saved, we find that they have learnt nothing and still don't lift a finger to help themselves. Susannah York was Lady Loam and Koo Stark had a small part as the housemaid Lord Loam runs off with.

I have particularly fond memories of filming *The Admirable Crichton*, quite apart from the fact that it's not every day you get to run off with Koo Stark and get paid for it. Everything about it looked magnificent, from the wonderful autumnal scenery of the New Forest to the magnificent animated rubber crocodile that was built for Ronnie B. to wrestle with in a most spectacular scene. Sadly, there is no Best Animated Rubber Crocodile category in the BAFTAs. Seriously, a lot of good work by dedicated professionals goes unsung in our business.

There were also scenes shot outside a very handsome house in Eaton Square in London. We rode around in elegant, open-top vintage Bentleys, and we wore plus fours, Argyll socks, two-tone shoes and jaunty eight-piece caps, those caps ribbed into eight sections, which are so popular with golfers, hunters and shooters. I have several of these. I love them for playing golf, when I like to look slightly tweedy, because I'm a Scotsman, I suppose. Anyway, even just filming this gracious style of living felt good.

Mostly, however, we were in the countryside, often in

deep countryside, often on private estates. Our location seekers were clever in finding places where we would be free from the attentions of a watching public, which can slow things down terribly.

Perhaps this is as good a moment as any to mention our attitude to the fact that, more and more, we were recognized by the public, wherever we went. I've never minded being recognized. I've never resented it. In fact I'm quite pleased about it, and I try to respond in the right way, though it isn't easy if I'm asked for my autograph when I'm in a curmudgeonly mood at the airport having lost my luggage. Ron, I think, felt much the same. I am unusual in that I am recognized in three different ways – by my height, my glasses and my voice. Other people can pass much more unnoticed in a crowd, even if they are even more well known than me.

I remember doing a summer season in Paignton, and Val Doonican was in nearby Torquay. I was emptying my theatre, he was filling his. We used to play golf every day, and if we went to a strange course I had to introduce Val to the pro, because if he had a hat on and dark glasses, nobody would know who he was, whereas I am recognized the moment I walk in anywhere, so it's just as well that I don't mind.

Anyway, on location, in the deep countryside around Chagford, there was nobody to recognize me. The serials that we filmed there, in idyllic weather, were two of the most popular ones we ever did. They were called 'Done to Death' and 'Death Can Be Fatal', and were spoofs on detective films. We played a couple of really inept detectives. I was Charley Farley and Ronnie was Piggy Malone. The first seven episodes of 'Done to Death' all ended with the words 'Only one thing was certain. There would be very little sleep for anyone that night.' For 'Death Can Be Fatal' the endings were more

Me as Charley Farley and Ron as Piggy Malone.

on exaggerated Dick Barton lines: 'Is this the end for our two heroes? What of Madame Cocotte? Is she in some bedroom somewhere, lying in wait with a silencer? Or lying in silence with a waiter? Find out next week in another exciting episode, "Villa of Villainy".'

We also parodied several other series of the time – *Colditz, The Regiment, Star Trek* and *Upstairs, Downstairs*. One joke that I will never forget was in the spoof of *Colditz*. I am waiting outside a lavatory for Ronnie to come out. He can't get out. There is much rattling of the door handle and banging on the door, and at last he emerges.

'Hello,' he says. 'I'm James. I'm the escape officer.'

The boldest of our serials was undoubtedly 'The Worm that Turned', set in a futuristic Britain in 2012. It was a story of a land dominated by women, with Diana Dors playing the Commander of the State Police. Men's clubs were abolished, gentlemen's toilets closed, creating widespread distress among thinking and drinking men everywhere. Big Ben had been renamed Big Brenda. The Tower of London was now known as Barbara Castle. The Union Jack had become the Union Jill. Men were forced to go around in dresses. I played the worm that turned. I think this was a far from safe and cosy subject even at the time. It might create an uproar now that we are so much closer to 2012.

This is probably as good a moment as any to bring up the question of drag. Ronnie and I did appear in drag quite a lot, especially in 'The Worm that Turned', but also frequently in our musical finales. Ronnie in drag was always funny and often inspired, but he claimed to hate doing it. I can't say I particularly enjoyed it, but I had become used to it over the years and by the time we got to *The Two Ronnies* I had no hang-ups about prancing around in dresses just so long as it was really funny. The moment it wasn't funny at all, or was only slightly funny, it became an embarrassment. But you can't create good comedy without taking risks, and it was a risk worth taking. I have to point out, though, that the vast majority of the items in which we appeared in drag were written by Ronnie – our other writers rarely touched on it, and I have the impression that he wrote more roles for himself in drag than he did for me. And then he threw himself into the roles with such abandon and skill. Did he really hate it as much as he claimed? That claim is perhaps the only thing he ever said to me that I am uncertain whether to fully believe. That's not bad in forty years, is it?

Joy absolutely hated seeing Ron in drag, but Anne didn't mind seeing me in drag at all. She had appeared so much with the Crazy Gang and Max Wall and had become thoroughly used to seeing men dressed as women for laughs. She recalls, when I was playing one of the Ugly Sisters in pantomime in Glasgow, going into Marks & Spencer's with our two daughters, Emma and Sophie, and saying to one of them, who was being naughty, 'Will you please behave yourself? I'm trying to buy some tights for your father.' The lady shop assistant looked shocked even in Glasgow. And it was lucky that we were in Glasgow. An Edinburgh assistant at the time would probably have fainted.

Back to the serials. As I say, Ronnie supervised every aspect

As Elizabeth Taylor and Richard Burton.

Asian lovelies.

of them, despite which, towards the end of his career, he expressed just a little dissatisfaction with them.

'I always think now, seeing the serials,' he said, 'that they were slow. We used to wait for laughs in places, and sometimes you didn't get them, so I look at them now and I think they could be faster. They weren't tight enough.'

It's perhaps a bit sad that Ronnie was not entirely satisfied, but then that was him, the perfectionist, and I think it's reassuring that he never lost the ability to be as critical of himself as he could be of other people. He never just accepted what he was given. Dick Vosburgh recalls that when Ronnie was in an early Ayckbourn play, *Mr Whatnot*, he queried quite a few things, and when he did Tom Stoppard's *The Real Inspector Hound* he suggested line changes. The important thing was that he was only doing it to try to make the piece work better, and his suggestions must have been constructive, because neither Ayckbourn nor Stoppard took offence.

We didn't do many other items on film, although at some stage Ron introduced a couple of new characters in the form of the two yokels, and their exchanges were always shot on location.

'You know old Cyril Harris, the one with one eye?'

'Yes. You don't see much of him lately.'

'No, well he don't see much of us either.'

'Where did you see him then?'

'Up the pictures. He went up to the girl in the box office and says, "With one eye, I should think you'd let me in for half price." But she wasn't having it.'

'Oh. Did he have to pay full price?'

'He had to pay double.'

'Double? Why was that then?'

'She reckoned it would take him twice as long to see the picture.'

'Oh.'

Ronnie made no bones about the fact that the yokels' gags were taken from an old joke book that he came across in his guise as a collector.

When we were out on location, if we were staying in the same area for any length of time, we would begin to get invitations to go to dinner in people's houses. Some of these invitations were tempting, but we never accepted them. For one reason, filming was tiring, we didn't have the surplus energy. But the more important reason was that actually, away from the work, without our scripts, we aren't particularly funny. I don't mean that we can't tell the occasional amusing anecdote, but we didn't perform, in everyday life, like we did in our work.

Our hosts would expect a riot of humour, we felt, with 'it's thank you very much from me' and 'it's thank you very much from him' at the door on the way out. We couldn't provide this, and even to try would wear us out.

Some comedians are naturally funny all the time. Eric Morecambe was. He was never not funny. I think it may have been what killed him. Although I have to say that when I was at a do with him, he wouldn't even get to his feet to hand out a prize if Ernie wasn't there, at his side. But if you got in a lift with him, he would be joking the whole time.

Ronnie had a great example of Eric's wit and playfulness. He and Joy invited the Morecambes to dinner. It was the first time the Morecambes had seen their very nice house in Pinner. Joy had taken great pains to be at her most glamorous. Eric entered, took in the scene, turned back to the door and mouthed an instruction to his taxi driver, just loud enough to be heard. 'About an hour.'

Ted Ray was another great ad-libber. Barry Cryer remembers, after the recording of an episode of *Jokers Wild*, sitting with Ted and the other comics in the lounge of a hotel and listening to a pianist murdering a popular song.

'What would you gentlemen like me to play now?' smarmed the pianist.

'Dominoes,' said Ted Ray.

Frank Carson never stops either. A friend of mine told me how, after a hard day in the studio on a comedy programme, he went down to breakfast in his hotel, slightly hungover, and saw that the only person in the room was Frank. A lovely man, but not if you like a quiet breakfast. My friend went to the far end of the room, furthest from him, and buried himself behind his *Daily Telegraph*. He ordered his breakfast, hidden behind the sports reports. He held his newspaper in front of him till his arm ached.

Then a crowd of suits entered. (We always call the management 'suits'. 'The suits won't like it.' 'The suits will think it's too expensive.' 'Don't worry. The suits won't understand it.') These were businessmen on a conference. As they streamed in my friend could see out of the corner of his eye that they all had name tags pinned to their jackets, and that they seated themselves at a long table in the middle of the room, between him and Frank Carson. Now, he thought, I'm safe. He lowered his newspaper.

'Oh hello,' said Frank immediately. 'Did you hear the one about the nun and the caravan?'

And he started to lob jokes across the room, over the heads of the businessmen. Literally a bit 'over the top'.

We just weren't in that mould. You wouldn't expect Ron to have been, with his background in rep, but with my times in panto, summer seasons and night clubs you might perhaps have expected me to be more of a gag merchant. In fact I think Ron made more of a stab at being funny than I did, but it didn't come naturally to either of us.

In any event, we were usually too busy to accept social invitations. The filming schedule was tight, and Ron and I also had work to do in preparation for the time when we went into the studio to record the shows in front of an audience. Our regular writers would be commissioned to deliver their material well in advance, and while we were on location we would set aside two or three evenings when we would read the material and decide what we thought worked for us and what didn't. Usually the hotel in which we were staying would be able to provide a small function room where we could sit round a table – we always liked to be round a table – and assemble running orders for the studio recordings. It's amazing how rarely we disagreed. We truly were on the same comedy wavelength.

Occasionally we would read a very funny sketch, but decide, reluctantly, that, while it was very good, it wasn't for us; it was more suited to, say, Dick Emery. It was possible, we felt, once or twice, that we were being sent a sketch that had been turned down for another show, or that had been written for a comedian who had died in real life before he could do the sketch.

In fact there is a well-known instance of a writer, who shall be nameless, doing just that and getting caught out rather badly. Eric Nameless was commissioned to write some sketches for Dick Emery, accepted the commission despite being very busy and asked his secretary to send in some old Tommy Cooper sketches that hadn't been used, changing Tommy's name to Dick throughout. Dick was actually very easy-going, happy to come into rehearsals on a Monday morning and say, 'Right. What have we got, then?', but even he smelt a rat when a sketch ended: 'Dick gives his characteristic laugh, and his fez falls off.'

That reminds me of the writer who was very proud, in the early days of word processors, to use his 'global search' facility. He had decided that he wanted to change the name of his main character from David to Nigel. Easy. A few seconds typing, and the job was done. Imagine his mortification when the book came out, and he realized that the main character now took a girlfriend to Florence, where they admired Michelangelo's Nigel in all its magnificence.

Back to those two or three evenings, during our location

With the great Tommy Cooper.

filming, when we chose the items for the shows, the material that we really liked, the cream. In one evening we would assemble enough for two or three shows, so by the end of the filming, after several of these evenings, we had the eight shows ready for rehearsal.

It's time to go back to the Acton Hilton, pearl of the A40.

10

'The world's untidiest man died yesterday. He is now lying in a state.'

'And now a message from the police in Finchley. There's bad news about the two rabbits stolen from Peter's Petshop. Only fourteen have so far been recovered.'

The Two Ronnies are at work, solemnly reading out the news items for the week's show. Sitting with them are the script editors, Ian Davidson and Peter Vincent.

The scene is a rehearsal room high up in the BBC rehearsal block in Acton. The wind is howling and the building is swaying slightly. Apparently this is as it should be and is in fact a safety feature.

There are lines of tape all over the floor. These represent the walls, doors, stairs, etc. of the sets for the various sketches in the show. This is where the rehearsals will take place. They are not taking place at the moment.

It's later in the week. Outside, traffic is snaking slowly along the A40. Inside, the Two Ronnies are at work. Or are we? We're sitting at a table, looking quite serious. In front of us are lots of little cards. Some of the cards are pink, some green, some yellow. We are moving the cards around. Are we playing some kind of game? No, we're beginning to assemble the finished shows, ready for transmission.

There are still lines of tape all over the floor. This is where the rehearsals will take place. They are not taking place at the moment.

The truth is, you see, that the thing Ronnie and I disliked most about rehearsals was the rehearsing. We loved the rest of it.

We loved playing with our little cards of various colours. They were index cards. They represented the various items in the show, pink would be my chair spot, green would be Ronnie's lecture item, yellow would be the musical finale, etc.

We were in a powerful enough position at the BBC, or far-sighted enough, or both, to have insisted that all eight shows were recorded before any of them went out, so we did not need to compose any of the finished shows until we had recorded all of them. So by the time we had completed a few of the rehearsals, we were able to move items around in order to create the actual shows that the public would see. We would say, 'Now this sketch doesn't quite go with that sketch as we're cockneys in both, so we'd better move that one out and replace it with that one in which you're a Scotsman and I'm an American.' That sort of thing. We fiddled around until we got the balance absolutely right. It was an ongoing process, and we would do all these ongoing processes rather than get to our feet and rehearse. We were quite loth to do that.

The truth was that we didn't need to rehearse very much. We were very quick learners and the actual mechanism and the putting together of the shows took precedence over the rehearsing. When at last we did rehearse we would decide that we would learn, say, three sketches on a particular night, and the next day we would come in and we would know these three sketches. There was no question of one of us saying, 'I stopped at the Beehive on the way home, had a few jars, then watched the football match and, bugger me, I wasn't in bed till one.' We were totally professional. We relied on each other and we trusted each other. We both also felt that you can rehearse comedy too much. You can rehearse all the fun out of it. You can stop finding it funny and add new bits to keep it fresh. They seem funnier because they're new, but in fact they spoil the thing.

The only snag, I always felt, was with visiting guests, whose roles would never be big, but despite that they might still be worrying about it and nervous. Our method meant that they wouldn't get as much chance as they might have liked to go over it again and again. We'd probably rehearse it four times on a Wednesday, and twice on a Friday and once on the Saturday, and then on the Sunday night we would do it.

Busy actors would welcome our light schedule, but it's an overcrowded profession, and occasionally we might have somebody in a sketch, somebody really good whose first job this was for months. If at half past eleven they were suddenly told, 'Right, that's it, you can go. See you ten-thirty to-morrow', they were really disappointed. They had hoped at least to hang on till lunchtime, go up to the canteen on the top floor, maybe meet a few old chums, be a part of it all for a few moments, but no, they were in the tube train returning to their silent home where the phone never rang. Not many directors understand this.

Towards the end of the week's rehearsals, shows have a 'technical run'. The representatives of the various departments – camera, lighting, wardrobe, make-up – watch a rehearsal, discuss with the director what he needs and chat to the actors about costumes.

We didn't really need to rehearse the items that were done straight to camera – the news items and our two solo spots. And the serial was already safely in the can. So the only items that really needed to be rehearsed were the sketches and the musical finales.

As I've said, our particular contribution to the sketch genre was the party sketch. These would usually come immediately after the opening news items. It was good to get straight into the party mood.

Peter Vincent, son of an air vice-marshal, was a prolific writer of party sketches. There was the two-man party with the very mean host and only one guest, and he was a gate-crasher. 'One tiny niggle, Wilfred. You are rather wearing out the carpet. Would you mind awfully standing on one leg?' There was the party in wife-swapping circles, car-keys-in-the-middle-of-the-floor territory. 'I've been hearing a lot about you. Still, I don't believe a word of it.'

Most of the party sketches were two-handers, but 'Party Names' involved quite a crowd, as new arrivals poured in, and the host's efforts to remember all their names foundered, despite his little efforts at helpful mnemonics. For instance, in the gathering chaos Alison Pinrut – that's turnip backwards – becomes Alison Pinsrap – that's parsnip backwards.

There was one very curious incident regarding this sketch. Early on in the piece a man is introduced as Neil – Lien backwards, which sounds like 'Lean backwards' – and the party guests all say, 'Oh, all right,' and lean backwards, then realize their mistake, and laugh. Well, somewhat amazingly, this sketch was bought by Swedish television and recorded in Swedish. A copy of the sketch, in Swedish, was sent over, and one has to say it does lose a little in the translation. However, this might be due to the fact that not one single member of the whole production team spoke even one word of Swedish – what a condemnation of British education. The extraordinary point is that at the moment when, in the English sketch, everybody leant backwards, exactly the same thing happens in the Swedish sketch: all the Swedish actors lean backwards. So what we've always wondered, for all these years, is, 'How on earth can the joke "Lean backwards. Oh, all right" work in Swedish?' Answers, please, on a postcard, in Swedish.

Another of our party sketches made physical demands on us of the kind that usually only affect synchronized swimmers. We played two total strangers wearing identical ghastly check jackets and uttering identical social chit-chat simultaneously. That isn't easy, not at all, and it just wouldn't be funny unless it was done perfectly. Well, we soon fell into a perfect rhythm, but there was one very awkward moment, when we both paused for quite a long while, as if to get rid of this infernal curse of saying everything at once, and then of course we started off again at exactly the same time. And it had to be *exactly* the same time, or the moment would be ruined. Well, Ronnie could always be trusted to come up with something in situations like that. Out of sight of the camera, he placed his left foot just next to my right foot, we paused, he touched my foot with his, and off we went again, to the end, where we walked away from each other, both muttering in unison, 'Frightful bore.'

Sometimes our sketches involved amazingly unlikely premises, as in another party sketch, called 'Repeats'. This had me playing a man who has a compulsion to repeat what the other person has said. He does this three times, then doesn't do it for one reply, then does it three times again. Likely? No. Funny? Yes. The sketch is really geared to play on our particular strengths, Ronnie's amazing verbal dexterity and my sense of timing.

Ronnie's character suspected that my character was making a fool of him deliberately, that I was being a fraud, so after a few examples of my repeating everything three times and then not repeating one thing, he set my character a little test. He said, 'I'll fox you. To escort an orang-utan from

Baden-Baden to Wagga Wagga via Addis Ababa or vice versa is enough to make a Ghurka Sherpa commit hara-kiri.'

I repeated it perfectly.

Now he tested me rather more severely, his third remark being 'Rumanian Dalmatians hate Tasmanian Alsatians and Tasmanian Dalmatians hate Rumanian Alsatians. Tasmanian Alsatians hate Rumanian Dalmatians but Rumanian Alsatians like Tasmanian Dalmatians. Tasmanian Alsatians hate Ruman-ian Alsatians. So Tasmanian Alsatians hate Rumanian Alsatians and Dalmatians but Rumanian Alsatians don't hate Tasmanian Dalmatians or Alsatians.'

It was clearly impossible for me to repeat all this. I was caught.

'Sometimes I only repeat things twice,' I said, after a pause.

That pause had to be of exactly the right length. Nobody can tell you how long it should be, it's all down to instinct, and truth. Even in a sketch as bizarre as that, one needs to play the characters utterly truthfully.

I needed to call on all my experience in a very funny sketch written by John '*Only Fools and Horses*' Sullivan. I told Ronnie B. that I had bought a racing pigeon that was going to earn me a fortune in bets. I showed it to him, plonking its cage on the table. In the cage was a beautiful male mallard. He was also a perfectly trained mallard. He understood that it was important, for the comedy, that he remain deadpan. It would also be much funnier if he didn't move at all, since I was intending to race him. He needed to be a lazy, inert duck. He did it brilliantly. This was no ordinary duck. This was the Buster Keaton of the duck world.

We were into a routine then, with Ronnie insisting it was a duck and me maintaining, increasingly desperately, that it was a pigeon.

Eventually, Ronnie asked me if it had a name.

'Yes,' I admitted cautiously.

'What is his name?'

I paused. I didn't want to admit this. My little world was collapsing around me.

'Donald.'

I think it's one of the funniest lines ever written. But again, the pause had to be just right, and truthful.

I would like to quote one of our sketches in full, so that you will get the full picture of their character. It was a sketch called 'Hello', and it was written by Michael Palin and Terry Jones.

Party music.
Ronnie Barker standing with a drink. Ronnie Corbett comes up to him.
RC: Hello.
RB: I'm sorry?
RC: I just said, 'hello'.
RB: Sorry? Sorry? I didn't catch it again.
RC: Hello.
RB: What?
RC: Hello!
RB: And?
RC: And what?
RB: And what else did you say besides 'hello'?
RC: I didn't say anything else. I just said 'hello'.
RB: Not 'Hello, you boring old git, who the hell invited you?'
RC: No, I didn't say that.
RB: Oh! I don't mean those exact words . . . I was only using them as an example . . . It might have been more on the lines of 'Hello, you fat, ugly, mealy-mouthed sadist, I wish you were dead.'
RC: No, I didn't say anything apart from 'hello'.
RB: Huh! I've only got your word for it.

RC: Look . . . I was over the other side of the room, I saw nobody was talking to you, and I thought I'd just come over and say 'hello'.

RB: I never did!

RC: What?

RB: You implied that Dorothy and I were having a relationship.

RC: When?

RB: Just then! All that stuff about my car not being in the garage.

RC: I didn't say anything about your car.

RB: Oh no . . . but you *implied* it.

RC: All I said was 'hello'.

RB: Oh yes, but look at the way you said it!

RC: What?

RB: You said it in that 'Hello! His-car-wasn't-in-the-garage-at-11.30-and-he-left-the-light-on-in-the-study-to-make-the-wife-think-he-was-working-late' kind of way.

RC: It wasn't meant to sound like that. It was just a 'Hello, how are you?'

RB: Oh, I see! 'Hello-how-are-you . . . going-to-explain-the-hotpants-in-the-glove-compartment-when-the-wife-gives-the-vicar-a-lift-on-Sunday?'

RC: It was only 'hello'.

RB: Listen, sonny, if you go around talking to everybody the way you've been talking to me, I'm not surprised you haven't any friends.

RC: I've got lots of friends.

RB: Oh yes . . . but they all ran out on you, and you had to come over and pick on me to heap abuse on!

RC: I only said 'hello'.

RB: I mean, how was I to know it was loaded?

RC: What?

RB: The gun! The gun you said.

RC: I said 'hello'.

RB: Anyway, I was going to throw it away and never use it . . . it was Dorothy who wanted to have a look down the barrel and see how fast the bullets came out.

RC: I just said 'hello'.

RB: I tried to stop her . . . But before I could, she'd pulled the trigger, jumped out of the car and buried herself under a bush on a lonely stretch of the A47 outside Stafford.

RC: I was only using the word 'hello' to start a little conv . . .

RB: And now I come to think of it, I was in Glasgow at the time in any case – no, Frankfurt! . . . No! Even further away . . . er . . . Istanbul: I was in a cellar – chained – all by myself . . . (*Pause*) except for the witnesses . . . lots of witnesses . . . Turks . . . but they *write* in English . . . *They*'d testify . . . you could write to them . . . unless they're dead . . . oh, come to think of it, I think they are dead! Yes, I think I read about them being dead . . . pity . . . You've got to believe me! You've got to!

RC: (*Embarrassed*) I only came up to him and said 'hello'.

RB: In any case I didn't mean to . . . but she kept on about the money and the divorce and the gambling and the bad breath . . . I just *had* to. (*His voice rising to a crescendo*) All right, I've been a fool! A bloody fool! I admit it!

RC: A perfectly ordinary 'hello'.

RB: (*A manic glint in his eye*) But you'll never take me alive!

He whips out a phial, tears off the top with his teeth and slips it in his martini and swigs it down, dying with many contortions and assorted terrible death convulsions. At last he lies dead at RC's feet. RC looks over him anxiously.

RC: Hello? (*Cautiously*) Hello? Hellooo? (*No reaction . . . RC stands up*) Tut tut! . . . Can't have a decent conversation with anyone nowadays . . .

Pull out fast to reveal RC standing alone amidst a room full of dead guests. All have glasses, some are draped over tables, most are on the floor.

Frost on Sunday panto, 1969.

Under the covers with the lovely Josephine Tewson.

Undressing for dinner.

Getting into a bit of a fix.

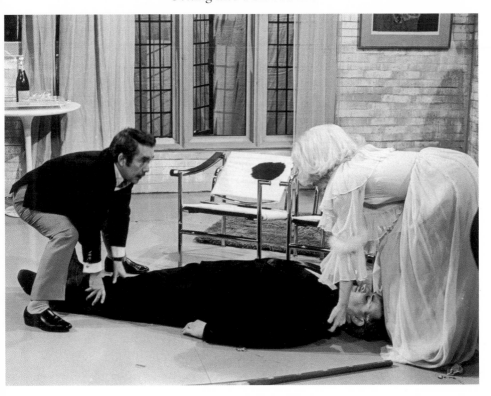

Some classic party sketches . . .

We spent a lot of
time in the pub.

I must have said
something rather
funny – I hope!

A common market.

Defending our
country.

Ronnie Barker as Queen Victoria and me as her dutiful friend and servant
John Brown.

RC starts to pick his way through them, picking up the odd head with his foot, saying 'hello' hopefully and letting it drop again. Fade.

That sketch shows how we could begin from a very mundane premise, a man saying 'hello' at a party, and end up with the most fantastic conclusion. It also shows the strength of our working relationship. I didn't say, 'Hang on a minute. Ron has all the funny lines. All I seem to say is "Hello!" and "What?"'

Later I'll quote a sketch, one of our best-remembered, in which I have all the funny lines. And I'll also come to the most famous sketch we ever did, but it's time to get back to the subject of rehearsals. I mentioned that in *Twang* I was directed by the legendary Joan Littlewood. Well, in *Irma La Douce*, Ronnie was directed by the even more legendary Peter Brook. Neither experience proved happy.

Twang proved unhappy because it was such a failure, and the fact that the failure proved lucky for me did little to diminish the pain of being part of it. *Irma La Douce* proved unhappy for Ron because it was such a success. He had to stay in it for two years – people were forced to stay in long-running shows in those days – and it drove him up the wall. But they both proved unhappy because we neither of us really got on with the two legends. I suspect that a lot of it was due to this business of rehearsal. Both Littlewood and Brook believed that rehearsal was a period of discovery. I have to say that they both seemed to think that, the more painful the discovery, the more rewarding it was.

Ronnie and I weren't right for this at all. We understood what our part entailed very quickly, we learnt it very quickly, we found we could do it without searching into the depths of our past and our motivation. I think Joan and Peter thought all this was very shallow, but I do believe, on the whole, that we were just as good as the people who were more at ease looking into the murky depths.

The rehearsals are finished. We are as ready as we will ever be. It's time to move into the studio for the actual recording.

The shows were recorded in front of a studio audience on Sunday evenings at the BBC Television Centre in Wood Lane, London. The main part of the building is entirely round, with a continuous round corridor on every floor, and until you get fully used to it, you tend to find that you are making the wrong decision as to which way to turn. You find yourself doing 83 per cent of the circle, when you only needed to do 17 per cent. There is a rather dispiriting air in these endless corridors, but that is gone the moment you step into the studios. They are huge, and hanging from the high ceilings are vast amounts of technical equipment.

On the Saturday evening, we would record the musical finale of that week's show, without an audience. This was because it was often a very elaborate set-up with a large chorus, but mainly because there just wouldn't have been any room for the set in the studio. These items took up a great deal of space.

Although there was no audience there on the Saturday, we would still feel an inextricable mixture of excitement and nerves as we began the show. Seeing the set that had been built in some warehouse by unknown people, we suddenly thought, 'My goodness. All this stuff we've had in our heads, it's real.' Of course we grew less nervous as series succeeded series, but we never lost that feeling entirely. You can't perform successfully without it. It's what keeps you up to the mark.

Dick Vosburgh created quite a few of our musical finales

over the years. Among the earliest was a follow-up to his Sousa marches sketch. This time it featured Julius Caesar to the music of Strauss. He also wrote, with Bill Solly, a parody of Gilbert and Sullivan and a piece entitled 'The Short and Fat Minstrel Show'. Dick and Bill had intended them to be short and fat instead of blacked up, but we did it blacked up, so if we did it now we'd upset societies for the short, the fat and the black, though I have no doubt that most short, fat blacks would still find it funny.

Many of our musical items involved us being members of a chorus, backed by quite a large group of singers and dancers, usually including several attractive young ladies. There was a sense of opulence about these items.

One week we were two members of a pipe band, singing to the tunes of 'Amazing Grace', 'The Bonnie Bonnie Banks of Loch Lomond', 'Blue Bells of Scotland', 'Over the Sea to Skye' and the 'Ball of Kirriemuir'.

Another time we were an Irish folk group, Peter Cutter and the Boggers. Ronnie was the violinist. I was the guitarist and clog dancer.

'Twas on a Monday morning, in the middle of the night
I dreamt that I had woken up, it gave me such a fright.
I thought I'd got insomnia, it nearly made me weep.
But luckily, when I woke up, I found I was asleep.
Etc.

If you haven't seen me clog dancing, I'm sorry to say that you just haven't really lived.

We couldn't leave the Welsh out: they're very sensitive, always on the lookout for a sight of the slightest slight. This time we sang to 'Sospan Fach', 'All Through the Night', 'The Ash Grove', 'Men of Harlech' and 'Land of my Fathers'.

As a couple of Welsh miners.

Marvellous. Enough emotion to raise the roof of a Millennium Stadium.

We were rarely impressionists, although Ronnie did think highly of his Patrick Moore, but then Patrick Moore always looks like a man doing an impression of someone even more eccentric than him and slightly overdoing it. And when we played two burglars once, we played them, just for the hell of it, as John Gielgud and Noël Coward. Nobody noticed, which may be why we only did it once.

We did occasionally, though, venture into caricature, and that gave rise to one of our funniest finales, with Ronnie as

Nana Moussaka and me as Charles Azenough. You see what I mean about drag. He was Nana and I was Charles.

Then there was the women's guild choir, all fa la la and including the following lovely lines, to the tune of 'Nymphs and Shepherds':

> Cynthia Shepherd's gone away.
> Where's she gone?
> Her mother won't say.

Particularly popular was Ronnie's take on 'Bold Sir John', sung by the two of us with quite a large chorus and a tenor soloist with a high-pitched voice. We were all dressed as folk singers who took ourselves terribly seriously. It contained some classic Barker word play. One verse will give you the feel of the thing.

ALL: Now bold Sir John he met a maid
As on her back she lay.

SOLOIST: Please show respect, and come not near
For I've seen many a maiden here
Get lost among the new-mown hay
So doff your hat, I pray.

RC: Get lost

RB: Get lost

ALL: Get lost
Get lost
Get lost among the new-mown hay:

RC: Sod off

RB: Sod off

ALL: Sod off
Sod off
So doff your hat, I pray.

Throw in a brass band, a pinch of Hinge and Bracket, add some pearly kings and a load of Cossacks and you've got a picture of some of the variety of cheery parodies that regularly brought our ninety-seven shows to what I hope was a rousing finale. Recording them certainly cheered up our Saturday nights.

After the recording, we might go to the BBC Club for a drink and a chat. After all, the Television Centre was becoming a kind of second home for us. The club was on the second floor, probably still is, and it was a large, airy place to which all the staff belonged. Members could sign guests in, and it was a pleasant way to unwind.

However, it is not for nothing that some people dub the

Me and Ron about to burst into song in a sketch called 'Ball and Socket'
(our version of Hinge and Bracket), from the Saturday night show.

BBC the British Bureaucracy Cock-up, and poor Ronnie B. fell foul of this. He was refused membership of the club. Why was he refused membership? Goodness knows.

Was Ronnie downhearted? Not in the least. He just gate-crashed. But, being Ronnie, he didn't leave it there. He added a flourish. He took guests along and signed them in. 'Just signing my guests in,' he'd say, and it would all be written down in a book. Nobody ever refused him. In fact he even got to the stage of signing in people who worked full-time for the BBC. Ronnie loved to get away with harmless deceptions like that. It was rather like a minor version of the Gerald Wiley story.

By the time we arrived on the Sunday morning, the sets were just about up, and there was anticipation and a touch of tension in the air, even more so than on the previous day. The realization that people had been working through the night, bringing in through the huge doors of the studio all the sets and scenery that people had been building for days in some workshop, gave us a sudden feeling of responsibility, a sense that this wasn't just comedy, it was a grown-up commercial enterprise.

When we arrived on the Sunday morning the sets would usually still be looking rather bare, but steadily throughout the day they would be dressed with all the fine detail that can make all the difference. I always felt it to be important that the set looked absolutely real. If it was a sketch set in a doctor's surgery, it needed to look exactly like a doctor's surgery in real life.

A man called Bobby Warans was the buyer for all our *Two Ronnies* series, and he was brilliant. I mentioned the spectacular rubber crocodile that we used in *The Admirable Crichton*. He would have had no trouble with that. He was never fazed. If you asked him for a chocolate bowler hat, he'd say, 'Plain or milk?' without turning a hair.

The studio rehearsal began at about half past ten, and the rest of the day till mid-afternoon would be a struggle, as the director attempted to get the best results on camera. He would have written what's called a camera script, which stated which of the five cameras would be filming what at any given time, but these never proved easy to follow in practice, and we would stop and start in the most painful manner. You just had to be patient, go through the motions and switch off while the technicians struggled. You had to remind yourself that some of the best technicians in the world were busting a gut to get the best results for your show. There were occasional moments of difficulties with the unions, moments when there was resentment of some matter that was nothing to do with us, but in my experience they were far outweighed by all the quiet and generous support that we regularly received.

Then there would be a dress rehearsal. This is the moment to pay tribute to Mary Husband, who created all our costumes and did so with unfailing brilliance. It was quite a challenge too, with the variety of roles we played, especially in the serials and the musical finales, but she never let us down. We used to get a lot of our clothes, including all our jackets for the news items, from a tailor in Fulham called Dimi Major, who I believe was Ukrainian.

Ron and I were lucky to have the same dressers for long periods. I was dressed by Dennis Adoo for the whole of the run of all the series, and Ronnie was dressed by Derek Sumner, an ex-actor, until his untimely death. They were two splendid men who would do all sorts of things for us, without complaint, including, as I mentioned earlier, getting our lunches on location. They were very very helpful, supportive, sweet and kind. They were great fans of the business, and they knew the business thoroughly. My Dennis had been a professional ice skater. They became good friends. They knew our foibles and what to talk about and what not to talk about. All this was invaluable, especially on recording days, when people would get tense and excited and nervous, and everything had to be done fast yet calmly. We were very lucky.

There were always a few people watching the dress

rehearsal, but it didn't do to take much notice of their laughter, as they would not be at all typical of the sort of people who would be in the audience that night. There would be an anthology of writers, or whatever the collective term should be – a gaggle, I suppose, for comedy writers – and there would often be a small group of people who didn't crack the faintest smile even once throughout the whole rehearsal. There was no need for us to panic, however. They might well be a delegation of Bolivian lighting engineers who were being given a tour of the studios and who didn't speak a word of English.

After the dress rehearsal, the director would come down from his control box to give us notes – usually there wouldn't be a need for many, as it was such a well-drilled operation. There was still about an hour and a half before the show, and people would go off to relax in whatever way they found best. Ron and I both went to our rooms for a few moments of peace and quiet; it was important to us to remain focused. We would both have a light snack, mine, I suspect, being lighter than his.

Between seven and seven thirty, the audience would file into their seats, and an atmosphere of anticipation would build. We would be feeling the tension. When we did our very first show, we were probably just a bit too tense, but from that moment onwards, while we still felt that tightening of the nerves, that sinking feeling in the stomach, it was never to a destructive level. In fact you had to feel it. Once you lost that tension, you would lose all your sharpness, all your adrenalin, all your style and energy. It comes with the territory, as the Americans say. But we were helped, of course, by the fact that we had prepared so thoroughly and so professionally.

Some of you, as you read this, will be remembering your

visit to a studio audience for a TV show, but the majority of you won't. That is a certainty, because the number of people in an audience is not much more than 200, and the shows were regularly watched by audiences not far short of twenty million.

It is a very strange business, doing a show live to just over 200 people, when the real targets of the programme are the millions of viewers around the country and indeed around the world. You have to play the humour for the viewers, who will be seeing everything in relative close-up, but if you have a live audience to laugh at you, you must get their laughs, so you must do the comedy with enough vigour and panache to reach out to an audience who are quite a long way from you and are watching you through a forest of cameras and lights. And the cameras are moving around all the time, distracting them. You are helped by the fact that there are a few TV monitors situated in strategic places above the audience's heads. ('What did you think of the show?' 'It was over my head.')

But, although the audience are getting a free show, they aren't going to be terribly happy if they just sit and watch it on the monitors. They might think that it hadn't been worth coming, they might as well be at home. We took great pains to make sure that they wouldn't feel like that. We gave them a proper show.

For variety shows like ours, there isn't much argument about having a studio audience – you need it. But Ron and I both also did our situation comedies with an audience; and I think we both felt that the knowledge that it would be played to a live audience sharpened us up, and the writers too. It had to be really funny. Smiles don't register on a sound track.

Most people believe that a great deal of canned laughter

is used in TV comedy. This is not so, in our experience, and I am quite certain that, in this country, canned laughter is used extremely rarely, if at all. Just occasionally, if a retake is needed, and if there isn't quite as much laughter on the second take, the editors might take the laughter off the first take, but it is still a genuine laugh, at that particular joke, by that particular audience, so I don't think that can be regarded as cheating. In fact the reason why people suspect that there is a lot of canned laughter is probably because the end of the laugh sometimes has to be removed in the editing, because it simply went on too long – if it was allowed its full course it would make the show too slow at home – so the laugh is suddenly cut off in a way that doesn't sound quite natural.

Nor do fierce men hold up boards saying, 'Laugh'. They will give a cue for applause, so that everybody claps at the same time, but there aren't any dreadful devices in the seats to give the audience electric shocks if they don't laugh.

In America it was very different. On our way to Australia, in the late seventies, Ronnie and I once stopped off to do a show in LA. It was called *The Big Show*, and was intended to be a huge spectacular series on three elements: ice, water and the stage. It was hosted by the great Victor Borge, creator of the wonderful line 'My uncle was a doctor, and he was very clever. In fact he invented a cure for which there was no disease.' Loretta Swit, Hotlips of *M.A.S.H.*, was on the bill, and Ronnie prostrated himself and kissed her feet, much to the audience's approval.

But that was the problem. There were very few people in the audience. They let people into the studio at seven, and by the time we went on to do our piece it was past midnight. The audience were free to come and go, slip outside for a meal, and at that late hour, not surprisingly, the place was almost deserted. There were hardly any laughs, and Ronnie and I were a bit depressed.

'Don't worry,' said the producer. 'There'll be plenty of laughs when it's transmitted.'

And there were. They had a machine like a synthesizer, only it played laughter and applause rather than music. The man who played it was a virtuoso, and told us that the laughter tracks were so old that half the people laughing must be dead.

If the show had caught on, things might have been very different, and we might have spent much more time in America, but it didn't catch on, and I must say that didn't really bother us. I don't think either of us fancied a long stint there.

As I say, we took good care of our live audience. We took great pains over the warm-up, which precedes all studio shows and gets the audience in the right mood.

The warm-up was started by an actor called Felix Bowness, whom you'll know best as playing the jockey in *Hi-de-Hi!* He was funny and sweet, and he was lovely because he was funny in an old-fashioned, kind of slightly naughty, camp way, and he mingled with the audience: he used to go up the aisles, he was sort of tactile with people, and quite confident with the audience, and he created a lovely rapport with them. I can't resist telling you that Felix called his house Strugglin'. I haven't seen him for a while now, so maybe he's retired and moved to another house, Dunwarmin'.

Next, our producer would go on. Usually nowadays there are credits for the producer and director, but at that time the word 'producer' covered both. Our first producer was Terry Hughes. He represented the handsome face of the BBC. He was always smiling. One of our writers once described him as a smile on legs. I think sometimes people were suspicious of him, when they first met him, because of all the smiling (are you reading this, Mr Blair?), but as you grew to know him, you realized that Terry's smile wasn't concealing anything. He was a clever, good-looking man who was producing, and producing extremely well, a very successful television show. Why should he not smile? He had plenty to smile about. We both got on very well with Terry; we would have dinner with him frequently when we were on location. He would be involved with us in the selection of the material and he was an extremely good judge of material.

Terry would talk to the audience very pleasantly, very fluently, very charmingly, not putting a foot wrong, and, in the audience, Anne would be counting silently to herself. We would invite various friends to the show, and Anne was counting up to the moment when our guest that week, whether male or female, would turn to her and whisper, 'Who's that lovely man?' They always asked the question before she had counted to ten.

After Terry, I would go on. I would do four or five minutes of patter, the same each week, I have to say, and there in the audience would be our dear wives, and Joy and Anne would laugh heartily, right to the end, at jokes they had heard eighty-eight times before. Occasionally, if there were any problems with the microphones, they would call out, 'Can't hear,' and the rest of the audience would wonder who those bossy women were.

My final joke, when I introduced Ronnie, would always be, 'Well you've seen me, looking like a Greek god. Now for a man who looks like a Greek restaurant.' Latterly, I had to alter my introduction, because Ron had become so slim, but you can't waste a good laugh, so I'd say, 'I used to say . . .' and do the Greek restaurant gag, and then I'd use a little joke that I sometimes use for myself in my act: 'But nowadays he's much trimmer because he's invested in a little treadmill he's got at home – he's only doing widths at the moment.'

Then Ronnie would come on, and do a short routine in the manner of McGill and the postcards. He would say to the audience, 'I've got three questions here. I'll read them out to you, and then I'll count three, two, one, and you all shout out the answer and we'll see how it goes. What are all men who mend shoes called? Three, two, one . . .'

'Cobblers,' shouted the audience.

'If doors don't have bells, what will they have? Three, two, one . . .'

'Knockers.'

'If a farmer has sheep, cows and bullocks on his farm, and the sheep and cows die, what would he have left?'

'Bullocks.'

Simple stuff, but brilliant in the context. Here was Ronnie, uneasy at making jokes to an audience, so what did he do? Gave the audience the tag. It let him off the hook and gave the audience a warm feeling of being part of the show.

We now moved seamlessly into the show itself, and here again we were very thorough. We worked out the running order in such a way that there would be the minimum of gaps, and we had material, like a sketch from the previous week's show, to keep the audience entertained if there should be a gap.

Nevertheless, things sometimes did go wrong, but you could use this to keep the audience on your side. In fact, one of Britain's most famous practitioners of situation comedy, Leonard Rossiter, always made a deliberate mistake early in his shows. He would deliberately fluff a line. Round about the third or fourth line that he had, he would make his mistake, and then he would curse, and everyone would laugh, and he'd say, 'Now we've got to go right back to the beginning,' and he would go backwards very fast as if rewinding himself, and there would be a great round of applause from an audience who believed that they were seeing a spontaneous reaction and had no idea that it was a little routine done each week. Now the audience relaxed and thought, 'They're human, they're like us,' and the laughs came much more quickly.

With our detailed warm-up, and the fact that our first jokes were the news items, we didn't feel that we needed anything like that, but when things went wrong, Ronnie would be very good with the audience, much better than he ever gave himself credit for – he would be very funny ad-libbing. If I said something slightly funny, by accident, he would say something funnier, as if by accident. But he wasn't confident that he could do that, so when he went on *Wogan*, or something like that, he used to hate it, although he was much better equipped for it than he ever allowed himself to believe.

I think that this was all because there is something very, very important in your early years of development in the business, in the theatre. Your early experiences are critical, and if you've been somebody who always had to learn the text verbatim of a Shaw play or Shakespeare or any of the classic roles in rep, you're not comfortable leaving the text and you don't have that sort of confidence. If you're somebody who's been in a sort of revue and night club like me, making little bits up every now and again, you're a little bit more confident. If you're somebody like Tarbuck, who's worked in Butlins from the age of about seventeen, you're very confident with fresh words, but not so confident with a script.

Anyway, we got through these moments pretty well, and I think that our studio audience would have to say that they had been given non-stop entertainment.

At the end we would take care to thank them, to make them feel that we hadn't just forgotten them now that we'd used them, and we would end with a little joke, the same every week: 'If you've enjoyed the show, tell your friends. If you haven't, don't forget, our names are Little and Large.'

Everywhere, in the control box, in the dressing rooms and the make-up suite, the tension would subside. Mary Husband always had a glass of his favourite Fleurie ready for Ronnie. 'It didn't touch the sides,' he would say of it.

After the studio shows, on the Sunday evenings, we didn't go to the club. We had a little party. We used to get three dressing rooms, one for Ronnie B., one for me, and one in the middle for Gerald Wiley. In this middle room we would host a small gathering, at which wives, guests, producers and some of the writers would chat over red and white wine, gin and tonic, beer and salted nuts.

Another person to help us substantially over our long careers – my goodness, how we've been helped – was a man called Ron Waverley. It was Ron who brought in the drinks in an 'Esky', and it was Ron who dispensed them. Ron came from Kelso in the Borders, but it wasn't in Scotland that I met him. I met him in pantomime in Bristol.

One particular year, fairly early in my television career, I was offered pantomimes in Manchester and Bristol. I chose Bristol because, as I said to Anne, 'You never know. Cary Grant might visit his mother in Bristol and pop in to see the show.' Ha very ha. Cary Grant had been born, named Archie Leach, in Bristol, and his mother still lived there. But, lo and behold, he did see the show and he popped round afterwards in his black and white Glen Urquhart tweed and his tortoiseshell glasses, accepted a gin and tonic, said he'd enjoyed the show and told me there had once been plans for him and Fred Astaire to play the Ugly Sisters, with Mickey Rooney as Buttons. Now that would have been something.

In our pantomime the Ugly Sisters were played by John Inman and Barry Howard. Later John Inman went for auditions for *Are You Being Served?*, and Barry Howard landed the part of the ballroom dancing instructor in *Hi-de-Hi!* So things would soon look up for both John and Barry.

Would things look up for Ron Waverley? He was a member of the chorus in the pantomime, and very Scottish. His real name was Ron Elms, and he changed it to Waverley because of the Walter Scott novels. He had a great phrase about people who came in from the country to see the shows. He said they were 'fresh in frae' fair oot'. His mum had been a nanny for the Duke of Roxburghe, and he was very proud of the fact that he had sung in the choir for the Duke's son's christening.

Ron's career wasn't really taking off, and he was contemplating giving showbiz up before it gave him up. Knowing this, and knowing that he was besotted with cars, I asked him if he would like to come and work for me, doing the mail and the driving and so on. And he did. Eventually he left, and I got somebody else, but during the run at the Palladium Ronnie B. began to think that it would be a good idea to have somebody to drive him around, and Ron came back to work for Ron. This is getting to sound like the three Ronnies. Ron was a deeply unassuming man, as opposed to a deeply unamusing man, of which I've met several.

If Ron had a catchphrase, it was, 'It's all right. It's only me.' That was what he would always say when he gave his diffident little knock on the door. He became far more than a driver cum dresser cum dispenser of drinks. He was a slim, rather attractive boy, and after he worked for Ronnie we saw a lot of him – he became a great family friend, and a friend of the girls. His home was in Eastbourne. I'm pretty sure he was gay, but he married a very rich Moroccan lady who'd had a baby by a Moroccan aristocrat who wasn't going to marry her, so Ron married her to make the baby legal, although they never lived together. They became dear friends, and she bought him a big second-hand Cadillac, so it was all rather lovely, as it benefited them both and they were very sweet to each other. He died, sadly, of cancer, much too young. When he was buried, at Eastbourne, Anne and I went down to the service. A friend of his had arranged a little table in his memory, with a picture of his Alsatian dog in Kelso and of the three cars that he'd owned in his life. It was rather a sad little memorial for a kind man.

After the party, Ron and I, with Joy and Anne, had another final unvarying routine. The four of us went off to an Indian restaurant in Westbourne Grove. In the very early days we would invite friends to come with us, but by the end of such a long day we found that we were really too tired to have to keep up the social chit-chat, and just the four of us used to go. It was always the same restaurant. We all got on so well. Joy and Anne had become firm friends, in a friendship that underpinned my friendship with Ron. We were so relaxed together, the four of us, sitting undisturbed with our curries. It was a great way to end a great day, and if Ron and I were too exhausted to make much conversation, nobody would have noticed. Anne and Joy could talk for Britain.

It was always the same restaurant, the Star of India. And it was a very comfortable place to be. The star in the name outside the restaurant wasn't a word, it was a star. It wasn't very brightly illuminated, and on our first visit Anne didn't notice it and said, ' "Of India". That's a funny name for a restaurant.'

It was always the same restaurant, but we didn't always order exactly the same food, of course. What do you think we were, creatures of habit?

12

Fun and fear – you need a bit of both, in comedy, and we had a touch of both with *The Two Ronnies* in the early seventies.

The fun came on the way back from Montreux. We had gone there because *The Two Ronnies* was up for the Golden Rose award. This time, unlike on *Frost Over England*, we were the stars of the show, and it was we who went.

I have to say that the visit did not go quite as we had anticipated in our dreams.

In the first place, we travelled out there economy class. I hope that our relatively humble beginnings and the fundamental decency of our families had ensured that we never became utterly spoilt, but we were pulling in audiences not far short of twenty million, we were up for a prestigious award and we did think the BBC just might have managed to be a bit more generous.

Never mind, we thought. They're sure to upgrade us when we win.

That was the second disappointment. We didn't win. We came second. I'm not a petty man, but, honestly, who were those judges? I jest. We were beaten not by some German sketch show or arty compilation by men of French letters, but by our very own Stanley Baxter, with whom we had both worked, I in pantomime in Glasgow, Ronnie in the revue *On the Brighter Side*. Stanley was brilliant, and we couldn't possibly resent his success. Besides, it was a great one and two for Britain, confirming that comedy was one of the increasingly few things in which Britain still led the rest of Europe.

In the evening the BBC took us up to a little restaurant in the mountains for dinner with some of Britain's best-known television journalists. Surely if you do that you are embarking on a good-will public-relations mission? We couldn't believe what happened at the end of the meal. The BBC asked the journalists to chip in for their share of the bill. It was one of the most embarrassing moments of my life. We joke about the meanness of the BBC, the awfulness of the canteen, etc., but that is really just a joke, an abiding tradition of BBC comedy. Only this wasn't a joke, it was real. It angered me, and I had a right old go at them later – not in front of the journalists, of course.

We were in economy class again on the way home, though Stanley was in first class. We were, I admit, in the first row behind the curtain, so I suppose we were spoilt a little bit, but still. Michael Grade and Cyril Bennett were in first class, and we were sitting there, good boys, not complaining, taking our punishment for only getting the silver, when a note was brought from Michael Grade in first class, and the little note said, 'Out front and loving it.' We had to laugh.

I've mentioned that we weren't the sort of comic actors who had everybody in stitches all the time. In fact I can only remember one occasion when we did, and it was at the end of this same trip. We arrived at the airport and filed down the gangway on to the tarmac, where one of those long, bendy airport buses was waiting to take us on the five-and-a-half-mile journey to the terminal. The bus was filling up as we approached with our hand luggage. Ronnie just managed to step on, but just as I was about to step on the doors closed right in my face, practically slicing off my nose and, incidentally, curing my deviated septum. Well, everybody fell about. The timing was absolutely perfect, and the 120 or so people on the bus thought they'd seen the best comic moment of their lives; they thought we'd done it deliberately, with brilliant, split-second timing. They must have thought we did that sort of thing all the time. We often thought of everyone going off to their homes all over the country saying, 'Well, dearie me, we saw the Two Ronnies at the airport, oh dear, it was so funny. Big Ron got on the bus and just as Wee Ron was about to get on, the doors closed. Oh dear, we did have a laugh. They timed it absolutely perfectly. They must do things like that all the time.'

And none of them ever knew – well, maybe some of them will read this and find out – that it was the only time in forty years that anything remotely like that happened to us.

I have to admit too that, even in an accident, the casting was perfect. It would have been funny if Ron had been left on the tarmac and I had been in the bus, but it wouldn't have been *as* funny.

The fear, and it was a very real fear, came early in 1972, when we were still basking in the favourable reaction to the first series of *The Two Ronnies*. We had a great shock. Far, far greater for Ronnie than for me, but still a shock for me. Ronnie had an enormous health scare.

We were still carrying on our policy of maintaining our separate careers alongside our joint ones, and Ronnie was offered the part of Falstaff in a musical adaptation of *The Merry Wives of Windsor*. The weekly theatrical newspaper *The Stage*, with its usual stunning accuracy, reported that the part of Falstaff would be played by Ronnie Corbett. Now that would have been a challenge. It could have been rather like a joke we once did. 'Ronnie Corbett will play the very important part of Henry VIII, and Ronnie Barker will play the rest of him.'

Jimmy Gilbert, our trusted producer, had teamed up with Julian More, who'd helped write *Irma La Douce*, to create the show. It was a very free adaptation indeed, set just after the turn of the century. Falstaff would be known as Good Time Johnny, and that would also be the name of the musical. Joan Sims, whom Ronnie knew well from radio, would play Mistress Ford. The plan was to open at Birmingham rep and hope to take it into the West End when it had bedded down.

After about three weeks Ronnie's voice began to go. It seemed like no more than an irritation. He'd sung in our show, but he'd never sung every day for three weeks or with such intensity. He assumed that he was misusing his voice. One of the actors in the show had a brother who was a doctor, and this gentleman had a look at Ronnie's throat the next day and said he would like a friend of his to look at it the following day. Ronnie was still fairly relaxed about the whole business, but then the second doctor looked down Ronnie's throat for a worryingly long time, and said, 'Sister, come and take a look at this.'

Sister went and took a look at . . . what? Suddenly Ronnie was worried. Suddenly he knew that it was serious.

'Interesting,' said the Sister, in a carefully non-committal tone.

This second doctor turned out to be a specialist, and he told Ronnie that there was a growth which might be pre-cancerous. It wasn't too bad at the moment, but when the Birmingham run of the show ended he would trim a little piece off Ron's vocal cords and have it tested.

Just to be on the safe side, he asked Ron to go back to see him the following week.

By the following week it had got worse, and the specialist decided that it couldn't wait. Someone else would have to play the part of Falstaff, and Ronnie was whipped into the

Queen Elizabeth Hospital in Birmingham, to have a microscopic slice taken off his vocal cords. There was a risk, said the doctor, that it might affect his voice. Ronnie was frightened. Cancer held such a special fear in our hearts then. It was the disease you didn't mention, the *Macbeth* of the body. It's still dreadful, but today it is talked about, and that very special, deep, communal, secret fear has gone.

The doctor asked Ronnie if he smoked. He did, heavily. He'd smoked twenty a day for a long time, but he had found that it helped his concentration, and in the last few years, the years of increasing success, it had gone up to sixty. That really did seem to add up to quite a heavy addiction. At that time he would have packs of 200 in his briefcase.

The doctor told him that he was to have an operation the next day, and a nurse advised him to have a hot bath to relax him, so that he could get a night's natural sleep before they started sedating him the next morning.

As Ronnie ran his bath, feeling pretty scared about things, he remembered that for some months his agent, Peter Eade, had asked, when he rang him, if he was suffering from a cold. The telephone, which exaggerates voices – don't you hate hearing your own voice on the answering machine? – had picked up a slight roughening of his tone.

I don't think Ronnie feared that he was going to die, although it must cross your mind that if the biopsy is positive, it might be the beginning of the end. What he really feared, though, was that he'd never be able to sing again.

So, as he lay in the bath, he began to sing. He sang all his favourite songs, then any song he could think of. He sang for an hour and half in that hospital bath, lying in the soapy, increasingly tepid water, just in case he could never sing again. I'm sure that, if there were any flies on the wall, Ronnie put a few moments of pleasure into their rotten, monotonous lives.

Well, the operation was a success, but Ronnie still had to wait a few horrible hours while the tissue was tested. Good news. They had got it in time. But Ronnie claimed that his singing voice *had* changed. It had improved!

When the surgeon made his round after Ronnie's operation, he chucked Ronnie's remaining cigarettes out of the window, plus a lighter and a good-quality cigarette case which had been a present from Joy. Ron never smoked again. He used to chew dummy cigarettes instead.

When Ronnie told the surgeon that giving up smoking was making it difficult for him to go to sleep, the surgeon advised him to drink a bottle of wine a night. Years later, when he was opening a bottle, Ronnie suddenly smiled. He had remembered the words of that surgeon, and he had realized something. The man was an ear, nose and throat specialist. He didn't mind what happened below the neck, it would never be his department's responsibility.

For at least a year, Ronnie found that he couldn't concentrate well enough to write, and he was a bit irritable at times. Once he suddenly stormed out of the rehearsals and went home, but on the whole he was very good about it.

The incident had scared me too, and not long afterwards I gave up. I too found it very difficult. In fact I became very short-tempered. I think my personality changed for six or seven months.

We got through it. We remained friends. A happy and smokeless future lay before us.

13

The making of a series of *The Two Ronnies* involved about a month of location filming, another month of preparation, and then eight weekly studio recordings, so altogether it took up a third of our year. The filming would be done in the summer, when the weather was good and the days long, and the studio recordings would be in the autumn, finishing in time for me to do a pantomime. During those four months Ronnie and I would be in each other's pockets. In the rest of the year we didn't see a great deal of each other.

We didn't make a conscious decision about that. Neither of us said, 'Look, old chum, let's not see too much of each other till the next series begins, in case we get tired of each other'! I'm sure that most of you have friends, lifelong friends, really good friends, whom you only see about once a year. We were like that. We both understood, I think, that, in our very British friendship, we needed to preserve our own individual space.

Apart from the normal fact that good friends don't live in each other's pockets, there were three reasons why we didn't meet all that often.

The first reason was that we lived a long way from each other, as I've already described. Pinner to Addington both ways is not an undertaking to be entered into lightly.

A second reason was that in the time between series of *The Two Ronnies* we were both extremely busy with our individual careers. It's the right moment, perhaps, to consider those separate careers.

Ronnie's aim after the success of the first series of *The Two Ronnies* was to find a really good situation comedy for himself. His first effort was a return to one of his old characters, Lord Rustless. But it wasn't a second series of *Hark at Barker*. It was called *His Lordship Entertains*, and it featured an entirely new situation for His Lordship, even though once again Ron was supported by Josephine Tewson and David Jason. Ronnie and David had struck up an instant rapport from the start. In the BAFTA tribute to Ronnie, many years later, Ronnie stood flanked by me and by David and called us his two greatest friends.

In *His Lordship Entertains*, Lord Rustless was running a luxury hotel, Chrome Hall. It wasn't a very good hotel, and Ronnie later referred to the series, jokingly, as 'Fawlty Towers, Mark 1'. The series was fine, but it is very difficult for an aristocrat to win the hearts of the television public. I think people admired the series rather than identified with it, and both Ronnie and the BBC felt that it was not the vehicle for which he was searching.

Ronnie now repeated his tried and trusty formula of doing a series of one-off programmes, partly in celebration of his versatility and partly for the more practical reason of trying to find a hit situation comedy for him. His intention was to do two series, called, in true Ronnie style, *Six of One* and *Half a Dozen of the Other*. This was scuppered when the BBC decided to do seven shows in the first series, not six. They went out, therefore, under the meaningless umbrella title of *Seven of One*. In fact there never was a second series. There didn't need to be. In the first series Ronnie found not one, but two superb vehicles for his talents.

The seven shows featured a fanatical football fan named Albert Spanner, who struggled to bring his local football team up to scratch; an old man who refuses to leave his soon-to-be-demolished house; a criminal who takes a train to prison, accompanied by two prison officers; a man forced to go on a crash diet when his wife hides his clothes so that he can't leave the house for food (I wonder which overweight writer/actor penned that one?); the penny-pinching owner of a northern c-c-c-c-corner shop; a story about a family of compulsive Welsh gamblers; and a story in which Ronnie and Roy Castle became Ronnie's beloved Laurel and Hardy (what perfect casting). Two of the shows became series.

Porridge turned out to be one of the greatest of all our television sitcoms. It was written by those fine writers Dick Clement and Ian La Fresnais. Ronnie's performance as Norman Stanley Fletcher was magnificent. While making Fletcher a very individual character, Ronnie also turned him into a universal prisoner. There is something in the nation's temperament – I say that, but I don't really know much about other nations' temperaments, maybe it occurs in all nations, maybe it's in the human temperament the world over – that identifies easily with petty crooks. So many of the famous Ealing comedies featured petty crooks. We'd be really indignant if Norman Stanley Fletcher burgled our home, but put him on the screen and we call him the underdog and identify with him against the very authorities of whom we complain in real life that they aren't doing enough to protect us.

Ronnie was brilliantly supported by Fulton Mackay and Brian Wilde as warders, and by Richard Beckinsale as his cellmate, Godber. There was also, at one stage, a superb cameo role for David Jason as a very old man. The series was filmed at Ealing Studios, with Slade Prison built in a drained water tank.

It was a huge success. Ronnie was amazed, at a royal film premiere, when the Queen Mother said, 'Oh, they've let you out, then.'

Ronnie once appeared with Fulton Mackay at a big charity do in a vast tent, early on in *Porridge*'s history. Being Ronnie, he couldn't, of course, talk directly to the audience, so a little incident was arranged. It was announced, between acts, that Fletcher had escaped, and later Ronnie appeared on a bicycle, riding furiously round and round the tent, a job that he didn't enjoy, as Fletcher didn't wear glasses and he could hardly see a thing. Then there was the sound of a police siren, and a van with flashing blue lights appeared, Fulton Mackay jumped out and barked, 'Nobody move!' The audience erupted, and Ronnie said that in that one moment Fulton realized for the first time just how popular he had become.

Ronnie believed Fletcher to be his finest character, and I'd go along with that. There is a view held by a few people . . . well, quite a lot of people . . . damn it, almost everybody, except perhaps my mum . . . well, and perhaps my dad . . . that Ronnie was more gifted than me, and I have no worry at all about that. In some ways, our relationship was a bit like an open marriage. What I mean is that, whatever Ron did separately, I knew that he would come back to *The Two Ronnies*, and come back yet more loved than he had been before.

I can't leave *Porridge* without mentioning, very briefly, a stunt that went wrong, when Ronnie and Fulton Mackay enacted another little scene together, on the occasion of the Water Rats, that great showbiz fraternity, making Ronnie their personality of the year. Unable to be himself, he came handcuffed to Fulton. Ronnie was staying for the dinner, but Fulton Mackay was going off to another engagement, They couldn't get the handcuffs undone. Well, you'd think if you were going to be trapped in handcuffs, the Water Rats might be one of the best places to be, and, sure enough, a Water Rat said, 'Don't worry. I'm a member of the Magic Circle.

You just have to know where to tap them.' Alas, the man's magic had deserted him. They were unlocked in the end, but it took forty minutes, and poor Fulton was late for his next appointment.

There were only three series of *Porridge*. Ronnie didn't want to do any more, because he didn't want to get typecast. He didn't want to hear cries of 'Oh, look, there's that man who plays that prisoner.' Also, he was deeply affected by the tragic death of Richard Beckinsale, loved not only for *Porridge*, but also for *Rising Damp*, perhaps the best situation comedy that ITV ever made.

Ronnie and I saw Richard on the evening before he died. We had done a stage version of *The Two Ronnies* at the Palladium, and we were taking it to Australia. There was a farewell party at Langan's Brasserie. Richard left early, to go to another function, saying cheerfully to Ronnie, 'Cheerio – see you in a year's time.'

Ronnie did not see him in a year's time. He never saw him again. Richard died in his sleep that night. The cause was believed to be sky-high cholesterol. He was thirty-one.

Ronnie did do one series of Fletcher that wasn't set in the prison. He was back in civvy street. It was called *Going Straight*. If *Porridge* had never happened it might have been considered quite a success, but without the authority figures against whom Fletcher had schemed, it just wasn't the same.

The other series from *Seven of One*, the one with the stuttering owner of a corner shop, was of course *Open All Hours*. It was written by another of TV's great sitcom writers, Roy Clarke. It starred Ronnie as Arkwright, the shop's proprietor, David Jason as his nephew Granville, and Lynda Baron as the trusty, not to mention busty, Nurse Gladys Emmanuel.

It was almost as successful as *Porridge*, and almost as loved by Ronnie. The clock moves on, and Ronnie is meeting HRH the Queen Mother again, this time at a royal gala at the Palladium. He is dressed in flunkey's uniform (so that he doesn't have to be himself) and is handing out programmes.

'Your puh-puh-programme, Your Majesty,' he says.

'Lovely, Mr Arkwright,' she replies.

'That'll be two guineas, please,' he jokes.

The Queen Mother looks at her pretty evening bag and says, 'I don't think I have any money on me.'

'I'll send you the bill,' says Ronnie/Arkwright. 'VAT added.'

I do feel that there was one other person in Ronnie's life whom I must mention, that if Ronnie was looking down on me, he would whisper, 'Don't forget Glenn.'

Glenn was Glenn Melvyn, and Ronnie never forgot him, as you will see. Glenn was the company's leading man at Bramhall in the early days of Ron's career in rep, and Ron said of him, 'He was to teach me everything I ever knew about comedy.' Glenn became far more than Ron's mentor. He became a close friend. Ron was not a particularly social person. I don't mean that he wasn't sociable, but that he didn't much like parties and large gatherings. He was at his happiest, I suspect, apart from with his family, in the two-handers of life, just he and a friend, having a pint or two, or a bottle of red wine, and chatting, chatting about the business, the craft, and about everything under the sun. His friendships were few, but deep, and his friendship with Glenn was as deep as any.

The relevance of mentioning Glenn at this point in our story is that it was from Glenn that the famous Arkwright stutter derived. It wasn't in Roy's script. It was the stutter that Glenn Melvyn created for a character in a play wot he

Enjoying a pint, in character of course . . .

wrote, called *Hot Water*. The part was written for Arthur Askey, but he couldn't go on tour with it, and Glenn Melvyn played the part, complete with stutter, and Ronnie played the other main male part and watched the stutter closely every night. It was, it has to be said, a comedy stutter, but done so brilliantly, and so consistently, that it developed that quality of truthfulness without which comedy just doesn't work for any length of time.

Ronnie's career was full of highlights, but nobody can avoid a few disappointments along the way. Ronnie did work in films, but it never quite happened for him on the big screen. Actually I don't believe this worried him much. He felt that television was his natural home. However, he was excited at the prospect of being directed by Dick Lester in *Robin and Marian*.

He played the role of Friar Tuck, with Sean Connery as Robin Hood and Audrey Hepburn as Maid Marian. According to the script, Friar Tuck was to ride a horse. Ronnie freely admitted to being terrified of riding horses. He was told there would be no need to ride a horse, a double could do it. He demanded, even so, that it be written into the contract that he would not be asked to ride a horse. It was. But this was the film industry, and, in the end, Ronnie had to sit on a horse, terrified. The horse wasn't too thrilled either. Ronnie did not have a jockey's build.

More serious was that he just wasn't happy working with Dick Lester. Ronnie needed everything carefully prepared and structured. Dick would say, 'Do something funny.' Ronnie couldn't be any good working like that.

Another disappointment was a sitcom called *The Magnificent Evans*. Ronnie played a Welsh photographer whose eye roved more than his camera. It was written by Roy Clarke again. I suspect that the Welsh character is even harder to capture than the Scottish character if one is a Sassenach (if there is an equivalent Welsh word for an English person, I don't know it), and this may be why the show didn't really catch on. And so it is forgotten, and the good ones are remembered.

But Ronnie's greatest disappointment was that he was pipped by Michael Hordern for the role of narrator for the children's television series of *Paddington Bear*.

And what was I doing? Well, a lot of my time between series was taken up with pantomimes. They were hard work, but I enjoyed them when I was younger. I've done a trapeze act on a Kirby wire – that takes courage – with a wonderfully funny double act called the Patton Brothers. They had a great routine on the trapeze and they started throwing me around.

I was on a wire, of course, and the climax of the act was when they sent me flying across the stage to land sitting on a platform that they were holding up for me. Of course they got it upside down and I landed on my backside on the handle of the thing. I did that piles of times.

Stanley Baxter and I developed an extraordinarily messy whitewash act. The traditional pantomime slosh is created by grating sticks of shaving soap and whisking them in a bucket. The water has to be at a particular temperature or the stuff doesn't really slosh. It's not very nice even when it does. The stuff gets in your eyes and makes them sore. During the run you are sloshed twice daily. In the interval, while *you* are wishing you'd ordered your drink before the show, *we* are removing our costumes and make-up, having a shower, putting on our costumes again and doing our full make-up again. It's hard work. So why do we do it? The answer is in the laughter of the children. To hear that laughter is to experience true joy.

A much less messy routine was a pastiche . . . well, more a travesty really . . . of *Swan Lake*. I had great fun doing this with Stanley, he was so very funny, and then I adapted it to do on my own. I was the cygnet at the end of the line, on my teetering points and in white tulle, getting into a worse and worse mess. The laughter was tremendous.

But I was still looking for a television vehicle, and didn't in fact find my ideal one until a long while later, in the mid-eighties, I did a pilot of a sitcom about a married couple, just divorced and getting together again. Or were they just married again and getting away from each other? To be honest, I can't remember, because in the end this sitcom wasn't the one that we developed.

I was carrying another script of a possible sitcom vehicle around with me. It was called *Sorry* and it was written by Ian

Davidson and Peter Vincent, writers and script editors for *The Two Ronnies*. I didn't look at the script until we'd finished the pilot, as I didn't want to be distracted, but a BBC executive saw me with it and commented, rather disparagingly, 'I don't think you need bother to read that.'

How lucky his comment was. If he'd said, 'That's the one you should be doing,' I might not have found the time to read it. After all, the pilot of the show I can barely remember had really gone rather well. But I was a bit irritated by the executive's dismissive tone, and I decided I jolly well would read it and make my own mind up, and when I read it I liked it immediately. I thought it was a very good idea.

Judging the potential in a comedy is not easy, and, as I had such great respect for Ronnie's judgement, I gave it to him to read. He read it straightaway. He was always very punctilious about giving me help if I asked for it, and he agreed that it was the perfect script for me.

I played a character called Timothy Lumsden, a sad 41-year-old anorak, totally dominated by his mother, who was a monster, a domineering control freak. The father was also bullied, and they were in timid rebellion against the mother. The mother was played by Barbara Lott, and the father by William Moore. It was all exaggerated, of course, but it was an exaggeration based on truth, and in any case it may not have been as exaggerated as we thought, because I got many letters from viewers who said that there was a Timothy at their work.

Timothy was pathetic, but he wasn't a complete wimp. If he had been, there would have been no pleasure in playing him. He could be almost brave on occasion, although, ultimately, that 'almost' would be the defining word. But he was capable of being, at times, cheeky and humorous and resilient.

I thoroughly enjoyed making *Sorry*, which vindicated

Ronnie's judgement of its potential by running for five years. We rehearsed in a church hall in Kensington, in an area with antique shops and good sandwich bars. What a paradise it would have been for Ronnie, far nicer than the Acton Hilton. The sandwich bars used nice multigrain bread. Well, once a baker's son, always a baker's son. There was also a superb cake shop in Church Street (halfway down on the right – I hope it's still there). Dave Allen lived near by, and he thoughtfully left me a little present in the cake shop. It was an apple charlotte, tied up with a bow and with a message on it, saying, 'Welcome to the district, happy rehearsals – Dave Allen.'

Timothy had elements of Walter Mitty in him. (Did you know that Walter Mitty was created by the American humorous writer James Thurber in a short story that was just six pages long? What brilliance, to create in six pages a character who would become a comic reference point for more than half a century.)

Timothy worked as a librarian, and we got into trouble for that. I got lots of letters from librarians saying that they were trying to improve the image of libraries and I wasn't helping. This sort of thing is always a problem. One of our writers in *The Two Ronnies* wrote a sketch about a dentist who blackmailed his characters in the chair, when they were terrified that he wouldn't give them injections. When the writer went for his next check-up, his dentist snarled, 'You've set back our public image ten years.'

It's always said that the key to audience appreciation is that the audience must be able to identify with the character. Well, in the late eighties I met one fan of *Sorry* who, it seemed to me, might have difficulty in identifying with poor put-upon librarian Timothy. He was the Prime Minister of Bahrain. I had been doing a turn at the opening of a golf course near the new airport in Hong Kong, and Anne and I had a stop-over between Dubai and Abu Dhabi. We were lolling by the pool when a friend of ours, who used to run the Bahraini royal family's flying squadron, told me that I had a fan who was longing to see me.

I wanted a fan at that time like a hole in the head, and we had only an hour before our onward flight, but you don't turn down prime ministers, and I agreed. The sheik, for such he was, agreed to meet us in our hotel. We met him in a room with three thrones. He sat on the central throne, dressed in a beautiful cream silk robe. We sat on the thrones beside him, in our towelling dressing gowns and flip flops, dripping water on to the marble floor.

And there, in that bizarre scene, the sheik revealed that he could actually recite most of the plots of *Sorry*. Then he waved over an officer from the armed guard, and he presented Anne and me with little boxes containing gifts. He gave Anne a Bahraini pearl necklace and me a Rolex. Such are the strange rewards that television brings.

There was a third reason why Ronnie and I didn't see each other very frequently when we weren't working together. Although we had so many similarities in our temperaments, we had very different leisure interests. He was a collector, a hoarder. He loved to go round little antique shops, even in Australia, where there weren't many antiques, and everything you bought in an antique shop in Australia had come from here in the first place, and you were taking it all the way back again. And in the limited touring we did with the stage show before we brought it into London, he would spend the days going round the shops, antique shops and bric-à-brac shops, and getting little bits of tea sets, and teapots, and teacups and little saucers; the *Antiques Roadshow* would have been right up his street.

He loved to collect illustrated books, prints, objets d'art, posters, anything that cast a bit of nostalgic light on a vanished Britain. He particularly loved the Victorian and Edwardian eras. Most of the stuff was small and easily stored, although he did buy three American pin-tables when he was in Australia.

Ronnie always felt that collecting was in his blood. He had in his possession a postcard sent to his mother from hospital before World War II, and a King Edward VIII Coronation souvenir handkerchief (not a product destined for huge success).

Chance played a great part in feeding Ronnie's collector's appetite. In the fifties, when he was working at the Apollo Theatre in Shaftesbury Avenue (at the time when he was in two shows every evening), he had to pass a little book barrow near the stage door. In the end he stopped to take a glance, and he was hooked. He picked up a little book crammed with illustrations of times past, found that it had been printed in 1815, and forked out a whole sixpence for it. 'Well,' he said, 'it had to be rescued and given a good home.'

One purchase led to another, of course, and in the end Ronnie was invited to have a look at the storeroom of the man behind the barrow. He went up the stairs to that musty wonderland, and came down a while later with thirty-nine Victorian picture books, for which he had paid two whole pounds. He was hooked. He was a collector.

But his main area of fascination was postcards, and his greatest pride as a collector was his superb collection of them.

This too began entirely by chance. In the late fifties he was appearing in *Lysistrata*, based on the Ancient Greek comedy by Aristophanes about peace-loving women in wartime denying men sexual favours unless they gave up fighting. A kind of 'No sex, please, you're brutish'.

He was sharing a dressing room with Peter Bull, and as

ancients they had to darken their bodies. They did this with an earth-based liquid make-up called Armenian bole, which was once used as an ingredient of antiseptics. Now, if you belong to that vast majority, the non-Armenian-bole-users, you won't know that it has to be painted on very thoroughly.

So there were these two large gentlemen – let's face it, these two too large gentlemen – trying to apply their Armenian bole at the same time in their little dressing room. The inevitable happened. Things that shouldn't have been painted got painted. Among them was a postcard (ah!) which Peter Bull had tucked into the mirror.

Peter Bull didn't seem too concerned about the ruination of one postcard, but Ronnie wanted to make amends, and went searching for postcards along the King's Road. He soon found a box of them on a tray outside a little shop. There were scenic postcards, comic postcards, all kinds. A few minutes later, Ronnie was the proud possessor of a hundred of them, bought for a few shillings.

He intended to give the lot to Peter. He was the card enthusiast, after all. Ronnie began to sort through them, and found that he liked them. He wanted some of them.

He decided to give only half of them to Peter.

His long run in *Irma La Douce* sealed his fate. There was another barrow in Cambridge Circus, run by a former ballet dancer and specializing in postcards. These were a bit pricey – fourpence each in old money – but over the long, long run of the play they formed the basis of Ron's collection.

He began by specializing in comic cards and bygone sweethearts, especially Edwardian and twenties glamour girls, but in the end he widened it to take in old views, which were often the only surviving records of old buildings and streets that had since been razed to the ground.

From those humble and chance beginnings, Ronnie built

a collection of 53,000 postcards, some so valuable that they had to be stored in vaults.

One instance of Ronnie's collecting habit occurred when we were performing our stage show in Bristol, polishing it before going on to the Palladium. It involved my old friend Ron Waverley

Ronnie found, through a small ad somewhere, a lady who was selling a collection of dolls, and he found out where she lived, and he told me how he went along to see this lady in her little house.

'She took me up the stairs,' he said, 'into this attic that she'd had converted, and there were what looked like hundreds of period dolls.'

It was a magnificent collection, and Ronnie was so taken with it that he offered her ten grand for the lot, and she accepted; she was very thrilled.

He took away, as a token, just one doll, a sailor doll, which he carried back to his digs, and he was going to arrange for the transit of the rest of her magnificent collection two days later.

The next day she rang up in tears. She said, 'I can't let you have them. I cannot part with them.'

He was very disappointed, of course, but he said, 'That's no problem. Just tear up the cheque and we'll forget the deal.'

But then she said, 'And would you bring the sailor back? I do miss him.'

The doll was a china doll some three feet tall. Ronnie wrapped it in brown paper, and then in a blanket, and handed it to Ron Waverley, who was in his car at a crossroads. Unfortunately the blanket had red paint stains on it, so the whole thing must have looked most suspicious. Poor Ron Waverley found it really embarrassing waiting at traffic lights, worrying that people would look in and see his sinister bundle.

I've shown how Ronnie enjoyed his food, but I don't think he took a particular interest in it in the way that I do. He enjoyed good restaurants, but he wouldn't seek them out. And I don't think he cooked.

I enjoy cooking, and especially baking. It's in the blood. And I love taking pains. I think there's a bit of my father in me when I do this. I recall him in the bakehouse in Edinburgh, preparing his vanilla slices, iced buns, chocolate sponges and lovely Madeira cakes. He would take me to the bakehouse at the weekend and do his jobs with the various doughs he was setting up, and I was able to run wild in this Aladdin's cave. I loved the wonderful rolling ovens and the trays piled with cakes and doughnuts and breads and rolls and pies and tarts and short pastry and puff pastry and rough puff pastry and marzipan and decorated cakes. All this comes back to me when I bake my bread or make my Béarnaise sauce – I'm particularly proud of my Béarnaise sauce! I like to do it as carefully as he did.

When I was in the kitchen, being very precise with my ingredients and my timings (timing is important in the world of bread as well as in comedy), I used to think of Ronnie poring over his old books and cards, and I can see in us both a careful, meticulous, almost finicky approach common to our hobbies as well as our professional life.

I don't think Ronnie was ever terribly interested in cars. They were things that took you from one antique shop to another. I've always been keener, and in 1973, after *Cinderella* in Bristol, and with *The Two Ronnies* going into its fourth year, I decided that I was doing well enough to be able to splash out on a Rolls-Royce. I had already owned a second-hand Rolls, but now I fancied a new one. Anne and I went to the Rolls-Royce headquarters in Crewe, where they made a fuss of us, gave us lunch and invited us to choose our colour. I don't mind admitting that I thoroughly relished every moment, after my modest beginnings and my years of struggle.

We chose one in Le Mans blue, with a pale cream roof. Le Mans had such an irresistible ring about it for a motoring man. The whole family gathered in Eastbourne, where I was doing a summer season, for the arrival of this splendid status symbol. There was only one snag. No car.

It turned out that the chauffeur bringing the car to Eastbourne for me had decided to pull in to a layby to straighten his cap. Quite right too. If a thing is worth doing, it is worth doing properly. Unfortunately, however, what he pulled into wasn't a layby. It was a pit of gravel, for vehicles to escape into if their brakes fail. The poor man found himself sinking in my magnificent new Rolls. Imagine him sitting there, up to the hub-caps in gravel. I shouldn't think he even had the heart to straighten his cap. The car had to be pulled out and taken back to Crewe on a lorry.

Never mind. The following week it did arrive, and the cap was straight, and the car looked magnificent, and we were soon setting off for London in it. On the way we tested its many features. How smoothly and silently the windows slid open. How smoothly and silently they . . . remained open. Only a minor electrical fault. Nothing to worry about. Nice to feel the fresh air on one's face.

I can't remember now whether the rain was forecast, but it came. How it came. We reached London soaking wet. Was somebody trying to tell me not to be flash? Anne and I never thought of ourselves as flash, and I hope we never were. In the seventies it seemed natural to us, if we could afford it, to buy a Rolls. Things seem different now.

Motoring was a pleasure, but not a hobby. My hobbies are mainly connected with sport, especially golf. While Ronnie was in his antique shops, I'd be out on the golf course. I number several sporting personalities among my friends and acquaintances.

I'm keener on watching cricket than would be expected of a Scotsman, though perhaps not of a Scotsman who won a cricket bat at St Andrews at the age of five, and I thoroughly enjoy racing. I used to go a great deal more than I do now, because I was a very good friend of Geoff Lewis, the jockey, now retired, who rode for Noel Murless, and won the Derby and the Coronation Cup on Mill Reef, who was a bit of a legend in his own nosebag. I used to go to Lingfield and Folkestone with Geoff, and I even had half a horse with him – Ta Morgan – and I also had a half share in another horse, which we called Chatty Dolly, after Anne's mother. Unfortunately it kept breaking away, and once it was hit by a car as it ran away, and had to have thirty-seven stitches down its front. Rascal! Racing didn't make me a millionaire.

I've always been keen on football. I mentioned the Television All-Stars earlier. The full name was actually the Television All-Stars and Showbiz XI. And in my palmier days I used to play for them alongside Tommy Steele, Anthony Newley, Lonnie Donegan, Mike and Bernie Winters and others. We used to gather at what seemed like an unearthly hour outside Broadcasting House on a Sunday morning and be driven to the match by coach. It was all for charity, but we took it pretty seriously on the pitch. I was a rather nippy right winger, though I say it myself. Tommy Docherty was our trainer. Sometimes he even played for us. From time to time he refereed. Occasionally, being Tommy, he did all three at the same time.

A cousin of mine actually played for Hearts (that's Heart

of Midlothian for those of you south of the border) and he played alongside Tommy Docherty in the Scotland side in the World Cup in Sweden. His name was James Murray. If I wanted to impress people in my young days in Edinburgh, I would say, with a deceptively casual air, 'I don't know if I've ever mentioned this, but James Murray is, in fact, a cousin of mine.' I didn't say it so much after I moved to Surrey. It didn't seem to have the same effect.

Naturally I was a very keen supporter of Hearts and indeed I still look for their result, but for the last thirty-eight years or so I have also been a Crystal Palace supporter and indeed I went regularly to matches for most of that time. I would be picked up at home by another great sporting friend of mine, Brian Huggett, the Welsh golfer and former Ryder Cup captain, who lived at Limpsfield. He would also bring Colin Cowdrey's two sons, Graham and Jeremy (not Colin, he was a Charlton man), and the four of us would have a grand afternoon out at Selhurst Park. Then Brian moved to Ross-on-Wye, and the little outings ceased, and I must admit I don't go on my own, though I still watch them on the box whenever I get the chance.

Once, in the mid-seventies, I took Ronnie B. to Palace as my guest. Palace had a promotional idea with the slogan 'Bring a Pal to Palace'. As a rather well-known supporter I felt I had to do my bit, and it would have seemed strange if I had invited anyone other than Ronnie. The speculation would have begun that we didn't really get on. So I invited Ronnie, and the poor man had to come. It was a long journey across London, and I'm sure the last thing he wanted to do was to come all that way to see a game of football in which he had no interest and the result of which was a matter of supreme unconcern to him. I can just imagine his heart sinking as he woke up, and him thinking, 'I wish I could go in character. Could I be Fletcher or Arkwright today?' But he came, and of course once he was there everything was fine and he passed it all off with great aplomb.

Yes, I loved football, but golf was *the* game, as it is for so many Scots. My dad was a good golfer, who played off a handicap of three or four, and my brother Allan is an excellent player too. I'm not as good, my handicap is sixteen, but I don't mind, I just love the game, and I love to be on a golf course, whether I'm playing or not.

I was twelve when my dad first took me on to a golf course, in the Braid Hills in Edinburgh, and I've been captivated by the game ever since.

My best friend at school, Tom Fell, took me to see the Open Championship at Muirfield in 1948. I rode on the back of his brand new black Triumph 500 motorbike, and we saw Henry Cotton, perhaps the greatest of all British golfers, sweep to a great triumph. I can see him clearly to this day, looking so stylish in his dark grey flannel trousers, paler grey cashmere cardigan, an even paler grey sports shirt and white buckskin shoes.

Little could I have dreamt, in those exhilarating teenage moments, that one day I would become a member at Muirfield, have a house there looking out on to the course and get to know Henry Cotton well enough to borrow his caddy on one best forgotten occasion.

It was from Henry Cotton that my dad had his one and only golf lesson. It was in 1936 and he was giving twenty-minute lessons for ten shillings a time. He told my dad that his swing was perfect and he shouldn't tamper with it. My dad thought that this was well worth ten shillings.

My dad actually died on the golf course. He was playing the fifteenth hole on the Prestonfield course in Edinburgh and he just collapsed and died. He was seventy-five. There can't be a much better way to go, but it was a great shock to my mum, waiting at home with his tea, and to me. Anne actually took the phone call, just as I was about to go out to do an engagement in Hornchurch. She said it was nothing important – what an actress she would still have been – and only told me the sad news when I got home at midnight. I felt an awful bleakness. I had never felt far away from him, even when we were hundreds of miles apart. I thought about how even when we were on holiday he would drop in on the local bakery, ostensibly to buy bread and cakes, but actually to stand and chat about the more abstruse corners of the baker's art. I recalled how, despite having a job that involved working all night long, he had found the time to take me to see the big parades which were a feature of life in Edinburgh, and to teach me golf. He also found time to be an elder at the church. He never thought of himself first.

My golfing life saw me become a member of the Stage Golfing Society, and I played in the *Celebrity Golf* series on television. I once played with that great comedy actor Jack Lemmon in a foursome with Lee Trevino and Sevy Ballesteros. I liked Jack Lemmon a lot, but I think he was even more nervous about the event than I was. Lee Trevino, of course, wasn't nervous at all, and kept up such a stream of wisecracks that any outsider would have assumed him to be the comedian. I wonder if he ever played with Frank Carson.

I could go on and on about golf. Golfers can, as you probably know only too well. But I must end with the great Henry Cotton, my hero after his win in the Muirfield Open in 1948 and all the more so because of the link with my dad and my dad's great admiration for him.

In 1969 we took a villa on the Algarve, and it was very near to the golf course at Penina, which Henry Cotton had designed himself. I discovered that Jimmy Tarbuck was staying near by, and the two of us decided that we would like to play Penina. We rang Henry to ask if we could play the course, and ended up being invited to drinks at his house, followed by dinner in a hotel.

The great man was wearing a wild-silk Nehru-collared jacket and a cravat, and his house was as elegant as he was. There was a reason for this. He was a great gambling man and used to play serious gambling golf matches with Bond Street dealers. He would play for a Chippendale table, or a pair of Louis XIV chairs. Not unnaturally, being a brilliant golfer, he had a very well-furnished house.

His wife, Toots, didn't appear for drinks or at the hotel, but he didn't seem the least put out. We learnt later that they had had a blazing row. Their relationship was always rather volatile. I just hope it hadn't begun when she said, 'You've not invited that bloody man Corbett!'

After dinner that supremely stylish man told streams of such racy stories that even Tarbuck had a job competing with him. It was a long night, and Jimmy and I have felt better in our time than we did the next morning at the course.

Henry was there, dapper as ever, and he said, 'As a special favour, I'm going to give you the services of my caddie, Pacifico.' Pacifico turned out to be a donkey. We just couldn't believe it, but Henry assured us that he knew all the rules and wouldn't walk on the greens or the tees. It turned out that the great man had rescued the donkey from a cruel farmer and spoilt him something rotten, feeding him Polo mints and all sorts of treats.

Our golf bags were strapped to Pacifico, one on each side, like panniers, and off he ambled towards the first tee. We had selected our clubs for our opening drives when we became aware of a loud gushing noise. We looked round, and saw our caddie behaving in a way that we had never seen from a caddy before. Pacifico was having a pee on the edge of the first green, not on the green itself – this was a donkey with a feeling for golf courses. And what a pee it was. It went on for a very long time, and we watched in awe and humility.

I prepared carefully for my first shot, rather foolishly aware that I wanted to make a good impression in front of this donkey. My shot skimmed off to the right. Did I detect just a touch of contempt in Pacifico's attitude?

Jimmy played his shot. His ball, like mine, did not go straight down the middle. It went to the left. I watched Pacifico carefully, and, yes, I think there was disdain in his demeanour.

He performed his duties perfectly, though, ambling with just a hint of arrogance towards my ball, and then, when I had chosen my club for my second shot, he ambled over to Jimmy's ball.

I was preparing for my second shot, when Jimmy called out. Pacifico was trotting off into the woods in the distance, with our golf bags. He had caddied for the great Henry Cotton. He wasn't going to caddy for the likes of us.

I said that I'd end with that story, but I don't think ending is one of my talents. Portugal reminds me that in Spain, which is quite near Portugal, I met that great actor and bon viveur Stewart Granger.

The first time I met him was actually in Edinburgh. He was with Jean Simmons. I use the word 'met' rather loosely. I saw him getting out of a taxi and going into the Roxburghe Hotel. He was in Edinburgh with Jean Simmons to appear in a play, *The Power of Darkness*. I shouldn't think he even saw me.

Anyway, we'd taken a holiday house in Spain and were in a supermarket, and there he was, just next to the special offer on stuffed olives. (I remember Gerald Wiley adding three lines to a party sketch – 'Have an olive.' 'Are they stuffed?' 'No, you eat them.') I recognized him, of course, but . . . he recognized me. Yes, this time I actually met him in the sense of meeting him. Not only that, but he even invited Anne and me to dinner the next night at his hacienda. He was dressed almost as he had been in *Bhowani Junction*. Only Ava Gardner was missing. Two delightful Oriental girls were cooking for him. He was a superb host. He made very stylish cocktails, and we had two legs of lamb for three people, so that we could all have the choicest cuts.

I didn't tell you that story in order to drop names. Honestly. I told you it because it struck me as a powerful symbol of how very, very fortunate I have been in my life, to go from seeing him getting out of a taxi to being invited to dinner at his hacienda. I had to pinch myself to believe that it was true.

14

No decade is short of bad news, and in the seventies there was plenty, including unemployment at its highest level since 1940, and two pub bombings by the IRA in Birmingham. But there was some good news too. The Americans finally withdrew from Vietnam. Democracy returned to Greece after the rule of the colonels, to Spain after General Franco, and also to Portugal. And in Britain there were two wonderful hot summers in succession.

The seventies were proving good news for us too. *The Two Ronnies* was firmly established in the ratings. The arrangement was that alternate series would begin either on BBC1 or on BBC2, and then be repeated on the other channel. Both channels paid for the series, and, as the BBC's faith in us rose, so did our budgets. If we wanted sixteen gorgeous girls in crinolines behind us, we got them. We were able to make the show look glossier, richer, more expansive, without ever sacrificing its original feeling of homeliness.

Our children were growing up. Ronnie had got over his health scare. The fact that we spent so much time apart meant that we were always really pleased to see each other on our occasional evenings together. The Barkers would invite us occasionally for a nice dinner, and we would do the same. Just occasionally one of us would give a party, and then of course the other would always be among the guests, and very, very occasionally we would go out for an evening together.

When we did go out, perhaps to the theatre, Ronnie would always be a bit tense about it, asking lots of questions. 'Where shall we go? What shall we do? What shall we have?' as if it was all really a bit of a problem, and then, when we got wherever it was, he would suddenly be very confident, and he'd take over.

What did we talk about? It's hard to remember. Nothing earth-shattering. Trivia. Gossip. Showbiz. Family. Clothes. Food. We instinctively avoided the controversial issues. I don't say that we would have found any major disagreements. I think we were both somewhere slightly to the right of centre in our political views, both more humanist than religious in our beliefs while subscribing to, and being influenced by, the moral principles of the Christian society in which we had been brought up. I do remember, though, that there was always a lot of laughter at our meetings. I've said that we weren't funny men off the screen, but what I meant, I suppose, was that we weren't gag merchants, acting up to our role as comedians. Ron, though, was a very witty man, and Joy too has a wonderful wit and humour. She and Anne can't be together for five minutes without laughter.

Nothing could have been more typical of Ronnie than the evening he came to see me in a Feydeau farce, *The Dressmaker* (you see, I didn't just do summer shows and pantos), directed by Patrick Garland. It was quite funny, but not one of Feydeau's best, and Ronnie said, 'I'd quite like to have a little go at it, because I have a feeling I could improve it.' Not many people would have the confidence to say that about a master of the medium of farce, as Feydeau is acknowledged to have been, but Ronnie thought he could, and he did. He wrote a very funny new scene which fitted perfectly into the play.

But when he sent it, it was far more than a funny new scene. He had adorned the script with apposite little drawings and sketches, all taken out of appropriate books. He had gone

173

to great trouble, and spent a lot of time, to help with the play but also to decorate his efforts with all these beautiful little touches. That was Ronnie. You asked for a little bit of help, and you got all that.

But it was *The Two Ronnies* that dominated our lives. Even at home, in our family life, it was ever present, in a way. I always think it's difficult for children to have parents who're well known. There'll always be somebody at school saying things like, 'My mother thinks your father's a little squirt' and 'You think your dad's funny. I don't think he's funny at all.' We couldn't take Emma and Sophie to the zoo or football matches, or even have a picnic in the park. There were bonuses like nice holidays but inevitably the children were cosseted, and they would have to lead a quiet life because we didn't go anywhere. And it wasn't always easy for me either. They'd bring a lot of friends to the house, and they'd all want to have a look at me, and I'd be hiding away because they were daft.

We did lots and lots of sketches over the years, but there are three that stand out for particular, and very different, reasons. One of them was called 'The Howling Brothers of St Wilkinson', and was written by Peter Vincent and a gentleman. Terry Hughes enthused about it, as a sketch with philosophy, but the reason for its inclusion here is that it was the only sketch that we were never able to complete, because we had uncontrollable attacks of corpsing while attempting to record it. I've mentioned corpsing before, but it occurs to me that you may not all know the derivation. It comes from the fact that very often in a play a person has to lie utterly still, like a corpse, and there will always be people in the audience who spend all their time looking at the corpse to see if there is some movement, a sign of breathing, or, worse, of amusement. And so inappropriate laughter is known as corpsing. Well, on this occasion somehow we just couldn't help ourselves.

Maybe I just looked so very funny as a novice monk, or maybe it was the fat cigar in the mouth of Ronnie B. as the abbot, or maybe the sketch was just so very funny, or maybe we didn't quite share Terry Hughes's enthusiasm for it and were a bit embarrassed.

I'll quote just a bit, so that you can make your minds up over its merit. Brother Cyril (me) was very surprised when the abbot said, 'Now you will find your cell furnished only with the bare essentials . . . a bed, a wooden chair, a picture of the founder and a washbasin. And a shower and a low flush toilet. And a fitted cupboard, three-piece suite, television, stereogram, and of course a cocktail cabinet.'

'Oh,' said Brother Cyril, taken aback. 'It's more than I expected, Father.'

'We rise early here,' continued the abbot. 'You will arise for early devotions at the crack of eleven o'clock. After devotions, that'll be five past eleven, you may return to your bed. Lunch is at one thirty. On Sundays, however, we all have a lie-in.'

'Oh yes, I see,' lied Brother Cyril.

'On *no* account,' continued the abbot, 'may you have a woman in your cell . . .'

'Perish the thought, Father,' exclaimed the horrified brother.

'. . . after midnight.'

The philosophical bit came at the end, after the abbot had said, 'Do finish this eclair.'

'No,' exclaimed the desperate brother. 'I don't want it. I mean I do want it but I don't want to want it. I mean I want to stop wanting what I want.'

The abbot stood and towered over the brother (not difficult) in righteous wrath (Ronnie could do a very righteous wrath) and said very sternly, 'It isn't as simple as that. You foolish vain little monk, what do you know of self-denial?

You came here because you *enjoy* denying yourself those things. Therefore I tell you that at this monastery you will learn to *deny* yourself that pleasure of denying yourself. From now on your life will be an orgy.'

'No, no,' exclaimed the horrified Brother Cyril. 'Not the orgy.'

There's more, but I've given you enough to judge it. Were we corpsing because it was so funny, or were we corpsing because we thought it was silly? Anyway, there it is, the one we never completed, the one that was never shown.

The second of the three sketches was very successful, and has been shown several times. Again there was a moment in it when I couldn't help corpsing, but that's not why I'm mentioning it particularly. I'm mentioning this one because of what it led to in a very different context.

It was called 'The Complete Rook', and it was set in a restaurant that only served rook. The restaurant was also called 'The Complete Rook', and it was awful, in fact it was a complete rook, but the customers felt that they couldn't complain because, after all, it had announced this by calling itself 'The Complete Rook'.

The menu included roast rook, grilled rook, steamed rook, braised rook and *la corneille bouillie à la mode de Toulouse* (boiled rook).

I played a character imaginatively described by the author as 'man'. A lot to go on there. I was with a young lady, and we were described as 'a well-heeled couple'.

'This doesn't seem to be the sort of restaurant to come to if you don't like rook,' I said.

'It isn't the sort of restaurant to come to if you do like rook,' said the waiter.

'Oh. Why's that?' I asked. (This was one of the sketches where I didn't have the funniest lines.)

'Because we use bloody tough old rooks,' said the waiter.

It was a very funny sketch. It wasn't written by Gerald Wiley, but Gerald Wiley was to play a part in its success. He often claimed to be a better rewriter than a writer. Some writers may have felt that he changed too much, but he never did it for its own sake, only to attempt to make the material stronger.

Here he made only one change. The writer had written the stage direction, 'The waiter looks round the empty restaurant.' The waiter's line then, in the script was, 'I think I can fit you in over here.' Ronnie/Wiley came up with the much stronger line, 'Have you booked?' This was his perfectionism at work, his taking of pains, his determination to improve even what was working well.

Ronnie also invented one bit of inspired business in this sketch. After he had brought us our menus, which were shaped like rooks, he sat down at our table with us. This simple bit of business was what caused me to corpse every time he did it.

But the real point about this sketch is Ronnie's performance. Funny though the sketch was, it was made much funnier still by his inspired performance and appearance as the slovenly, unfriendly waiter.

This led directly to a moment at a Water Rats' celebratory lunch, at which I was asked to say a few words. With these sort of things, the invitation always came for both of us, and it was always quite tricky, in a way, to decide how to play it, because I was up for doing something, but I didn't want to be seeming to be much more comfortable at something when Ronnie was either not going to take part or would take part but feel ill at ease with it. It was quite a big do, and the Prince of Wales was a guest, on the top table with Tommy Trinder (it *was* a long time ago). Well, I talked to Ronnie, and I said,

'I can do something, how about you?' and he said, 'Well, if they want me I have an idea. You can do your speech and after you've been doing it for about six minutes, I can shuffle on from the back, dressed like the waiter from the rook sketch, with the moustache and the terrible hair down the sides.'

So I would be standing up and saying, 'So the whole point was . . .' and then this man, the waiter, would be going round the tables, moving glasses, and he would approach me, flicking my table plan, and even picking up my wine and sipping it.

They had to warn the Prince of Wales and his security people, because Ronnie did look distinctly dodgy.

At first, in fact, the audience thought there was a nutcase waiter and they were embarrassed, but then they realized, and of course it got roars.

The Water Rats lunch.

And at the end of it, when I had finished my speech, we both said a little poem that Ron had written.

It was the perfect example of how determined he was not to have to make appearances as himself, and of how ingenious he was at getting round the need to do that.

Members of the public often used to send us ideas for jokes and sketches. Very few of these ever proved of any value to us, maybe just half a dozen in the whole ninety-eight programmes, but we always made sure that one or other of us read them, and it was lucky that we did, because it was out of a letter from a member of the public that Gerald Wiley got the idea for the most famous sketch we ever did.

A couple who ran a hardware shop in Hayes, not that far from Ronnie's home in Pinner, wrote in and mentioned funny things that happened in their shop. People often wrote about funny things that happened in their shop, but somehow they were never quite funny enough. This was different. Gerald Wiley had itchy fingers straightaway.

They wrote about a couple of misunderstandings that had taken place in their store. A customer had come in asking, as they thought, for four candles, and they had presented him with four candles, but what he had actually asked for were fork handles.

Somebody else asked for what the shopkeeper thought to be garden hoes, as in utensils, but the customer actually wanted hose, as in watering.

The possibilities rang a bell with Ronnie immediately, and he set to work on the sketch, always known as 'Fork Handles', the credits for which should perhaps have read 'By Gerald Wiley and an Ironmonger'.

As the sketch opened, I was serving a woman with a toilet roll. 'There you go,' I said. 'Mind how you go.' It's quite important sometimes, especially in a new or unusual setting, to give the audience a beat to take in the scene before the comedy begins. On this occasion we needed to establish that we were in an ironmonger's shop, a very old-fashioned shop of the kind that sells virtually everything, and that I was not too bright.

Then Ronnie entered, in workman's clothes, and he wasn't too bright either. It was very important that the audience should know that we were not too bright before the fun started.

'Yes, sir?' I began.

'Four candles?' began Ronnie.

'Four candles? Yes, sir.' I got four candles from a drawer, and plonked them on the counter. I use the word 'plonked' deliberately. It was such a definite gesture, as if all the man's problems had been solved.

But the workman just stared at them in bemusement, unable to believe what he saw.

'No,' he said. 'Fork handles.'

'Four candles,' I said. 'That's four candles.' I was utterly confused.

'No, fork handles – handles for forks.'

'Oh. Fork handles.'

I got two garden fork handles from the back of the shop.

'Anything else?'

The workman consulted his list.

'Got any plugs?'

'What sort of plugs?'

'Bathroom. Rubber ones.'

I fetched a box of bath plugs, and held up two different sizes.

'What size?'

'Thirteen amp.'

'Oh, electric plugs.'

I got an electric plug from a drawer.

'What else?'

'Saw tips.'

'Saw tips? What you want, ointment?'

'No, tips to cover the saw.'

'Oh. No, we ain't got any.'

'Oh. Got any hoes?'

'Hoes, yeah.'

I got a garden hoe and did a bit more plonking. Ronnie just stared at it disbelievingly.

'No – hose.'

'Oh, hose. I thought you meant "hoes".'

I got a roll of garden hose.

'No. Hose.'

'What hose?' I got a packet of ladies' tights from a display stand. 'Pantie-hose, you mean?'

'No. "O"s. Letter "O"s. Letters for the gate. "Mon Repos".'

'Why didn't you say so?' I climbed up a ladder to a cupboard high up on the wall, and got down a box of letters. 'Now, "O"s.' I hunted through the box. 'Here we are. Two?'

'Yeah.'

'Right.' I took the box back up the ladder, and descended. 'Next?'

'Got any "P"s?'

'Oh my gawd. Why didn't you bleedin' say while I'd got the box of letters down here?' I set off again on my long journey to the top of the ladder, grumbling as I went. 'I'm working my guts out here climbing about all over the shop, putting things back and then getting them out again.' My lines weren't funny. They didn't need to be. The situation was funny. Everybody knew that what I was coming back with would be wrong. Only Ronnie and I didn't know that. By this time I was back. I opened the box. 'How many? Two?'

I plonked two letter 'P's on the counter. Ronnie just stared at them.

'No. Peas. Three tins of peas.'

The misunderstandings continued through foot pumps, which turned out not to be pumps that you worked with your feet but brown pumps, size nine, and washers. By now I was thoroughly exasperated.

'Windscreen washers? Car washers? Dishwashers? Hair washers? Back scrubbers? Lavatory cleaners? Floor washers?'

'Half-inch washers.'

'Tap washers!' My self-control snapped, I grabbed the list, said, 'I'm not serving you any more,' and thrust the list into the hands of an assistant.

He looked through the list, calm and unruffled, and said, 'What sort of billhooks did you want?'

This tag was unworthy of the sketch, and Gerald/Ronnie knew it. The double entendre was too contrived. It was lame. Later, when we did the sketch in our stage show, Ronnie adapted it, turning the new assistant into a young lady with a spectacular figure, who read through the list and said, 'Yes, sir, what sort of knockers were you looking for?' It was still a get-out rather than a classic tag, but it was less contrived. We did come in for criticism from certain quarters for our reliance on jokes of that kind, but to Ronnie they were an embodiment of a great British tradition, a robust tradition if I may be permitted to use a word with 'bust' in it. The Gerald Wiley who loved such jokes was the Ronnie Barker who collected seaside postcards, and I think that the level of criticism that we sometimes received is a bit strange when we are also praised for having created something that is almost impossible to find these days – a comedy show that the whole family can happily watch together.

So, the letter from the hardware store in Hayes was the seed from which our most famous sketch sprang. There was still a lot of work to be done before the finished article emerged. Ronnie/Gerald had to think up a whole lot of misunderstandings, then he had to add the little touches of business, the ladder in particular adding enormously to it all, as I went on long, frustrating journeys. Also important was the utter seriousness of our performances. This was a playlet about the anger and frustration of two not very bright men for whom the simplest acts in life were fraught with difficulty.

It was an occasion when one twinkle, one hint of corpsing, would have sent the whole edifice tumbling down.

Pace is very important in comedy, and it is not to be confused with speed. Sometimes speed is necessary, and we've seen that Ronnie felt that our serials were sometimes too slow. Nobody could say that about 'Fork Handles'. Its slow speed was of the essence, it whetted the appetite of an audience happily awaiting the next misunderstanding.

On 1 January 1978, in the New Year's Honours, Ron and I were awarded the OBE (one each).

On 31 December 1977, I was extremely glad to know that, in the news the next day, it would be announced that we had been awarded the OBE.

I was in Bahrain, entertaining an audience of 500 Saudis. I use the word 'entertaining' in its loosest sense. I was standing in front of them, and I was being paid to tell them jokes.

I imagine that, every time a comedian walks on stage, he has, somewhere, even if he doesn't admit it, the fear of a nightmare in which, suddenly, he gets no laughs at all. The nightmare became real for me that night in Bahrain. It wasn't entirely my fault. I shouldn't have felt bad about it. The audience of 500 Saudis could not have been expected to be interested in my gags. The wit of that very funny writer Spike Mullins didn't seem to travel. I'm not sure if that audience would have laughed at 'The Captain did confide in me that it was really his ship and not an iceberg that sank the *Titanic*, but he didn't say anything at the time because he didn't want to lose his no-claim bonus' even if they had understood a word of English. The fact was that they had only come over to Bahrain because they could get a drink there.

I told myself that it wasn't my fault. The audience were drunk and they didn't speak English. It was the fault of the people who had booked me. Wasn't there a Saudi act called the Two Mustaphas that they could have booked?

I told myself that it didn't matter. I would very probably – in fact, almost certainly – never see any of these people again. What did it matter if they didn't laugh?

None of this helped. Nothing much does help when you're dying on your feet. But one thing really did help on that occasion. One thing got me through that evening with my spirits intact – the knowledge that the next morning, in Britain, it would be announced that Ronnie and I had both been given the OBE, the fact that I must, at some stage in my life, have been funny, or I wouldn't be being honoured in that way.

Ron and I were both thrilled to get the award. It felt, coming so relatively early in our careers, as if it was a reward for genuine achievement, not just for survival.

We received our OBEs from Her Majesty at Buckingham Palace in the following February (1978). I was determined to do the whole thing properly. An investiture at Buckingham Palace demands something a bit better than Moss Bros, I decided, so I went to get my top hat from a shop called Patey's, near Newington Butts, in South London. They put a metal gadget on my head to measure it. I hoped that my head hadn't swollen, but unfortunately nobody had measured it when I started out in the business, probably because nobody ever invited me to anything that required a top hat, so there was no way of telling. I loved Patey's, the smell of the lacquer and the glue, and the wooden blocks on which they made the hats. There was that same sense of exact craftsmanship that I knew from my father and his cakes and that I felt Ron and I had in our very different world.

The actual investiture was a lovely occasion. I think the public were touched to see us getting our joint award, and I

know that this meant a lot to us. It was like getting an OBE for our relationship. So joint was it that the normal strict protocol of alphabetical order was dispensed with, and the Queen gave us our medals together.

She asked us what we were doing now, and Ronnie

replied, 'We're at the Palladium, Your Majesty. You ought to come and see us.'

'I very well might,' she replied.

But she didn't. One can hardly blame her. She does have rather a lot to do.

Afterwards, we celebrated with our families at Walton's restaurant, in Walton Street. The whole day was delightful, and I think Ron and I both had to pinch ourselves to believe that it was true, that our two stuttering careers had led us all the way to this.

I never flaunted my medal. I never said, 'Hello, I'm Ronnie Corbett OBE, let's not be formal.' In any case there aren't many events in the comedy world at which medals are worn. But I was proud of it, and still am. There wouldn't have been much point in accepting it if I wasn't. And I did put it on

some of my letterheads, which had an unexpected effect earlier this year.

I had a cable asking me to send a message to a charity golf day in Sydney, and I sent the message, unthinkingly, handwritten on a bit of notepaper that happened to be headed Ronnie Corbett OBE. Soon I had the message back, 'Congratulations on your OBE, long overdue,' and I had to write back to say that I'd actually been awarded it twenty-eight years before.

15

I mentioned, at the end of the last chapter, that Ronnie told Her Majesty that we were at the London Palladium. The impresario Harold Fielding had been attempting to persuade us to do this for a few years, and eventually by 1978 the prospect seemed irresistible.

Ronnie was very nervous about the show. I was a bit nervous too, of course, but I had done lots of variety in night clubs and in my summer shows in Margate and Yarmouth and the like. For Ronnie, brought up in straight theatre, live variety was a new departure.

'I'm very proud to say that I'm the only person who's ever started their variety career by topping the bill at the London Palladium,' he once said.

I should imagine that every performer suffers from nerves, and we all evolve our own ways of dealing with the problem. I know that before every episode of *Porridge*, for instance, Ronnie used to lie down for half an hour in a darkened room, to get his brain going and calm his nerves.

Terry Hughes, the director of our first few series of *The Two Ronnies* on TV, was overseeing the show. We made our entrance through two doors, one large, one small. Of course I came through the large door, and Ronnie through the small door. Such a simple gag, but one that set the tone for the show perfectly. Then we descended a huge staircase, and began the show, which followed the format of the television show pretty closely, though with more in the way of variety acts to support us.

The wall of noise that greeted us as we made our first appearance was astonishing. I think it surprised us anew every night.

The show began with our usual very untopical news items, and thus thrust us straight into the middle of Ronnie's problems and the main reason why he was so nervous. He couldn't come on to the stage as a newsreader. It wasn't like being seen already sitting at the desk. He had to make an entry as himself, as Ronnie B., and begin the show as himself, and this was what he just couldn't do.

In the end I made a suggestion – that he should play himself as a character. It's what I do in the chair. All right, my intonations and throwaways and controlled waffling are a bit like the real me, but I keep making jokes as if Anne is a gorgon, and our children horrid, and our home a tip, and nothing could be further from the truth. It is a fictional version of me. So I suggested that Ronnie play a fictional version of himself. It had to be just a little bit more removed from the reality than my performance, just a bit more of a performance, in fact. So he developed a more chummy, more outgoing, more avuncular version of himself. Uncle Ronnie, in fact. It wasn't easy; it still took about a month before he was completely at ease with it, but he got there in the end. Being so close to him, I could tell that it wasn't quite natural for him, because his gestures were exactly the same every night, every movement of the hands precise and controlled and worked out. I mentioned that he hadn't known what to do with his hands in his early days on the stage. By now, of course, he had learnt, but his use of his hands had never become entirely instinctive.

Our main fear had to be that we would forget our words. There was no autocue here. There were no retakes if anything went wrong. And we hadn't done theatre work for such a long time. Probably television does make you a little bit soft. In our defence I would have to say that some of our words were a bit complicated to remember, to say the least.

We did a delightful musical item in which we were two Chelsea pensioners reminiscing about our romantic conquests. It began with Ronnie B. wheeling me in, and as we became excited by our memories, the sketch began to turn into one of our musical items. We sang parodies of 'Mademoiselle from Armentières', 'Daisy, Daisy', 'K-K-K-Katie' (did Arkwright ever sing that?), 'Just Like the Ivy', 'Mary from the Dairy' and 'Phil the Fluter's Ball'. I had quite a lot of words, but the parody on 'Phil the Fluter's Ball' became a solo for Ronnie, during which he did a little dance and got so excited that by the end he was saying, 'Here, Albert, my turn in the pram,' and it all finished with *my* wheeling *him* off. The sketch was full of typical Ronnie naughtiness, softened by its warmth and humanity. But in the song, Ron had to sing three verses giving the names of his conquests, all done very quickly, and while doing his little dance. If I just give you one of those verses you will see how complex it was and why he was worried about forgetting the words, which of course he never did.

There was Clare, there was Chris
There was Connie and Clarissa
And Cecilia and Charity and Caroline and Kate.
There was shrinking little Violet
Who doesn't want to marry yet
And bulging little Harriet
Who can't afford to wait.
Clarissa you could kiss her
You could meddle with Melissa and
Vanessa you could press her and

Caress against the wall.
You could have your fun with Nicola
But if you tried to tickle her
You'd end up with Virginia
Who wouldn't do at all.

The writer had given Ronnie a pretty difficult task, but he could hardly complain. The writer was Gerald Wiley.

The show contained some of our favourite sketches from the TV series, plus one or two new items to give it more variety. I donned my tutu and did my ballet performance from pantomime. Dick Clement and Ian La Fresnais wrote a *Porridge* sketch for Ronnie as Fletcher, and with a good supporting role for that very funny character actor, Sam Kelly. I suppose it was about ten minutes long, and it worked pretty well without touching the heights of the TV series, which existed on a rather more realistic plane than you could get in a variety show.

Among our supporting acts at the Palladium were an illusionist called Omar Pasha, who seemed to be able to take people's heads off and throw them in the air – no mean feat; a spectacular acrobatic act, the Kosiaks, from Poland; and a group of eight very tall, very glamorous black girls in white kid thigh boots, who did very exotic things and were called the Love Machine.

I can't help wondering what has happened to the world's speciality acts. There are still the circuses, of course, but at one time, in addition to circuses, there would be variety shows in every town and city, and indeed there were plenty of them in the early days of television, and there were ice shows everywhere, and in these shows there would be illusionists, mind readers, acrobats, trapeze artists, knife throwers, unicyclists, unicycling trapeze artists, knife-throwing skaters,

A couple of Cossacks, at the Palladium.

acrobatic unicycle throwers, skating trapeze artists, comedy
dog acts, comedy skating dog acts. Where are they now?
Performing their tricks, very slowly, in old people's homes?

Some of the critics were not very kind about the show.
I don't think we could have expected them to be. They
complained that it was little more than the television show
on the stage, and of course that was only slightly unfair,
though perhaps a bit of a harsh verdict on a show playing the
Palladium, which is essentially a variety venue. Anyway, our
audiences didn't worry, and they flocked to see us. The
original seven-week run was extended to three months.

In the end, Dick Clement and Ian La Fresnais contributed
much more to our stage show than their *Porridge* sketch. They
gave us an amazing piece of information about income tax.

They told Ronnie something that, frankly, seemed too good to be true – that if you went abroad for a whole tax year, resigned from your clubs, etc., didn't come back to this country at all during that time, the Inland Revenue couldn't raise an assessment on you for the previous year.

Nobody enjoys paying tax. Apart from anything else, so much of one's money goes on things of which one just doesn't approve. And we had already paid so much tax that we didn't have any qualms about evading it, legally, on this one occasion. Well, would you? In fact, Ron once wrote a little song called 'The Laughing Taxman'. The first verse went:

> I am a tax inspector,
> A jolly chap, that's me.
> I deal with your assessments
> And drink a lot of tea.
> You'll always find me laughing,
> You'll never see me cry.
> I find out what you're earning
> And then I bleed you dry.

It was nice to feel that it was our turn to laugh.

But before committing ourselves, we obviously needed to check up on the facts. Things do tend to change. It's in the nature of loopholes that they get closed. So we decided to go and consult a tax QC. We went to see a man called Mr Andrew Park.

On the way to see him we were busy casting the man, wondering what he'd be like. That's typical of the sort of gentle fun we would have together. We both decided that he'd be a John Le Mesurier type, a far-back Englishman, with perhaps a touch of the Alastair Sim, who had featured in both our younger lives. How wrong can you be? He was rather like a younger version of Alan Bennett, with the same accent, as flat as a cap.

He told us, quickly and simply, that our plan was indeed watertight and that he wished he was coming with us. How splendid and direct. It came as no surprise to either of us that he was knighted soon afterwards, although somewhat to our surprise the citation did not mention 'for his services to Ronnies'.

Well, we were already having a good financial year, in no small measure due to the stage show, so the obvious thing to do was go to Australia the following year, and take the stage show with us.

We spent the rest of the year trying to earn as much money as we could, knowing that this would be the last tax-free money either of us would ever see, and making plans for the move. We were going as families, of course, so we would have to find homes and schools for the children. It was a busy time.

For Ronnie and Joy it would be their first visit to Australia, but Anne and I knew it well. I worked out that we have visited Australia no less than seventeen times and that I have played on thirty-seven Australian golf courses. We love it.

Australia was actually the setting, about three years before our joint visit, for a very unlucky crime, a crime more fitted to Charley Farley and Piggy Malone than to real life. I had done a cabaret at the St George's League Club in Sydney, went out to supper afterwards and returned to my car to find that it had been broken into and my dinner suit stolen. I think it's quite funny now. I can just imagine the huge, brutish thief, with his great muscular thighs and arms, staring at his haul – my dinner suit. But it wasn't funny at the time. I had other engagements, and no suit. How could I get one? Easy. The *Sydney Morning Herald* showed a photo of me making an appeal for help dressed only in my shirt tails and a bow tie. Help came. British Airways flew my spare suit from London to Sydney in twenty-four hours.

On another visit, we were able to do two people a very good turn. I was booked to do a week's cabaret at a casino called Wrest Point, in Tasmania. Anne and I would always arrive a couple of days early for an engagement that required a long-haul flight. It's not much fun performing with jet lag, and pretty unprofessional. So we had a chance to see the previous week's show, and we were absolutely stunned by one of the girls in it. She was extremely tall but wore her clothes beautifully and was very talented.

Not long afterwards, we were in Paris, visiting a night club called Paradis Latin (what an exciting life we led in those far-off days!). We talked to the owner, and he said that he was losing his leading lady shortly. We told him that we knew the very girl for him, that he couldn't do better if he searched the whole world. That shows how outstanding we thought Lisa Murphy from Tasmania was. We would never normally stick our necks out like that. Well, the owner was so impressed by our enthusiasm that he tried to get in touch with her in Tasmania, but she had already moved on and was appearing in a big, glamorous show in Seoul in South Korea, dancing and singing Seoul music (sorry about that one).

That was that, we thought, but later, out of the blue, we received a postcard from Paris, which said, 'How sweet of you to think of me and mention me. Here I am, the leading lady at the *Paradis Latin*. Love and best wishes, Lisa Murphy.' I must say it gave us a warm feeling to have achieved this, but I decided to stick to performing rather than becoming an international talent spotter.

For our year's stay in Australia, Anne and I decided to take the family by the scenic route, via the Taj Mahal and other

Indian restaurants – no, via the real thing, and Malaysia, Phuket, Pattaya and Bangkok. We were accompanied and aided on this odyssey by a splendid girl called Debbie, who had never been abroad before, but stayed the whole year and turned out to be the most brilliant traveller. Whatever we suddenly needed, a piece of elastoplast, some sticky tape, an indigestion pill, a pair of tweezers, Debbie had them. And she only took one suitcase. Amazing.

Ron and his family went via New York, Los Angeles, Honolulu and Fiji. We went by different routes, but in Sydney we became near neighbours, having both taken apartments in the delightful eastern suburbs that run from Double Bay to Rose Bay.

The Corbett family's scenic journey hit the rocks while we were staying in the Oriental Hotel in Bangkok. I felt extremely unwell. The hotel doctor took some tests and discovered that I had hepatitis, which I must have picked up from an injection I had against the disease before I left London. The doctor said that I had to lie down in an air-conditioned room for at least a month, and preferably six weeks. The only good thing about this news was that I was already in an air-conditioned room, and I had a very big and comfortable bed to lie down on, but I was supposed to be going on to Hong Kong and doing a six-week cabaret engagement in the Pink Giraffe Club at the Hong Kong Sheraton. We contacted the general manager of the South-east Asia Sheratons, and he generously suggested that he would put the whole family up entirely free at the Hong Kong Sheraton if I would agree to do my cabaret stint when I'd recovered.

So for six weeks I lay in my air-conditioned room, moving just twice a day in order to have the sheets changed (a regular practice in the best Oriental hotels). The rest of the time I spent watching television. I became an expert on Chinese horse racing and could have written a dissertation on Chinese cartoons, had I had the energy.

But the only real excitement was the window-cleaning. The scaffolding these brave men used to clean the windows of the high-rise hotels was made of lengths of bamboo cane tied together. These huge structures swayed enormously in the wind, and those magnificent men on their window-cleaning machines were wafted to and fro most alarmingly. It was far more thrilling than anything on the television.

Our jockey friend, Geoff Lewis, was there to ride in several races and was most disappointed that we couldn't go out together, but to cheer me up he engaged a tailor, Richard Ha, to make a suit for me. It was a bit unnerving to be measured for a suit lying full length in a bed. It felt like being measured for a coffin.

Anyway, Mr Ha delivered the suit in record time, as they all do, and I wore it for my first night at the Pink Giraffe Club, with Mr Ha in the audience and becoming, I hoped, Mr Ha-Ha. The style of the suit was actually a bit stiff for me, and I never wore it again, but I didn't want to hurt Mr Ha's feelings. I was still not at anything like full strength, but nobody has ever called my cabaret 'action-packed', and the travelling didn't get me down – it comprised short walks along two corridors and an eight-storey ride in a lift. And the room would have cheered me up if nothing else had. It's not often you work in such a beautiful room with all the upholstery made of pink fake giraffe skin. I'm glad it was fake. I like giraffes.

Well, we reached Sydney in the end and lived in a lovely apartment on Wunulla Road. We had a great view over Sydney Harbour, a roof garden and a private swimming pool.

The whole area was delightful, with superb restaurants, chic fashion boutiques and well-stocked shops run by people from virtually every European country. The fishmongers were particularly good, but I always paused to have a little look at the patisserie shops . . . were they up to Dad's high standards? They most certainly were, and I got a thrill, on his behalf, as it were, when I stood and admired them.

Ronnie and I were now living close to each other, for the first time in our lives. Ron and Joy were really just up the hill from us, with a wonderful view over the harbour; we took lots of gorgeous photographs of sunsets, even though they were all exactly the same, and now we saw each other all the time.

Our girls were eleven and twelve, and were utterly happy in a very good girls' school called Ascham, run by a very modern headmistress named Rowena Danziger. In fact this was just about the only time that Emma was happy at school, and both girls found their schools in Croydon old-fashioned compared to Ascham. Sophie had been to ballet school, while Emma had been at a very traditional, old-fashioned school, run by a headmistress who was a bit of a martinet, and who had a limited vision of what a girl's education should consist of. Ascham was, admittedly, a privileged and expensive institution, but seemed to us to have none of the divisive class atmosphere that top English schools can have, and to Emma it was a revelation.

The Barkers' three were happy too. Larry got a job as a bouncer at the theatre where we were working, and Charlotte went to drama school. Like our two, Adam was happy in his school.

There were times when Ron and I were working, although we did have more time off than in England, and Joy and Anne were able, for the first time in our relationship, to spend a lot of time together. They went to see shows, and, once a week, went for lunch in some fabulous restaurant.

A gay half-Maori friend of Anne's called Alan Brown – he had been in *Annie Get Your Gun* with her and had kept in touch ever since – used to escort Anne and Joy, along with a gay pianist friend of his, to one of the fabulous restaurants around Sydney every week. He was very camp and an enormous fan of Ethel Merman. When she died, he telephoned the Barkers. Charlotte answered the phone, and he said, 'Tell Mummy to light a candle for Ethel.' Charlotte didn't know what he was talking about, and couldn't hear very clearly, and the message that Joy actually got was: 'Light a candle for Edward.'

It was a glorious year. The two lots of children got on well, in fact all the family friendships were cemented. We all agreed that, if we were ever to leave Britain – which wasn't practical, really, with our careers – Australia, and in particular Sydney, would be the place where we would most like to live. There was all that sunshine, of course, but it was the quality of life that attracted us as well. By day, when we weren't working, I went golfing while Ron swam a bit, wrote a bit, and visited antique shops a bit, but we saw much more of each other in the evenings than we ever had.

I think it was while he was in the pool in Australia that Ron had his first little heart flutter, a hint that perhaps all was not quite well in that department.

The stage show was very closely based on the English version, though with new supporting artistes, apart from Sam Kelly. In fact, it was planned to use the same costumes and sets, and they were halfway across the sea when the Australian union movement said that they wouldn't have them, so the clothes and sets had to be made in Australia all over again, at tremendous cost. That was Australian trade unionism at that time.

As the comedian Dave Willis. One of my earlier influences.

Ron as the Genie in *The Two Ronnies Christmas Show*, 1985.

Snivelling and Grudge.

An Australian outback sketch.

Charley Farley and Piggy Malone.

The Country
and Western duo
Jehosophat and Jones.

As Adam Ant and Buster Bloodvessel.

A couple of Swiss yokels.

American Indians.

Sid and George at the beach.

Steam-train drivers.

Canadian Mounties.

The Royal Command Performance at the Victoria Palace: making our entrance.

Ron and I with our lovely wives Anne and Joy.

With some old friends. *From left to right*: Bruce Forsyth, me, Ron, Jimmy Tarbuck, Michael Winner's son, Michael Winner, Michael Parkinson.

Anne and Joy wearing our glasses.

We made no allowances, in our material, for its being in Australia. We didn't need to. In those days we were almost bigger in Australia than we were here, certainly as big. There wasn't a great deal of Australian comedy then, and the audiences were delighted with our routines, because they still had a soul that related to the UK, and they were thrilled to find nice, wordy, finely presented stuff. The show played for four weeks in Sydney and four weeks in Melbourne. Those were the only appearances that Ronnie did during that year, though of course he was able to get on with a lot of writing. I did a variety series while I was out there, but, even so, it was a relatively restful year for us both.

The family took one short motoring trip from Sydney to Melbourne via the coast. I say 'short' because it only lasted about three days. It was actually a long way. Australia is vast. We thought that a nice little family trip round the coast would be really restful, and it was. Nothing much happened at all, except that at a place called Narooma the headmaster gave the school a half holiday, so that he could play a round of golf with me, and all the school came to watch and cheer. Oh, and then there was the cheese. Or rather there wasn't the cheese. Narooma is known for its cheese, and I was presented with one at a delightful little ceremony. Was the cheese nice? I haven't the faintest idea. I forgot to take it. I hope it was found before the next occupants moved into the room, and I hope that Narooma didn't think I'd left it deliberately. But apart from that it was very restful. Oh, except for the gaggle of geese, that is. I went back to our room the wrong way on the next night, and was chased by this gaggle. Don't laugh, geese can be really picky about making friends. They seemed to have a pecking order, and I was at the top of it – in fact I was worried that they would peck me to death, and was really glad to get back to the room.

Still, there was one last day to recover, and that was very restful, apart from locking ourselves out of the car and having to get the manager of the local McDonald's to pick the lock. An eventful trip, then, but all part of the fun of Oz.

At the end of that great year, Anne and I gave a rather grand outdoor party at our apartment. We used outside caterers, not a thing we had ever done before, but we didn't feel we had quite the depth of experience of Southern Hemisphere barbies to do it ourselves. Anyway, I thought it would be much more relaxing for Anne.

How wrong can you be? When she was organizing everything, she was as cool as a cucumber. Now that she didn't even have a cool cucumber to slice, she grew nervous, and started sipping champagne before the guests arrived, and by the time the guests did arrive she was so nervous and excited and so carried away that she collapsed into a rose bed, and indeed did have to be carried away, back indoors to lie down. But she soon recovered in time to enjoy the rest of the party, and after its unexpected start it was a huge success, and a great ending to a great year.

On one of my earlier visits to Australia, I had enjoyed the enormous privilege of being top of the bill in the Concert Hall of the Sydney Opera House. It was an exhilarating experience to play this famous and beautiful building, which is perhaps the greatest symbol of twentieth-century architecture in the world. I could not possibly have dreamt of appearing there when I was serving drinks in the Buckstone Club! Anyway, there I was, and I managed to fill it for three nights running. What I didn't manage to fill was my dressing room. It was a fabulous suite and looked almost as big as the Concert Hall. It was certainly a lot bigger than some of the clubs I'd played in my early days. I had to set off for the stage five minutes before I was called. There was even a seven-foot Bösendorfer grand piano in my lounge area, just in case I should fancy a quick tinkle on the way.

David Frost brought a party to one of my shows, and in the party were Kerry Packer and his wife Ros. You tend to meet people like that in David's parties. David took us all out to supper, and that was how I got to know Kerry Packer.

Now, towards the end of our year's trip, I suddenly had a great thought. I rang Ron immediately. Not just to boast that I'd had a good thought – they weren't that rare – but to tell him what it was. Why not try to do a series of *The Two Ronnies* for Australian television, on Kerry Packer's Channel Nine? This time we could do some extra material specially written for the Australian audiences. Ronnie was all for it. He was loving Australia too, and would be very happy to go back.

There is something very approachable about Australians. Traditional British reserve melts. I rang Kerry Packer that very evening. It was a Sunday. I don't think I'd do that in England. I'd think, 'He's probably watching *Midsomer Murders*.' Well, he was at home, and I put the proposition to him, and he said he was very interested, and could I go round and see him the next morning? I don't think a British media mogul would ever be so open and so immediate. Apart from anything else, they wouldn't want to give the impression that they didn't have a full diary for the next morning, and they wouldn't want to seem too eager, so that later they could drive a hard bargain. Kerry Packer just went straight for it.

I went to his office and he said, 'I'll have as many shows as you're prepared to do.' He told me that a man called Lynton Taylor would arrange everything. Our business had been conducted in no time at all, leaving him free to talk about golf. Kerry Packer was a passionate golfer and a great friend of many top golfers, but particularly of Jack Nicklaus. He had recently felt that his golf was in the doldrums and had asked Jack Nicklaus if there was anybody he could recommend to help him. Nicklaus had recommended the American professional Phil Rodgers. He had been flown over and put up in a hotel for a week just to help Kerry Packer with his golf. It must be nice to be so powerful, but at least Kerry Packer was spreading his money around and not hoarding it as a recluse. Anyway, he used his chipping iron and his putter in his large office that morning, demonstrating to me what he had been taught by Phil Rodgers, and then I went to see Lynton Taylor, and in no time at all the financial details for a series of six shows had been agreed, and I left their offices happy about the challenge of the new series and more confident about my golf! There was something very direct and very Australian about the whole process.

There hadn't been time to do the TV series during our year's visit, but soon we found ourselves in Australia again. This time Ron went out on his own first, before his family, so as to sort out arrangements before they joined him. Anne and I were already there, and we sent him a little gift of welcome, a straw hat and a wonderful sumptuous soft beach towel for him to lie on and dry himself off when he'd had a swim, because we knew that he had a lovely pool in his garden.

And we had the most sweet little poem back, which he'd set, as Ron was wont to do, in an Edwardian print cut out from an old book he would have had, so that it was framed in a pretty little etched drawing of Edwardian angels, sitting on clouds and playing musical instruments, with the little poem in the middle, which we have now framed and which hangs on our wall at home.

Your gift will be most welcome when
I strive for inspiration ~
The straw hat will protect my brain,
The towel, my perspiration

So I remain, dear Ron and Anne
Forever in your debt;
For though the work will be a slog,
It won't be such a sweat.

The whole thing, the poem and the presentation, were so Ron, so very Ron.

Another thing that happened before Joy arrived was that Ron used the opportunity to make a determined effort to lose weight. It was the right time, and a great opportunity. After all, eating is nothing like so enjoyable when it's a solitary activity. Well, Harry Secombe was also in Sydney, and he was also on his own, and also using the opportunity to have a serious go at dieting. Anne and I went out to dinner with the two of them, and we discovered the amazing fact that between them Ronnie and Harry had lost me – the equivalent of my weight – between them.

We did quite a bit of material that we'd already done in England, but which we hadn't allowed to be sold to Australia, because we knew that we had this commitment, and we wanted it to be fresh to them. We asked the BBC not to sell our shows to Australia for a year, so we were able to do bits and pieces that we'd already done in this country, but we also did bits and pieces with an Australian background, filmed in Australia, and feeling Australian, and we did news items on Australian subjects, so the shows were made on the understanding that they wouldn't be shown in England.

For instance, we did a song each week as our Country and Western duo, Jehosaphat and Jones. In England these would have been done live in the studio. In Australia we recorded them in exotic locations found for us by the production team. One of the songs was called 'Railroad Man'.

They said, 'Lay tracks for the railroad,
'Cos steam means speed and power.'
So I'm doing my best and I'm travelling west,
About fifteen feet an hour, oh Lord,
About fifteen feet an hour.

It was a chain-gang song.

Oh I crouched all night laying track down,
And the wind on my back made me choke,
And I felt that the bottom had fell out of my life,
Till I found that my braces had broke, oh Lord,
I found that my braces had broke.

We filmed that up in the Blue Mountains, on the railroad.

Someone had stolen my hammer,
But I still got to earn my bread
And life ain't so grand, when you're standing on your
hands

And driving in the rivets with your head, oh Lord,
Driving in the rivets with your head.

It was very picturesque, recording up there, and gave us another of our memorable Australian experiences.

There's a curve in the track up yonder,
I think it's the beginning of the end;
I've tried going straight, but sad to relate
I think I'm a'going round the bend, oh Lord,
I think I'm a'going round the bend.

That evening, after we'd recorded the song, we were all having dinner up in the mountains, and it began to snow, turning the Blue Mountains white. We had dancers up there, eighteen- and nineteen-year-old girls, and they had never seen snow before. They rushed out excitedly, and started to play in it, suddenly turned back into children, which was very sweet. The two of us had seen enough snow to last us a lifetime, and preferred to stay inside with a nice bottle of full-flavoured, robust Australian wine.

It beat Shepherd's Bush hands down.

The studio recordings were also extremely pleasant. The studio was quite near Sydney. It was a small studio, beautifully run, intimately run, with lovely food (are you reading this, BBC?), the same dressing rooms each week, beautifully furnished, with a bathroom, a relaxing lounge and a little reception room. We were spoilt in Australia, whereas the BBC didn't spoil us; the BBC dressing rooms were, for most of our time there, appalling. Only now have they cheered up six of them.

In fact we had a head-to-head conflict with the Controller of the BBC at the time, Alastair Milne, who came out to visit Australia while we were there, and we said to him, 'Really, just look at this dressing room, Alastair. How can you let people like Margot Fonteyn or Rudolf Nureyev go into those awful, lavatorial rooms you've got at the BBC?' Since then they have improved them, and the Television Centre is much better now; they've got these cafeterias, rather trendy little coffee shops and newsagents, proper things. I'm not actually suggesting that our meeting with Alastair Milne had anything to do with all this, but then again, who knows?

Back in England, we resumed the even tenor of our lives, and in 1983 we did our second stage show of *The Two Ronnies* at the London Palladium. Now it was my turn to have a problem. It was actually a very serious problem, a really traumatic experience.

We were seven weeks into the three-month run, and everything was going swimmingly. We were in the middle of a Saturday matinee, and we were doing a big musical number called 'Hello, Sailor', a typical Ron/Gerald romp. Ron and I were dressed as Wrens, and we were accompanied by a troupe dressed as naval ratings, who, I must say, were excellent – well, our shows always had very good ratings. See how I try to take refuge in a joke, because, even now, more than twenty years later, this is a difficult subject for me to talk about.

We were singing Ronnie's words to the tunes of 'A Life on the Ocean Wave', 'Hearts of Oak', 'Drunken Sailor', 'Bobby Shafto' and 'Rule Britannia'. It was one of those medleys that he so adored writing new words for, and it was swinging along merrily, but almost from the beginning I began to feel odd. The lights were affecting me. I could hardly stand the brightness and the heat. I began to feel very giddy. I carried on, of course:

Heigh ho, and up she rises,
She's got knees of different sizes,
One's very small, but the other wins prizes
Early in the morning.

A word of advice. If ever you have a tendency to giddiness,
don't wear Wrens' high-heeled shoes. I was feeling very
wobbly indeed. I was really alarmed. I could hear myself still
singing as if from far away:

Heigh ho, and up she rises,
They have suits of different sizes,
The pockets are full of little surprises
Early in the morning.

By this time I felt that I was going to fall into the orchestra
pit. It was all so sudden, and so terrifying, and still I ploughed
on:

Bobby Shafto's gone to sea,
He'll be back in time for tea.
He's in charge of the WC
On the Channel ferry.

At last it was over, I had the interval in which to recover.
I recovered a bit. I was able to go on and do the second half
of the show. But I don't know how I got through it. The
stage was spinning, the auditorium was swaying, the lights
were lurching towards me and then pulling back, teasing me.
I felt more and more panicky, and my hands were running
with sweat.

At last the show was over. But that was only the matinee.
There was an evening show still to do. Harold Fielding, the

producer, called in a doctor, named Martin Scurr, and he put me on a tranquillizer called Ativan. Half an Ativan. Then a second half if the first half didn't work. If the first half didn't work during the first half of the show, I would take the second half before the second half – no, stop it, this wasn't funny. This was really serious. It was getting worse, not better.

I was sent to a neurologist called Nigel Legg, and his diagnosis was that I was suffering from labyrinthitis, a benign infection of the inner ear which affects the sense of balance. The only cure was rest. He told Harold Fielding that they would have to close the show for a fortnight, which of course they did. Harold Fielding was insured and, luckily, for the first time in my life, I was insured too.

I went back to our lovely home, and I rested, and I continued to take my Ativan. Now if you're told to rest, you aren't supposed to do very much, but I took this to extremes. I did nothing at all. I just sat in my chair for hours on end, staring out into the garden. Anne was really worried by my behaviour. I was utterly unconscious of it at the time, but I think I must have been going through some kind of breakdown.

During my second week of Ronnie Corbett in the chair but definitely not telling gags, Martin Scurr came to see me, and told me to relax and forget about the show. 'Go out on Saturday night, have a lovely dinner and a glass of wine, enjoy yourself, then spend a quiet Sunday at home and start again refreshed at the Palladium on Monday.'

So, on the Saturday night, Anne and I went to a very nice place, the Old Lodge, in Limpsfield. I had more than one glass of wine, and I began to talk about Martin Scurr in rather extravagant terms. In fact I called him 'the Messiah' and said that he had saved my life. Both these statements were

Harold Fielding's stage production of The Two Ronnies *at the London Palladium.*

exaggerations. I hadn't been in danger of dying and I have it on good authority that Martin Scurr, excellent doctor though he was, was not 'the Messiah' and had never claimed to be.

I carried my mood of exaggeration into my choice of desserts. I ordered four puddings. Now I very often don't have one pudding, let alone four. What was going on?

Well, I did rest on the Sunday and I did go back to the Palladium on the Monday and I did complete the three weeks that remained of the run, but I wasn't really fit to go back, it was too soon, and I struggled through those interminable three weeks, no longer enjoying anything about the show or its comedy. I was so affected that I could no longer face making my entry through the large door at the top of the stairs and walking down that huge, steep staircase. I had to come on from the side, destroying the opening gag. I was very far from being my usual self. However, many years later, when I could bring myself to talk about it, I asked Ron if there had been any difference that he could see in my performances, and he said, 'None whatsoever.' I must emphasize, too, how wonderfully supportive and patient he was with me. It must have been frustrating and irritating for him, but he never showed it. He was as cool as a cucumber, a rock of support, never made me feel as if I was being a nuisance, just rode it all.

It's hard to sort it all out now. How much of a breakdown was I having? Why did I behave so oddly? I mean, I did have labyrinthitis. That wasn't an illusion. But why should it make me behave so strangely? Why did I order four puddings? Could the disease affect the balance of the mind as well as the body?

I think that perhaps it's part of the price we pay. It's a marvellously fortunate way to earn a living, but there is a price. When you read performers' books or look through their lives, I think you find it is part of the price, because it's such an unnatural way to live, such an unnatural way to behave, performing in front of a lot of people all your life, I think that it causes stress. Olivier had a period, when he was at the National Theatre, when he told everybody, 'When you're acting with me, you mustn't look at me.' They had to act away from him, slightly upstage of him, never looking at him. The moment he was looked at, his bottle went.

I've gone into this at some length, because it had such an

effect on my life. The scars lasted, certainly for the next ten years, but only in the context of theatre. I had no problem at all with television. But in the theatre, if I did anything remotely resembling a long run, the balance would begin to go as I tired, and the fear of it happening was never far away. Was I really suffering from labyrinthitis again, did I have a latent condition which only affected me when I was exhausted, or was this psychological? I couldn't be quite sure, but at times it got so bad that it even affected me when I went to see a show and was sitting in the audience. I would see an actor up there on the stage, with nothing to lean on, nothing to support him, and I would get quite distressed on his behalf. I've heard of stage fright, but audience fright . . . ?

I used to have to time it carefully so that I got to the theatre for my performances only just on time, and had no time to think as I prepared for my first entrance. And I needed to be sure that there was something around to lean on, should my balance begin to go.

Anyway, I struggled through, and I did another tour of Australia, but then I had another crisis. I was booked to do twenty-one cabaret shows, and I was sitting by the pool in this lovely house in Rose Bay, on a golden, sunny afternoon, before the first show, and I said to Anne, 'I cannot do these twenty-one shows. I just can't face them.'

We got on to the phone to a man called Ken Dyball, who was a psychiatrist to the Sydney police. His wife Karen answered – we knew them both quite well – and she said, 'Well, I'm afraid he's playing tennis down at the Royal Sydney Golf Club at the moment, but if you want you can see him down there after he's finished, if it's urgent.' And Anne said, 'It *is* urgent,' so we went down there, and it was like a Woody Allen film – we were standing outside the wire netting, behind a bush, waiting for an appropriate moment in the match, and when he came over to collect a ball, with his sweat bands and his knee bandages and ankle bandages (he played too much tennis and was always injuring himself), Anne went over to the netting, and he said, 'Oh hello, Anne,' not seeming at all surprised to see her there, and Anne said, 'Ron would like to have a word with you,' and he said, 'Well, right, I'll have finished this set in a minute.'

He came out, and we explained what the position was, and he asked me what I'd been on, and I told him I'd been taking half a milligram of Ativan, and he said, 'Go back and take one and a half.' I did, and three hours later the fear and anxiety left me, and with the aid of Ativan I did the twenty-one shows, although I did always make sure that there was a chair handy in case my balance did go.

Even in 1992, almost ten years after the initial attack, I still had a fear that the problem would return. I was in Australia with Donald Sinden, doing Ray Cooney's very funny farce *Out of Order*. I would wonder if I was going to be able to go on, and if there would be something I could lean on if necessary. The audience reaction was amazing, and I enjoyed it despite my fears, but fighting the fear was an exhausting business, and by the end of the tour, when I was really pretty tired, it got so bad that during the day I couldn't even bend down in a bookshop to look at the books on the lowest shelf, for fear of toppling over, and by the time I got back to England I couldn't even stand over a putt.

But I didn't have another attack on the stage, and in the end the fear did leave me, and I got to a point where I didn't need to take the pills any more, though I must admit that to this day I do carry a couple of them in my shaving bag, just in case. But I haven't needed them for more than ten years, and it does seem, touch wood, that the fear has left me at last.

16

Back in England, four months of each year was taken up with *The Two Ronnies*, and both of us continued to develop our own separate careers. Ron and his family were back in Pinner, Anne and I and family in Addington, and all London between us. Now, though, after Australia, I think we each missed the other's company, and we met more often.

We came back from Australia to a very different political landscape, the Conservatives under Mrs Thatcher having come to power while we were away. Prince Charles married Lady Diana Spencer, Ken Livingstone banned the giving of goldfish as prizes at fairs in Greater London, and there was a long, bitter, violent, divisive miners' strike. Throughout it all *The Two Ronnies* went on and on, four months every year, from success to success.

Ronnie and I received a lot of praise over the years, but occasionally we came in for some brickbats. There was only one instance that really upset us, and that was an attack on us, a parody of us, by Mel Smith and Griff Rhys Jones, in the BBC's own *Not the Nine O'Clock News*. Ronnie was even more upset than I was, but we both felt that it was very unfair. One of the accusations was that we used bad language. How strange that seems today. It seemed pretty strange then. We worked out that we had used the word 'bloody' three times, and that was the extent of it. One 'bloody' every 32.66 programmes. What an example to children! Of course, we used words that may have sounded like swear words, but that was in the great British tradition, and we made no bones about being in that tradition.

Someone said that Mel Smith and Griff Rhys Jones were going to be *The Two Ronnies* of the eighties, and Ronnie wasn't prepared to let this go. After all, it was already 1983 and we were still on top of our game. So Ronnie wrote to the newspaper in question and said, 'No, *The Two Ronnies* are going to be *The Two Ronnies* of the eighties; Smith and Jones may well be *The Two Ronnies* of the nineties.'

You may think that we were being a bit prickly and would have been wiser to let the attack on us pass, and maybe we would have been, but I think two things particularly upset us, and especially Ronnie. One was that it was on the BBC, and they were our employers, and the other was that they were fellow comedians, not critics. We had a great respect for and love of the comics of the past, Ronnie especially, with his fondness for all things old. We felt proud to be a part of that tradition and wouldn't have dreamt of criticizing our peers, even had we not liked them. We felt that respect for fellow comedians should still be observed, and it usually is. Honesty compels me to admit that Ron himself uncharacteristically failed to do so himself on one occasion, albeit in private, of which more later.

Another criticism came from a much more unexpected source – Mrs Mary Whitehouse no less. For younger readers I should explain that she was a retired schoolteacher who appointed herself as an arbiter of taste on television, which she felt to be riddled with sex and violence. If she thought that then, what would she think now? If she was still alive, she'd be turning in her grave.

It wasn't sex that she was complaining of, it was violence, and it wasn't actually about *The Two Ronnies*. It was about a silent film we had made, called *By the Sea*.

This was the second of two silent films that we made. Well,

perhaps it would be more accurate to call them almost silent films. There were grunts and mutterings in them, used almost as impressions of words. Not content with being a part of Anthony Burgess's paradigm, Ronnie was also a bit of a paradox. His greatest strength was his verbal dexterity and versatility, but he delighted in forgoing this (delighted except when he had to perform mime in Welsh schools) in favour of visual comedy.

The Picnic featured the characters, mainly aristocrats, that Ronnie had created in *Hark at Barker,* in which he played the bumbling aristocrat Lord Rustless. He had also made, a long while before – in 1970, in fact – a silent film called *Futtock's End*, featuring a character called General Futtock, who was really Lord Rustless in uniform.

By the Sea was more ambitious than *The Picnic*: harder, glossier, longer. It ran, originally, after Ronnie and the editor had worked on it, for an hour and forty minutes. Jimmy Gilbert felt that this was far too long, and wanted to reduce it to fifty minutes. This horrified Ronnie, but I think it was probably necessary. This was a bit of a special production for Ronnie. It was the seaside postcard brought to life, his tribute to the world of McGill, which had always so fascinated him for so many years. It was probably, therefore, his most personal work of all, and I think for this reason he had probably been a bit self-indulgent.

Jimmy was adamant, and fifty minutes it became. Then Jimmy suggested cutting it to forty, and Ronnie said, 'That's not cutting, it's murdering.' After much debate it remained at fifty.

The BBC produced a book of comic postcards to publicize the film, and in the end both Jimmy and Ronnie were very happy with the finished product.

Mrs Whitehouse wasn't, however. Two scenes upset her.

In By the Sea *with Debbie Blythe.*

In one, I got stuck in a revolving door, the lovely Rikki
Howard went wiggling past in a bikini, Ronnie trundled
round in the door to get another look at her, and I shot out
like a cork. In the other, the delightful Madge Hindle, acting
as companion to a rather grand lady played by Barbara New,
lingered rather too long over a rack of postcards on the pier,

and got a sharp prod from the grand lady's parasol for her pains. Prodding parasols and dangerous doors. *Quelle horreur*. Mrs Whitehouse said that these scenes were 'encouraging violence'.

Among the invitations that Ronnie and I didn't accept was one to be the two Ugly Sisters at the Palladium. Taken in complete isolation that might have been fun, but it went against the principles on which we had been building our careers. The silent films were fine, because they were a natural evolution from the style of the classic serial in *The Two Ronnies*. To go into pantomime together seemed a step too far, and I don't think Ron, although he had done pantomime and done it well, was as keen on the genre as I was.

As in our wider career, so in *The Two Ronnies* itself. The bits when we were apart in the show were as important as the bits when we were together.

Before I describe how *The Two Ronnies* came to an end, I should perhaps say a few words about our two solo spots.

I've already touched on the fact that Ronnie's and my solo spots on the show were very different, that he played his in character, and I played mine as myself, or as a fictional version of myself. But on reflection they were different in every way.

Ronnie's were precise, fast, impersonal. Mine were rambling, slow, personal. Often Ronnie had amusing visual aids, captions, charts, pictures. All you saw with me was me and a chair. It was a nice chair, a very nice chair, but its visual impact wasn't great from the start, and was non-existent by the end of the ninety-eight shows.

Every week I sat in this chair and uttered the magical words of a genius from Slough, Spike Mullins.

Spike – real name Dennis – had led a hard life. And we thought we'd had it tough. He'd worked as office boy, sweeper-up, messenger, builder's labourer, farm hand and steel erector. He'd been in the RAF in the war. He'd been a stevedore in the docks and gone totting with a diddicoy. That sounds picturesque, but have you ever gone collecting old scrap and selling it with an itinerant tinker? He'd spent many years as a galley boy on cargo ships and tramp steamers, visiting some of the most unlovely and insect-infested corners of the globe. He'd worked in the kitchens of the Grosvenor Hotel. Well, no, not *the* Grosvenor Hotel. *A* Grosvenor Hotel. He'd worked in all-night cafés. He'd even sold stolen ladies' powder compacts (the powder compacts were stolen, not the ladies. It might have been more fun if it had been the ladies). But he'd always hankered after a *really* tough life – writing gags for comedians.

He had a tiny bit of a breakthrough when he began selling gags to the comedian Vic Oliver, who paid him half a guinea (ten shillings and sixpence) per gag, but only if the audience laughed. Spike got a great thrill from hearing his gags getting laughs on the radio, but less of a thrill when he regularly felt that he was being paid for fewer laughs than he deserved. It all fizzled out, and he put his dreams on the back burner.

Spike was house painting when a chance remark by one of his fellow decorators, a young man with the suitably mournful comic name of Brian Goom, set him on the path that would change his life. It was 1963, and he was forty-seven years of age. Young Mr Goom read in *Reveille* that Max Bygraves was looking for writers to be trained in writing for television. I don't know where you are now, Mr Goom, and I don't know if you'll ever read this, but, if you do, thank you.

That night Spike wrote furiously in longhand, and his wife Mary typed the words on their old three-quid typewriter, and the next morning they posted the stuff off, and tried to forget about it.

Three days later an envelope dropped on to their mat. It contained a cheque and a letter from Max Bygraves.

'Dear Spike Mullins, Many thanks for the script received this morning, and I am elated with the way you wrote this. Of course it is not all usable but I think a good 40 per cent or 50 per cent is, which is wonderful from a seven-page script. So as you will not think you are wasting your time, I enclose a cheque for £25.0.0d on account of the script I will get when I have spoken to you and just given you a few more outlets for the comedy. Many thanks again for your kind interest.'

Spike had started, and he never looked back. He wrote for Max and for Harry Secombe and others, but life was still a bit of a struggle. His confidence in himself was growing, though, until he was bold enough to send that message that he thought he could improve my waffling!

He certainly could. It's a rare occasion when two talents come together and fit perfectly. Ronnie Corbett in the chair was a triumph for Spike and for me, and I must say that part of the pleasure I got from it was the knowledge of how much it meant to him.

'My great-grandfather was killed at Custer's Last Stand – he didn't take any part in the fighting, he was camping near by and went over to complain about the noise.'

'My old house was very nice – right next door to David Frost – a lovely neighbour. You could always send one of the children next door to ask, "Can Mummy borrow a cup of money till the morning?"'

'I actually found this joke in an old *Reader's Digest* in between an article called "Having Fun with a Hernia" and a story about a woman who brought up a family of four with one hand while waiting for Directory Enquiries to answer.'

'The crowd [at a church fête] at its peak was estimated to be somewhere in the region of sixteen. The beauty queen from the tyre factory – Miss Re-Tread of 1969 – sold kisses at 5p a time, and old Fred at the butcher's had a quid's worth and got a bit over-involved. However, disaster was averted thanks to the local fire brigade, four policemen and a chap with a humane killer. Then we had the Unusual Pets Competition, which, owing to lack of support, was won by my wife's brother with a tin of salmon.'

'My wife joined the East Grinstead Co-operative Vivisection Society – they meet in the Co-op and pull people to pieces.'

'I said to my wife last week – I met her at the chemist's, she's always there on Saturday mornings, it's her hobby, she collects prescription numbers – I said to her, "Our house is getting so dirty you have to wipe your feet to go out into the street." She said, "That's the trouble with that street – it marks so easily."'

'My Uncle Spyro was lost at sea under very unusual circumstances – he went up the mast to look for land and when he came down the ship had gone.'

'For some time now my wife's had this ridiculous idea that I'm playing too much golf. Actually it came to a head at about eleven thirty last night. She suddenly shouted at me, "Golf, golf, golf, all you ever think about is bloody golf!" And I'll be honest, it frightened the life out of me. I mean you don't expect to meet somebody on the fourteenth green at that time of night.'

When we recorded my spot in the chair, I never went straight into it. I chatted and joked a little bit to get the audience relaxed, and only then began the actual piece that was being recorded. Also, I have to admit that I played a little trick in order to ensure that I got good laughs. I would tell the audience that, if I wanted them to laugh more, I would touch my glasses and just move them slightly. They would be waiting for this, and it never failed when I did it. They loved it, of course. They felt that they were a part of it, that they and I had a little secret together.

I rarely needed these extra laughs, in actual fact, because Spike's monologues were so good. They might have seemed to be rather rambling, but in fact they were beautifully crafted. I think he deserves to have a whole one quoted. Pour yourself a drink, dim the lights, sit back in your chair, and watch me in my chair.

'This evening I'd like, if I may, to tell you a story about a chap who was cast ashore on a desert island. By the way, this is not the one about the two Irishmen on a desert island who found a lifeboat and broke it up to make a raft.

'I'm glad it's not that one because that is a bit ridiculous.

'This is about a chap who was a passenger on a jumbo jet flying to New York, and when they started the film he'd seen it before on the telly, and he was so disgusted he got up and walked out.

'And as soon as he lands in the water he realizes what he's done and he gets very depressed.

'"Bless my soul," he says, and "Help!" But they up in the aeroplane can't hear him because they're all watching Doris Day, and drinking their duty frees and shouting, "Shut that door!"

'So there he is being tossed about by the waves – that reminds me: a little wave – to my mum and dad.

'Actually my mother still thinks of me as her wee baby, and let's face it I was a wee baby – I spent the first three weeks of my life on a charm bracelet.

'Not exactly true, but if I told you the truth you'd never believe me.

'She's very proud of me. Just as I was leaving tonight she looked at me. Her face was radiant and her eyes were shining – I don't know what she's taking, but I wish I could get some of it – and she turned to my dad, who was sitting there sewing a button on his hat – he's had a lot of worry lately – she said, "Ty" – she calls him Ty, short for Titanic, because she thinks he's a bit of a disaster – she said, "Ty, can this be the same little boy who sang, 'It's My Mother's Birthday Today' and won the talent contest at the old Holborn Empire, all those years ago?"

'And he said, "No, that was Max Bygraves."

'Anyway, back to the chap in the water, who is now swimming strongly towards the desert island which was to be his home for the next fifteen years – all alone, nothing but the sea and the sand and the sky – it makes you wonder what he lived on for fifteen years – credit, I suppose, the same as the rest of us.

'So one day he's sitting there on the beach with nothing but his roughly hewn bucket and spade – and his eight gramophone records – waiting for the tide to come in and fill his little moat.

'Suddenly out of the sea there appeared an apparition. He was very frightened as it flapped its way up the beach towards him.

'"My God," he says, "it's Ronnie Corbett's wife!"

'No, he didn't, he didn't say that at all – I just put that in. I must stop saying nasty things about my wife, especially as today is our anniversary: just twelve years ago today when she said, "I do."

'Which, as I told you before, certainly surprised me, because I didn't think she did.

'Anyway, when it gets nearer, the apparition turns out to be a beautiful girl wearing a wetsuit, snorkel and flippers, and she removes the snorkel and says, "Hullo, what are you doing here?"

'He says, "Well, actually I'm a castaway on this desert island."

'She says, "Oh, you poor man, tch, tch, tch, well I never, fancy that, hm, hm, dog my cats, you poor man. How long is it since you had a cigarette?"

'And he says, "Well, actually, it's about fifteen years, and I'm seriously thinking of giving it up – starting tomorrow."

'Whereupon she unzips a pocket in the wetsuit – she was a big girl. She produced a packet of cigarettes, and he was overwhelmed.

'"I'm overwhelmed," he said – there, I told you he was.

'She said, "Buster, you have seen nothing yet. The best is still to come. How long since you had a drinky-winky?"

'She unzipped another pocket and produced a flask of his favourite whisky. A tear sprang to his eye – did I tell you he only had one eye? It doesn't matter – well, it matters to him, but it doesn't matter to us.

'"This is marvellous," he said. "I haven't had a drink or a cigarette in fifteen years."

'Then she started slowly to unzip the front of her wetsuit and said, "And how long since you played around?"

'And he said, "Good heavens, don't tell me you've got a set of golf clubs in there."'

Spike was a very funny man in real life too. He had white hair and a little white moustache. Well, he probably didn't always have them, but he did by the time I knew him. Or was it after our first meeting that he went white?

Spike once built an open vivarium in his garden. You don't get many of those in Slough. You don't get many closed vivaria (I assume it's a Latin word) either. In the unlikely event that you don't know what a vivarium is, I'd better tell you that it's a place where live animals are kept in conditions resembling their natural habitat. I know that for a fact – unless the person responsible for words beginning with 'v' in the dictionary was sacked and put in a few false definitions out of pique. Spike's vivarium was for lizards. He fancied having lizards, and bought six from London Zoo. They gave him great pleasure in the two days before they died.

Spike spoke in a slightly monotonous voice that was almost a whine, but what he came out with were gems.

On one occasion, one of the BBC governors was touring the building, as they do, and he stopped to speak to Spike.

'How long does it take you to get to work?' he asked – not very inspiringly, it has to be said.

'Well, I live in Slough,' began Spike. 'Well, when I say in Slough, a bit outside. There's a bus every half hour, ten minutes to the station, but the buses don't always coincide with the trains. Say a ten-minute wait at the station.' The poor governor was wishing he'd never asked that dull question, the answer to which was of no possible interest to him. 'Twenty-five minutes on the train to Paddington,' continued Spike remorselessly. 'Then it's the Circle Line to Notting Hill Gate, change to the Central Line for White City, five minutes' walk from there. Round about two hours in all, I suppose. Long time without a woman.'

'Yes, yes, jolly good, ha ha,' spluttered the governor. And he scurried off as fast as his legs would carry him.

In fact, Spike was making all that up about the journey. Once he began to enjoy this marvellous late flowering of his career, he decided to compensate for the rigours of his early life by being spoilt just a little, and he began to insist that a car was sent for him – wouldn't go anywhere without it. He even had a car sent to Slough for his script, which, right to the end, was written in longhand and typed by Mary.

Spike's was a very individual and often a very dry sense of humour, but it reached out to the twenty million people who watched the show at its height.

Spike wrote a monologue for me for my very first appearance on the Royal Variety Show. This was in 1969, after I had worked with him on *The Corbett Follies*, but before his humour had been proven in *The Two Ronnies*. Unfortunately, his style was not appreciated by the producers of the show. After rehearsals I was summoned to the Royal Box, to be interviewed by Bernard Delfont, the impresario, Dick Hurran, the director of the show, Billy Marsh of the Entertainment Artistes' Benevolent Fund and Robert Nesbitt, another director. They didn't understand the jokes. They asked me to explain them. It was impossible. How do you explain a joke? It shrivels and disappears.

Then Billy Marsh suggested I went on stage at that moment and did, for their benefit, the act that I had done when I'd stood in for Cilla Black at the Coventry Hippodrome. They wanted to select something appropriate from it.

This was awful, because I just knew that that wouldn't work. And I managed to stick to my guns, although the encounter didn't do much for my confidence.

On the day, I found that I was sharing a dressing room with Buddy Rich, the great American jazz drummer, and he developed severe toothache. A fashionable showbiz dentist was summoned (yes, there are such people) and I discovered that watching someone else's teeth being drilled is only marginally less disturbing than having your own done.

I was a nervous wreck by the time I went on stage, but everything seemed to go all right, and the audience had no problem with Spike's jokes. I never found out whether Her Majesty understood them.

Spike would always tell me that I needed to be more

laid-back in my delivery, that I was rushing it, and he was right. I was almost there, but it's only in recent years that I've felt that I am doing my material as he would have wanted me to.

I wish he was alive to see it, but he died in 1994. At his funeral at Slough Crematorium, behind the gravel pits, Dick Vosburgh made a very funny speech, for it was also a celebration of Spike's life and wit. His humour was often quite morose, which caused Dick to dub him the Despond of Slough, but I don't think he would have wanted to be sent on his last journey morosely.

'I'm very pleased to say,' said Dick, 'that today they have sent a very special car for Spike. They must have, because otherwise he wouldn't have gone.'

During the run, round about 1978, Spike began to feel that he was running out of steam. He'd done almost fifty of my monologues, and he just felt that he wasn't quite keeping up the standard he'd set himself. This was a very serious moment for me. What would I do if I couldn't do the chair?

Help was at hand in the shape of a young writer called David Renwick, whom I mentioned earlier. He had been one of the writers who sent in news items and got a few accepted, but unlike most of the others he used to come to the show on studio days, hang around, drink in the atmosphere, watch the dress rehearsal and the recording. Well, he lived in Luton, so you can understand it. He lived at the time, I believe, with his parents, and even when he moved, he didn't move very far, so that he could still go back for his Sunday lunch. Somehow, all that was encouraging. He seemed to be the sort of person who might fit into the Spike mould.

Much later, in a TV show after Ronnie's retirement, David, who by then had written *One Foot in the Grave* and

Jonathan Creek, said, 'Spike wrote the first fifty, and I carried on "in his shadow", I'm tempted to say. I have the most joyous memories of sitting there and watching you in the chair in the dress rehearsal. It just creased me up. I loved Spike's style. I loved the man. I revered him, and it became a labour of love to try and echo all that. Spike had established the tone, the character. They just oozed class, those monologues.'

Well, so did David's. He wrote almost fifty of them too, and the amazing thing is that you can't see the join. I was blessed, really blessed. It's extraordinary, really, that for all those fifteen years, I only had two writers for my solo spot.

Ronnie B., on the other hand, had a great many writers, and a great many characters. He would play spokespersons, government officials and newsreaders. Very often he would be appealing on behalf of people with some very strange complaint, usually speech-related. He would deliver them irresistibly, in an unstoppable tide of words. Sometimes these words were extremely complex. I don't think I'm giving away any secrets when I reveal that we had a device called an autocue, so that we could read the words, but this was more to save us from learning them than to make it easy. Reading aloud can actually be harder than speaking what one has learnt.

I'm going to try to recall a few of these monologues, in the hope that they will bring back memories of the shows.

One week Ronnie was appealing on behalf of the very clumsy, courtesy of scriptwriter Peter Vincent. 'Our society was founded in the sixteenth century by the executioner who beheaded Sir Thomas More . . . although he was actually aiming at Anne Boleyn.'

Another week, Barry Cryer and Peter Vincent wrote a parody of the news in which the newsreader discovers that his new electronic typewriter has developed a minor fault and has been typing 'o's instead of 'e's. Ronnie's performance as a lumbering, puzzled newsreader was inspired. Just one paragraph will give you the feel of it. 'Hor Majosty tho Quoon was at Homol Hompstoad today to unvoil a momorial to sovoral groat Onglish mon of lottors and poots, including Anthony Trollopo, H. G. Wolls and Hilairo Bolloc.' And to think that we were both given OBOs after that!

Barry knew a good thing when he saw one, and came up with another monologue in which the problem was that the letter 'G' was missing on a typewriter. To be successful this had to be brilliantly written, and of course it was. It contained the marvellous line, 'I met film stars like Reta Arbo, Rear Arson and Edward Robinson.' 'Rear Arson' was brilliant (Greer Garson in case you don't remember her) but Edward Robinson was inspired. Suddenly, shorn of his 'G', he seemed terribly ordinary. Enius. Sheer enius.

Ronnie's spokesmen were wonderfully self-assured, complacent and arrogant, as they came out with great streams of nonsense.

'Good evening. I want to speak to you tonight about the water shortage. Now, there have been rumours that the government are washing their hands of the whole problem. But we're not – because there isn't any water. But there has been this ridiculous rumour that the cows in the north-east are giving dried milk. Let me deal with that one straight away. It's true.'

'Good evening. I'm from the Ministry of Pollution. Now, a lot of people say to me, "You're not doing enough about pollution," and I say, "Rubbish," and they say, "You're not doing enough about rubbish," and I say, "Pollution."'

'Good evening. Equality. The government White Paper on the Equal Society was published today. Its main provisions were as follows: from April 1st, 1981, everyone must be of equal height.'

Bad news for John Cleese and me and the class sketch.

There was one monologue about statistics, written by Eric Idle. I haven't a script of that, but one gag comes back to me across the decades. 'This was the result of a statistical freak. He works in our Reading office.' Spike could have written that.

Spike, though, would never have written 'An Ear in Your Word', which was another vehicle for Ronnie's mastery of word play, written by a writer who understood him well, Gerald Wiley.

'A very good one to you all and evening. My name is Willie Cope. I am the president of the Getting your Wrongs in the Word Order Society, and I've been asked by the BCB to come a night too long to aim the society's explains, and picture you firmly in the put.'

One piece with a more topical theme was Peter Vincent's 'Doctors Anonymous'. There had been a controversy about doctors advertising themselves when appearing as spokespeople.

'Good evening,' began Ronnie. 'I'm a doctor. Now, I'm not allowed to reveal my name for reasons of professional etiquette. I fully agree with this, and so does my wife, *Mrs* Poncett-Wilberforce. And of course I am not allowed to reveal my address, but here is an eye test:

523

A Harley

Street W1'

I mentioned earlier that Ronnie did a rather good Patrick Moore. However, he wouldn't have claimed to be in the Rory Bremner class, and so he had the bright idea of being Patrick Moore's brother, so that he couldn't be criticized if it wasn't quite accurate. He made all sorts of weird drawings, explaining, 'Here is the famous Sea of Tranquillity, here's a mountain known as the Height of Absurdity, and here are two craters known as the Depths of Depravity.' That doesn't look particularly hilarious in print, does it, but imagine Ronnie as Patrick Moore, and it comes to life. That was one of the many things I admired about Ron. His energy. He gave his monologues tremendous energy, while I sat there in my chair being laid-back.

No wonder he needed to retire before I did.

17

Lulworth Cove, in the fair county of Dorset, is a renowned beauty spot. In fact it's a world-famous example of . . . well, of a cove. It has a very narrow entrance, but inside it is huge and perfectly round, as if a giant had taken a vast bite out of the cliffs for his breakfast.

Ron and I were having breakfast at the time, actually, in our caravan, on location. It was the summer of 1986. He was waiting for his two fried eggs and rashers and fried bread, I was waiting for something small and perfectly formed. We were both dressed as Vikings, and not even very nice Vikings at that. I mean, there must have been some nice Vikings, saying, 'Steady on, chaps. These people don't look too bad. It seems a bit of a shame to pillage them, on the whole.' But we weren't that sort of Viking. We were hairy and disgusting and not over-endowed with intelligence. We had huge horned helmets, not that we were actually wearing them at that moment. You don't eat breakfast in your helmet, even if you're a rather disgusting Viking. But if I tell you that our names were Mudguard the Mighty and Pith the Pathetic you'll realize what sort of Vikings we were. Not natty dressers.

Do I need to tell you which part I played? Yes, I think I do. For this sketch, we reversed the expected casting. I was Mudguard the Mighty, and Ron was Pith the Pathetic, and wonderfully funny he was being pathetic, really big and pathetic. The unexpected casting made this a very funny sketch.

I've often wondered why Ronnie chose that moment to

The Vikings at Lulworth Cove. Ron played Pith the Pathetic,
and I played Mudguard the Mighty.

tell me. Was it his innate sense of the ludicrous and the
incongruous, which is at the heart of almost all comedy? Or
was it just so that it wouldn't seem too serious, it wouldn't
seem too momentous an announcement, we could pass it off,
finish our breakfast, trot down to the cove and give our
wonderful, spellbinding performances as Mudguard and Pith?
(Mudguard and Pith – that could even be the title for yet
another new detective series.) Anyway, he did choose that

moment. He suddenly looked serious. I had an intimation that he was going to say something important.

'Ron,' he said, in the low voice of a newsreader moving on to something sad, 'I think I ought to tell you that the Christmas after next . . .' that was how far ahead we were talking about '. . . after the Christmas special, I am going to retire.'

I can't remember what I said. Nothing very much, probably. There wasn't much to say. I certainly wasn't upset with him. He had every right to make the decision, and I was grateful to him for giving me a year and a half of warning.

'I'm not telling anybody else,' he said, 'so please don't you tell anybody else yourself.' It would be a secret between us and our wives. He said that he would let the BBC know some time in the following year.

I knew, though he hadn't told me in any graphic way, that he had suffered one or two heart scares, first of all in a tiny way in Australia, as I've mentioned, and then a somewhat bigger scare later. He had told me that he had a problem, and he had told it to me in confidence. When Eric Morecambe went, and Tommy Cooper died on stage, I thought that he felt that, if his health was still suspect, what was the point of going on?

For a long time Ron actually denied that worries over health had played any part in his decision. He gave other reasons, more complex reasons, and I think now that all of them contributed.

He said later that he had actually decided to retire in the previous year, 1985, and that Peter Hall had been partly responsible. There was a kind of satisfying dramatic shape to that. Peter Hall had been the person who had brought Ron to London from Oxford, and now he was unwittingly persuading him to retire from London and go and live near Oxford!

What happened was that Peter Hall asked Ron to play the part of Falstaff (this time *The Stage* didn't get it wrong and say that it was me), and Ron started thinking about commuting to the National and back, and how long it would take with all the traffic, and whether he would be able to avoid the rush hour, and he thought that perhaps these were not the considerations that ought to come first to one's mind when offered a great Shakespearean role, and in that moment he realized that he was no longer hungry enough, he was no longer ambitious enough.

Peter Hall said later, 'He would have been a wonderful Falstaff, a wonderful Toby Belch; there are about fifteen parts in Shakespeare he could have done. And the parts that Molière wrote for himself – *School for Wives*, *Tartuffe*, *The Misanthrope* – he would have been wonderful in any of those. During my fifteen years at the National, I'd kept on asking him, offering him all these roles. But it never worked out because of the scheduling. I do think he's the great actor we lost. I really do think that.'

Well, Ron simply didn't have any burning ambition to do these things, because he did other things which he loved, and they filled his life. The important thing, to me, about his career, is that he never for one moment thought that he was dumbing down, or selling out, in pursuing a life in comedy. He always believed that comedy was as good and as important as serious work, and that making millions laugh on television was just as good as moving much smaller numbers of people to tears in the theatre.

The Falstaff offer, and his reaction to it, was just one of the factors that led Ronnie to plan his retirement at such an unusually young age for an actor. He was just fifty-seven when he told me that morning in Dorset. Come to think of it, it's unusual for an actor at any age. Retirement doesn't usually come into the equation. Old soldiers never die, they just fade away. Old actors never retire, they just forget their lines.

Another window on Ronnie's thinking was opened by Jo Tewson, the leading lady in so many of our sketches. Long before *The Two Ronnies* even began, Jo and Ron were both in Tom Stoppard's *The Real Inspector Hound*. They were going to the theatre together, and Jo was worried because the train was late. Ronnie asked her why she was worried. 'Because the show must go on,' she said. 'Why?' he asked. 'Why must the show go on? Nobody's going to bother if we're not there. The world isn't going to come to an end if we don't do the show tonight.' Sometimes Ron was too sensible, too ordinary even, to be a star. In the days of *Frost on Sunday*, right back then at the beginning of our work together, he turned down a good Shakespearean part because it would interfere with the school holidays, and he was, first and foremost, a family man. That might have been an excuse, because he did seem extremely reluctant to do Shakespeare, but I think there was truth in it. He was at heart, from the time when he fell in love with Joy, a family man even before he was an actor. So, deep down, his decision wasn't a total surprise to me.

There was another reason, I think, a more particular reason, and that was to do with *The Two Ronnies*. He had finished doing *Porridge* after just eighteen episodes, well before it ran out of steam. He had finished doing *Open All Hours* after nineteen episodes, again ensuring that it wouldn't run out of steam. We had already done about ninety episodes of *The Two Ronnies*. Ronnie didn't believe that we could keep up the standard. In fact he believed that the standard had already, imperceptibly, begun to slip. The main reason for this was that it was becoming harder and harder to get material. Gerald Wiley's well was beginning to run dry. The flood of good ideas had become a trickle. Some of our other writers had moved on to pastures new, to developing their own work, and were now simply too busy to continue writing for us. For all the writers, it was difficult not to run out of ideas after as many series as we had done. We must have done almost every party sketch that it is possible to conceive. Musical finales, serials, we'd done so many. David Renwick was coming up to fifty monologues for me in the chair. He was coming up to the point at which mental fatigue had set in for Spike Mullins. There are only so many jokes that you can make on my size and the producer's meanness. In Ronnie's monologues, too, every kind of verbal problem had been exploited.

It might not have been time to stop, but what was certain was that very soon it would be time to stop. One day, perhaps next year, perhaps the year after, the BBC would have said to us, 'Sorry, chaps. You've had your day. It's run its course.' Wasn't it better to tell them first?

Ron and I had discussed the possibility of giving the show a break, perhaps an extended break, but always in the context of our doing something else together for a while. We'd talked of doing a sitcom together, something on the lines of *The Odd Couple*, perhaps. That might have been interesting, but now it was not to be. We had also been looking, though not in an urgent way, for an idea strong enough for a film. It hadn't materialized.

I've talked, in the context of my illness, about the stress involved in regularly appearing in front of large numbers of people. Perhaps Ronnie's well of energy as a performer was drying up, just as his well of ideas was. With him there was an added stress in the claims of fame. I've emphasized how he never really became comfortable with the idea of performing as himself, but he was just as uncomfortable being seen in public as himself.

He recalled an August Bank Holiday in Littlehampton – why did he choose Littlehampton? Was he drawn there unconsciously because of its name, which had given rise to more than one double entendre in his career? The resort was crowded. It just wouldn't have been sensible for him to show his face outdoors. By midnight, he was desperate for a breath of air and set off for a stroll on the beach. Before he'd even closed the front door, a car had braked to a halt and four young people had exclaimed, 'Oooh, it's Ronnie Barker.'

He also recalled a visit to the Louvre, to see the *Mona Lisa*, on his very first visit to Paris. There was a big crowd in front of it, naturally (and, if you haven't seen it, it is surprisingly small. I like it. We have a lot in common), but the crowd happened to be a party of British tourists, and Joy nudged him, and pointed out that they were all studying him studying the *Mona Lisa*. Gratifying, perhaps, but nevertheless it wouldn't have pleased him. I don't think Leonardo da Vinci would have been too thrilled either.

All these considerations may have contributed to Ronnie's decision, but at the heart of it was the fact that he loved life at his mill and wanted to enjoy at least a few happy years there. The mill is a delightful place, tucked away off a leafy lane, a mellow stone old Cotswold building, unpretentious and private like Ron himself. Streams murmur peacefully through the lawns. Trees provide shade and secrecy. He and Joy bought it originally as a weekend cottage, but loved it so much that they sold the house in Pinner, and it became a true home, where the family enjoyed traditional Christmases and great firework parties on Guy Fawkes night. It was quite an extended family, too, at such times, with Ronnie's sisters and

Joy's sister and their children, and Joy's cousin and their children. In Joy's words, 'He had no desire to do a Tommy Cooper and die on stage. He wanted a bit of life off stage.' In any other profession this would cause no surprise.

Ronnie's announcement to me, so inappropriately made in the guise of Pith the Pathetic, was a bit of a shock at the time, but I took it calmly. We did the sketch just as if nothing had happened. And of course, from everyone else's point of view, nothing had happened.

I don't think the act of telling me was an easy one for Ron, but I tried not to make it difficult. He said that I was wonderful about it, but I honestly don't think there was really anything wonderful in my reaction. I had no choice. In a comedy partnership, as in sex, the one who says 'no' has to win.

We continued to make the series, nursing our great secret. I made certain that I enjoyed it all the more because I knew that time was running out, and I think that our sense that there wasn't long to go kept us on our toes, made us work all the harder to maintain the standards we had set ourselves.

The following year Ronnie told Michael Grade and our departmental heads at the Television Centre, Gareth Gwenlan and Jim Moir. None of them wanted to lose Ron, but they could see that he was serious and they didn't try to dissuade him. Michael Grade wrote to him a couple of days later and used a phrase that Ron loved. 'I know what it is,' he wrote. 'You just want to stop and smell the roses.' They too were sworn to secrecy, and the press never got a whiff of it.

We paid another visit to Australia in 1986, to do our second series of *The Two Ronnies* there. Once again it was an entirely happy experience. We still had a Christmas special to do in England, but this marked the end of our series together. Nobody knew, of course. Ronnie and I shook hands, and he said, 'That's it, then.' That was all. So very British, even in Australia.

While we were in Australia, Ron was writing the scripts for his new sitcom, which was called *Clarence*. This had been commissioned, of course, and put into the production schedules, before he announced his retirement to anyone at the BBC. The show had its roots in one of a series of programmes called *Six Dates with Barker* that he had recorded in 1971. It had been called *Fred, The Removals Person* and had been written by a very fine Irish writer named Hugh Leonard. As in the original, Ron was supported by Jo Tewson and Phyllida Law (Emma Thompson's mother). No doubt everyone concerned with it hoped that they would be in a long-running series. Ron couldn't tell them that they wouldn't be. The secret must go on.

Clarence was the most working-class of all Ronnie's characters, a rung or two down the social scale even from Fletcher. The main joke was that he was very short-sighted. What appealed to Ronnie most about the project was that he could film the exterior shots in his beloved Oxfordshire, not too far from the mill.

And so the year moved on, and we came to our very last show together, the Christmas special, an event steeped in emotion for us both, but an emotion that had to be completely hidden, because Ron was keeping his secret right to the end. He would have hated a long, lingering goodbye, a huge, sentimental farewell with all the crew. He was too private for that.

He did, however, as I learnt later, teeter on the edge of giving away the secret. He considered ending the show, after I'd said, 'Goodnight from me' with the words, 'And it's goodbye from him.' He knew it would be unwise, after keeping the secret for so long, to open the floodgates of speculation, which it surely would have done. But he *was* tempted. It was, after all, a very special moment.

Ron and I didn't talk about our feelings on that night. We couldn't. I know that I felt sad and had to work at keeping up the energy level without which comedy just doesn't work. Our eyes had to twinkle with humour, not glisten with tears. We had to make this a really good show.

In the show, playing a small part, was a childhood pal of Ronnie's, Ivor Humphris. In those far-off days he too had dreamt of becoming an actor, but in his case the dream hadn't worked, and he'd become a teacher instead. But he still had his Equity card, and so Ron had this idea of having him in his very last show. But he couldn't tell him that the reason that he was in it was that it was his very last show. How very Ron. A truly sentimental but very private gesture.

So we recorded all the usual items – our last sketches, Ron's last spokesperson, my last chat in the chair.

There was a particularly big set for our final item, called 'Pinocchio II – Killer Doll'.

'I was at one end of it,' Ron recalled, 'and I walked from one side to the other, through a glade and up over a little rustic bridge, and I was thinking then that this was the last time I was going to be on a set. I was very emotional. But all on my own. It was lovely, there was no one about. So I just lingered about a bit and said goodbye to it.'

And so to the final item at the news desk, and Ron's temptation, about which I knew nothing.

He resisted it, of course.

'So it's goodnight from me,' I said.

'And it's goodnight from him,' he said.

And it was.

So we held the usual party, with the usual drinks and nibbles, in the dressing room for Gerald Wiley, between our

In our last show, 'Pinocchio II – Killer Doll'. Ron as Geppetto and me as Pinocchio. Christmas Night with the Two Ronnies, 1987.

two dressing rooms. And we went off to our usual Indian restaurant in Westbourne Grove, Anne and me and Joy and Ronnie, and had our usual curry. I found it touching that we did it like that, so quietly, just the four of us, our usual routine, no histrionics.

We left the restaurant, and went to our cars. Then it really was goodnight from us, and goodnight from them.

18

For many years Ronnie had acted as his own agent, with a second telephone line, strictly for business only, at his country home in Oxfordshire. If you rang the line to discuss business, you were told that you were through to Dean Miller Associates, named after their home, Dean Mill. But you would never have got through to anybody. The line was permanently on answerphone. They would listen to the messages, and Joy would phone back as and when required.

On New Year's Eve 1986, just a few days after our final seasonal special had dominated the Christmas ratings, Ronnie decided to record a new message. Anyone who phoned after that evening was told, 'As of 1st January I am retiring from public and professional life so I am unable to undertake any more commitments. To those people with whom I have worked, I would like to express my gratitude and good wishes. So it's a big thank you from me and it's goodbye from him. Goodbye.'

People thought it odd that Ron announced his retirement in such a way, but I thought it was very Ron. Impersonal, yet not ungracious. Unemotional, yet rather touching. What else could he have done? He himself said that he didn't think he was important enough, or that the event was important enough, for him to make an official announcement. He was a comic actor, not a world leader.

One of the first people to hear this message was a representative of the *Daily Mail*. The secret was out. The speculation about Ronnie's true reasons began. Our life after *The Two Ronnies* began.

The BBC marked the retirement by bringing Ronnie back to do a one-off programme, recorded in front of an audience, to tell the story of our shows together. It was a discussion programme, hosted by Barry Cryer, with Ron and me answering his questions, and Ian Davidson, Terry Hughes, David Nobbs, David Renwick, Peter Vincent and Dick Vosburgh also chipping in. The set felt very cumbersome, with all the participants seeming to be a long way away from each other, as if it was a BO clinic, and to the participants there was a slightly stilted feel to it. Here there was no escape for Ronnie from being himself, there was no character role to hide behind, and I could tell that he was a bit uneasy, but I don't think the audience would have noticed, because he did this kind of thing so much better than he thought he did.

In the event, although we may have felt that it was stilted, the audience in the studio and the audience at home enjoyed this last look at the history of the ninety-eight shows. The discussions were intercut with scenes from our shows, a last nostalgic view before the realities of retirement.

There were a couple of typical news items.

'The pound had a good day today. It rose sharply at ten o'clock, had a light breakfast and went for a stroll in the park.' How silly is that, and yet there was a big laugh that went on and on. How would an analyst of humour try to explain the joke to somebody who didn't think it funny?

'We've just heard that there's a new rail service specially for people travelling to Brighton. It's the Have It Away Day.'

There were extracts from a couple of sketches. 'Sid and George', from 1979, was written by John Sullivan and Freddie Usher. The setting is a pub. Sid and George are discussing women over their pints.

Sid and George.

'They have these . . . er . . . they have these places, don't they?' says Ronnie, not without embarrassment.

'Places?'

'Yeah. You know. You've heard of the erosive zones, haven't you?'

'Well, I've seen pictures of them in holiday brochures.'

'No, erosive zone, that's the medical term for a place a woman's got, you see, where if you touch it she goes mad. Well, your Lil's got one of them.'

'Yeah. Her wallet.'

Another sketch set in a pub featured the man who finished all his friend's sentences. What I liked about this was that my character, and of course it was me who was interrupted, never ever seemed the slightest bit annoyed by this.

'They wanted me to change my . . . er . . .'

'What? Change your hours?'

'No. Change my . . .'

'Change your habits?'

'No . . . er . . .'

'Change your socks more often?'

'No. Change my duties. Of course I always worked with . . . er . . .'

'Pride?'

'No, with . . . er . . .'

'Within reason?'

'No, with . . .'

'With your overcoat on?'

'No. With Harry Hawkins. I always worked with Harry Hawkins. He used to give me . . .'

'His wholehearted support?'

'No, his . . .'

'His athletic support?'

'No. His ginger nuts.'

(And so on.)

The third sketch they chose to show a snippet from was called 'The Chute', and was written by Barry Cryer and David Nobbs. Ronnie was laundryman in a big hotel and I was an under-manager who kept coming down the laundry chute, because I was being shoved down it, a fact which I was attempting to hide. It was a very well-judged chute. I came down at exactly the right speed for comedy, quite fast but not ridiculously fast, and I attempted to preserve my dignity throughout.

'Well, the chute's certainly working all right.'

'Course it is. It's a chute, ain't it? That's why it's called a chute – you shove stuff in the top, it shoots down, that's why it's called a chute.'

'Well, I realize that, yes, but I'm just checking it, you see. I don't want you to think I'm being thrown down it.'

Whereupon I walked off with every shred of dignity I could muster, only to reappear down the chute a moment later.

They showed extracts from three of Ronnie's monologues. There was 'Tomorrow's Kitchen', by Peter Vincent and Ian Davidson. 'But what about the pests of the future? Here is the mousetrap of the future. It consists of a piece of cheese, a Jimmy Young record and a brick. When the mouse smells the cheese he comes out of his hole. Play the Jimmy Young record, and when the poor little so and so puts his paws over his ears, you creep up behind him and clobber him with the brick. Simple really.'

'Guru' was also by Peter Vincent and showed Ronnie blacked up as an Indian guru. 'What is my message to you? Oh my God, the cocoa's coming off. Some of you are saying, this man is not a genuine Indian Indian, he is from Basildon New Town with Irish father and mother from Arbroath who travels in cocoa. No, no, no. To these sceptics, I say, joss-sticks to you.' This was a portrayal not of a man who was an Indian guru, but of a man pretending to be an Indian guru. Despite this, in today's climate it would probably be considered politically incorrect.

The third extract from Ronnie's monologues was the original 'Pispronunciation' sketch, appealing on behalf of those who couldn't say their worms correctly. 'I remember twice a dong lime ago, an old angler exploded to me, "I haven't fought a king all day." Of course he meant, I haven't caught a ding all fay.'

There was also an extract from one of my monologues in the chair, and having quoted one of Spike Mullins's in full, I'd like to quote this one of David Renwick's in full also, in thanks for the fifty or so of these pieces that he wrote for me.

'Tonight I'd like to tell you a very, very funny joke. This is the sort of joke that will still be loved and enjoyed even when it's a hundred years old. A week next Tuesday. Why do I bother? Why do I carry on every week when you consider that for three times the money I could go and work for British Rail? Who says crime doesn't pay? If I'd gone into films, by now I could have matured into a huge, international sex symbol. You can laugh. Did they explain that to you when you came in? No, but for a strange quirk of fate I could have been the new Charles Bronson. If the old one had been a pint-sized comedian who wore glasses.

'Actually I'm being unfair to myself there – all these stories I keep putting around about being small. Like when I say that for three months I served as a shop steward on a silicon chip. That's all just part of my professional repertoire. The truth is, I've always been very sensitive about my physique, since that time I went into hospital. I took off all my clothes, and the doctor rushed over and gave me the kiss of life. I suppose really I should never have got undressed in the first place – strictly speaking, my wife wasn't even allowed visitors.

'As it happens I was admitted myself, shortly afterwards. I'd been feeling very weak and tired, and nothing the doctors did seemed to help. In the end they put me on a course of iron tablets, and I collapsed with metal fatigue.

'You see, people never take me seriously. Like the dressing rooms they gave me here at the BBC. You won't believe this, but until a month ago I was still classified as a glove puppet. Until the start of each show I was kept folded up in a biscuit tin with Basil Brush. Worst of all must be this set – a box with a chair on it. Well, this week my pride got the better of me, and I complained to the Managing Director of Television. He said, "Don't worry about a thing. As from this week I'm giving the whole set a face lift. More sparkle, more glitter, more razzamatazz," he said. "You won't even recognize it." '

. . . at which point I pulled down a solitary pink balloon and sat there, holding it.

'Isn't it pathetic? Little things please little minds, I suppose.'

. . . as I took out a long knitting needle.

'Shall I? If only it were that simple. Do you realize that one stab with this and I could cause a national walk-out by the National Federation of Balloon-Popping Operatives? Which could seriously disrupt Diana Dors's acupuncture course. So I won't bother. Why should I descend to their level? Minds like children, all of them. Oh, that reminds me, a little wave to my own children.'

I waved.

'Only things have been a bit iffy at home again lately. The riots in the hamster's cage are just entering their fifth week, and on Monday afternoon our little boy became very distraught when his piggy bank contracted swine fever. Added to which, last weekend our young puppy dog was sniffing around the front room and accidentally swallowed the remote control gadget for the TV. A bit unfortunate – now we have to twiddle his tummy to get BBC1. If we want ITV we have to twiddle the top of his left leg. Thank God we never watch BBC2.

'Anyway, on to the joke, which concerns this rather posh, well-to-do lady from Belgravia, who one day takes her young son for a day out to the local cattle market. And the son is all agog because he's never seen a cow close up before. Well, he's seen bits of them, you know, nestling by the Yorkshire pudding. But he's never seen what they look like all put

together. And as they're standing there looking at one particular cow, an old farmer comes up and starts feeling the animal
all along its flank, pressing the skin and kneading its muscles
. . . I think he was trying to get BBC2, actually. And the boy
turns to his mummy, and says, "Mummy". Because he knows
her quite well. "Mummy," he says, "What's that man doing
that for?"

'His mother says, "Well, he's got to do that, that tells him
how much meat there is on the cow, and if he thinks there's
enough he'll buy it, you see." It's quite educational this joke,
isn't it? That's about all it is.

'So a couple of days later the boy is sitting at the breakfast
table in the family's plush mansion, tucking into his quadra-
phonic Rice Krispies, and wearing a bit of a frown, so his
mother asks him what's on his mind.

'He says, "Well, you know what you told me the other
day about that farmer and the cow at the cattle market?" She
says, "Yes?" He says, "Well, I was just walking past the
kitchen a few minutes ago, and I think Daddy wants to buy
the cook."'

The same programme showed brief extracts from two
delightful film pieces that David Renwick wrote, one called
'Raiders of the Lost Auk', a skit on the Harrison Ford classic,
and the other, written with David Marshall, a stylish parody
of Poirot. This contained a marvellous sequence in which I
fell into an ornamental fountain. It really was very funny. To
watch. It wasn't funny to do. It was just wet. The key to it
was that I behaved as if I had meant to fall in. I lolled there
elegantly, attempting unsuccessfully to stem a flow of water
which looked as if I was relieving myself as prodigiously as
Henry Cotton's donkey in far-off Portugal. So it managed to
be a lavatory joke and an elegant joke at the same time – no
mean feat.

The last word on the programme should come from Ronnie himself. Barry questioned him on why he had retired, and he said, 'I'd done everything I wanted to do. I had no ambitions left, and I began to hate London more and more, so, off to the Cotswolds and my water mill.'

Our lives were now very different. I was still a working actor, and Ron was retired. But one factor that was similar in both of our lives was that our mothers lived on to a much greater age than our fathers. Ron didn't speak much about his family, he was very private in that regard, but I do know that his father left his mother for a German lady, coming back when that didn't work out, but only to be given rather a hard time, not entirely unnaturally, by Ron's mother. He died in 1972. Ron's mother lived in Cambridge for many years, but eventually Ron bought a house in Chipping Norton, with a ground-floor flat for her, and, at the age of ninety, after several happy years there, she moved in with Ron and Joy at the mill, where she died in 1994 at the age of ninety-four.

My mother continued to live in Edinburgh, and eventually moved into sheltered housing, where she lived a reasonably happy if rather lonely life for many years. We did think of bringing her south to live with us, but her whole life had been based in Edinburgh, her surviving friends were there, as were my brother and my sister-in-law, and so in the end we didn't. Then she started wandering out to post letters at three in the morning, so really she was suffering from dementia. My brother got her into a very nice, high-quality home, where she was well looked after. We visited her frequently, and she died there at the age of ninety-three. By that time she was seeing all sorts of visions. An hour or so before she died, I was lying on her bed beside her. I remember that for some reason I still had my cap on. Tears were streaming down my cheeks, and beside me she was sleeping peacefully.

Both Ron and I were to suffer an early disappointment in our new life. Ronnie was disappointed by the public reaction to *Clarence*. It wasn't a serious matter, as there could now never be a second series, but the character was rather close to his heart, and he would have liked to have gone out with a bang. It wasn't exactly a whimper, but the public reaction was a bit lukewarm.

I think there was more than one reason for this. Partly it was due to the fact that, by Ronnie's very highest standards, it wasn't as rich a piece as *Porridge* or *Open All Hours*. It was too reliant on the one joke, Clarence's short-sightedness. That on its own would not necessarily have been serious – after all, the fact that *Some Mothers Do 'Ave 'Em* was entirely dependent on the clumsiness and physical ineptitude of the character so memorably played by Michael Crawford didn't stop it being a major success. But the public knew that Ronnie had retired. It was not in their best interests to become too fond of this new character, as there would never be another series. Also, Ronnie had consigned himself to history. He was in the past. Later, nostalgia would set in, but it was too soon for that.

My disappointment was probably the greater, since I was still a working man with a career. Ronnie's retirement wasn't a fatal blow for me. It wasn't an amputation. I still had a busy career of my own. Nevertheless, *The Two Ronnies* was the undoubted highlight of my career, so Ronnie's retirement had to be a difficult moment for me. The second highlight of my career, after *The Two Ronnies*, was my sitcom *Sorry*, which had actually run for longer than either *Porridge* or *Open All Hours*. However, the BBC chose this moment to say, 'We've decided not to do any more *Sorry*. Sorry.'

But my disappointment didn't last long. Exciting new challenges would soon present themselves. In the meantime, instead of wallowing in a bit of self-pity, let's think of Ron in his retirement.

Of course I didn't see him as much as I had when we'd been working, but the friendship continued as it had always done and was all the more relaxed now that we were no longer working together. We'd go to each other's parties, meet in London from time to time, see the occasional show, and . . . well, meet at awards ceremonies and nostalgic tributes on TV more often than we could ever have dreamt.

In actual fact Ron wasn't strictly retired. He had retired from show business, but he and Joy bought a little shop, called the Emporium, in the rather severe little Cotswold town of Chipping Norton. It was an antique shop. He had moved from working with his greatest love (after Joy and the family), comedy, to working with his second-greatest love, antiques. It was hard work. Every two months they drove down to London and came back laden with objets d'art. One of the great attractions for Ron was that he could always take home whatever he wanted from the shop. If you own it, it isn't shoplifting. It does, however, rather tend to hit at the profits, and after ten years, working with Ron's younger sister Eileen and her husband, they decided that they would have to sell.

Ron didn't go to the local pubs or anything like that. It's virtually impossible when you're so well known. But in Chipping Norton itself people grew used to him, and he was able to become part of the furniture, as it were. He became a familiar sight, walking down the High Street. There was no longer any fuss. He could go into the Crown and Cushion, a smart little hotel in the square, or to a little Italian restaurant near by, and be himself.

A fascinating picture of Ron in this environment was given

by Bob McCabe, who wrote an authorized biography of him for BBC Books, sensibly entitled *The Authorized Biography of Ronnie Barker*, which remains the most complete description of his life and work.

In an 'Afterword' at the end of the book, Bob McCabe wrote, 'We would work in the morning and the afternoon, with a break in the hotel bar for an hour's lunch. I was pleased to discover that Ronnie has a taste for chilli con carne – as do I – and theirs wasn't bad. It was fascinating, though, watching him interact with the locals in the bar. He felt obliged to say something funny, and I'm sure I noticed him timing it by the moment he chose to put his hand in the pocket of one of those striped blazers he favours. It reminded me of *The Two Ronnies'* run at the London Palladium, when Ronnie Corbett recalls an incident where Barker invented a stage version of himself for fear of revealing his true self. My feeling is that Ronnie B. is both the man behind the mask and the mask itself – he knows how to play the character, and he knows that his audience expect to see him as well.'

Perhaps 'fear' is too strong a word, and 'unease' or 'discomfort' might be better, but it's beautifully put and a fine picture of my dear friend in his Chipping Norton days.

Sadly, health problems did come to mar Ron's rural idyll, but, luckily, not to ruin it. The problem, as always, was his heart. He had regular six-monthly tests and checks for blood pressure, and in 1994 they decided that he needed to have an angiogram, in which a catheter is inserted into the groin and a dye is introduced into the bloodstream. As it circulates, they can map the arteries and detect narrowing, furring and the other ills that arteries are heir to.

Ronnie needed a heart bypass, and this was done in 1996. The doctors told him that there was a 3 per cent risk of fatality, which is one of those statistics that somewhat alarm me, because if you do die 100 per cent of you dies, not 3 per cent, and it's no consolation to know that 97 per cent of people haven't died if the statistics are accurate. Anyway, the important statistic was that the doctors estimated that if he delayed until the following year, the fatality risk would be 30 per cent. Naturally, therefore, he had the operation.

The operation was a success, and Ronnie described his coming round after it rather memorably. 'When you wake up you think, "Who are these ghosts? What's happening?" Because everything's very dark. And it's the nurses. It's all the nurses in the night, silently walking about.'

Nine months later, on 1 April 1997 – a suitable date for a comedian, but this was no April fool – Ron developed a pulmonary embolism, which is very often fatal. It's a blood clot, and it can go either to the lungs or the brain. Ron's went to the lungs, which was probably lucky. It grew harder and harder for him to breathe, and he was rushed to hospital, where he was put on a wonderful new type of drug known as a 'clot buster'. It worked, and by that evening the specialist who had done the operation the previous year was convinced that he had turned the corner.

Ron realized, though, when he saw all his family round the bed, how close he had been to death. It's a difficult one, isn't it? Your family naturally want to be with you en masse if there's a risk if your dying, but the sight of them all there round your bed could precipitate the very event that they dread.

Anyway, Ron soon felt fine, and his heart was certainly immeasurably better than before the bypass, although, as Joy put it, 'He didn't obey orders. He never did. He was supposed to walk two miles a day. He just wasn't that sort of person. He had too much to do sitting at home,' and before too long he was persuaded out of retirement to do a couple of films. I have heard people suggest that this rendered the integrity of his retirement suspect. What nonsense. His return to work was in 2002. He had been retired for more than fifteen years. A long time for an insincere gesture! The shop had been sold, his health was better, he was rested, he was no longer tired; one of the biggest reasons for his retiring had been removed.

Fifteen years! Time, perhaps, to consider what I had been doing during those fifteen years.

In the theatre I had the great privilege, as I've mentioned, of being in Ray Cooney's stage play *Out of Order* with Donald Sinden, who is excellent company, and what a difference that makes, especially on tour. There's a lot of unemployment in the profession, and on the whole one can take one's pick of many excellent actors for any part, so throughout *The Two Ronnies* we would avoid people who were boring at rehearsals, or temperamental on the set, in favour of people who weren't, and were just as good actors. The thing I didn't mention about *Out of Order*, the thing that carried me through it despite the remnants of my fears about my labyrinthitis, was the laughter. I went to see the play at the Shaftesbury, with Michael Williams in the role I was to play, and I had never heard such a volume of laughter, especially in the second act. It beat even the laughter we got at the Palladium, and it was, I'm glad to say, the same in Australia with me in the part. What a joy it is to laugh like that, and what a joy and a privilege it is to provide laughter like that. Thank you, Ray.

My next TV show put a smile on people's faces too. It was called *Small Talk*. Yes, I know, but the title didn't actually refer to me, it referred to children. Well, I suppose it referred to me a bit as well. In fact, maybe they gave me the job because I fitted the title. No, they didn't. They gave it to me because I was supremely well fitted for the job, and the title was just a bit of luck, or serendipity if you're intellectual. Anyway, it was a programme with lots of children in it, being asked all sorts of questions, and responding with delightful charm and confidence and ignorance and making everybody laugh. There were also adult contestants who had to guess what the reaction of the children would be.

I have to admit that in a way it was a bit of a cheat. Most television is. The programme gave the impression that I had the children with me, but I didn't. They had been filmed in advance. We did three programmes in a day, and I would change my clothes to give the impression that they were all separate events.

Despite not being with the children, I took great pains to have a rapport with them, and I'd like to think that one of the reasons why I was chosen as presenter (and nothing to do with the title) was that I would be able to have my fun with, rather than at the expense of, the children.

What has given me particular pleasure in recent years is my involvement with some of the younger generation of comedians. This has given me enormous pleasure, as well as the reassuring feeling that I wasn't yet a dinosaur.

I was pleased to be invited to tea at the Ritz for a second time. It has to be flattering when this happens as often as every thirty years. I mentioned many chapters ago that the identity of the second person to invite me to break cucumber sandwiches with him was more surprising than the first. I can tell you now that it was Ben Elton. Did you have him down for a habitué of the Ritz and a lover of afternoon tea? No? Well, did you have him down for a quiet, sweet, warm human being? Wrong again. He is. The ferocity is in his act, and is an act.

Ben wanted me to do my spot in the chair from *The Two Ronnies* in his new series of *The Ben Elton Show*. Not once, but regularly. I was thrilled. In fact he was so involved with it that he actually wrote three of my monologues, and wrote them very cleverly, pushing me into the naughty areas that might be expected by *his* audience without ever pushing me that bit too far for *my* audience.

Both my teas at the Ritz had been productive, and if I'm still around thirty years after Ben's invitation, I'll be looking forward eagerly to the next one.

Harry Hill has the confidence to be original and quirky, and it was a great pleasure to be on his radio show with him. I felt that all this was keeping me young. It was an exploration, and I've always been happy to do a bit of that.

In 1999 I was asked to play an Ugly Sister in an ITV production of *Cinderella*. The other Ugly Sister was played by Paul Merton. Frank Skinner and Harry Hill were also in it, and Cinderella was Samantha Janus. Frank and Paul were schoolboys at the time I was doing *Sorry*, and to my amazement I found that they could still remember scenes from it.

I was delighted to do this show, as I had by now decided that doing pantomimes in the theatre was too much, too tiring; twelve extremely energetic performances a week was a bit much for me in my maturity. But I loved the genre and in this final outing I would throw myself into the style of the thing with verve.

Paul was up for doing the full 'slosh' routine as done by me with Stanley Baxter in Edinburgh and Glasgow more than thirty years before. I actually found a film of us doing the routine, and showed it to him.

Paul is brilliant, but I don't think he'll mind my claiming that in one department of the comic arts he had a lot to learn from a master such as me. I refer, of course, to achieving the right consistency for the 'slosh'. Imagine his surprise when I turned up to rehearsals with a plastic bowl, some sticks of

Erasmic, a whisk and a kettle. *Ready, Steady, Go*, eat your heart out.

Ronnie wasn't really a party animal, but on one occasion at a party in our house he very uncharacteristically read out a poem that he'd written many years before when he'd been on tour with, among others, Frank Finlay. It was one of his double entendre poems with a naughty rhyme, and you were expecting 'knickers' but got something completely innocent. It was very cleverly done, and it brought the house down. Well, it didn't quite bring it down, because we lived on in it until a couple of years ago.

In 2001, I was chairman of the Saints and Sinners Club of London. The Saints and Sinners is a charity club. It has a hundred members, and you have to be invited to join, you can't apply. Somebody has to approach you and say, 'Would you be prepared to become a member?' We have four club lunches a year at the Savoy, and a big Christmas lunch on the first Friday in December, which is a huge fund-raising event, at which we always try to invite two very good speakers. It's a nice mixture of show business, industry and politics, and we have a very good time and raise a lot of money for good causes.

With guests there would be about 550 of the great and the good gathered to hear the speakers, who were always people of high profile. Ronald Reagan spoke at the event on one occasion.

I'd got John Sergeant as one of my speakers, and it was absolutely natural to ask Ron to be the other. But would he come? And what would he do if he did come? He didn't do speeches. Well, I wrote to him . . . it shows how aware of each other we were even after thirty-five years, and how we respected each other's privacy. I would never have rung him and pressurized him. In fact he wasn't at ease on the phone, he wasn't chatty on it, and we rarely used it . . . I wrote to him and told him I was chairman and said what a blessing it would be if he would just come and read the poem.

He wrote back and said, 'Well, I will come and do it, but I don't want to be on the menu. I don't want my name printed, in case at the last moment my bottle goes and I can't face it.'

That's what a tender flower he was on that sort of occasion.

Well, on the day he did come, and really I had known that he wouldn't let me down. John Sergeant spoke and he was very funny, and then I got up and did my chairman's remarks, and I got a few laughs – I wish I could remember them now – and then I said, 'Gentlemen, now I'd like to introduce my dear friend Ronnie Barker.' I think they must have suspected that something of the kind would happen, because although he wasn't on the menu, they must have seen him on the top table.

Anyway, Ronnie stood up, and 550 people in the room stood up as one before he'd said a word, and applauded him long and loud. It was very touching, deeply moving.

And he paralysed them with the poem; it got roars. And then he had a cup of coffee and within ten minutes he'd put on his trenchcoat, his well-known trenchcoat, and was in his car and away home to Oxfordshire.

That was such a typical example of what Ronnie was like, of how difficult it was for him to do it and how triumphant it was when he did. He didn't want to be there early and he didn't want to stay long afterwards; he just came and did his duty as far as I was concerned, and did it fantastically. But the atmosphere he created just by being there is still talked about in the Saints and Sinners.

★

Meanwhile, back at the water mill, in 2002, Ronald William George Barker was at last tempted to return to acting. It was an offer to play a relatively small part in a film, but what a part and what a film. It was called *The Gathering Storm* and it was a story about Winston Churchill in the tense times before the outbreak of World War II. Ronnie played Churchill's butler, David Inches. Albert Finney was Churchill, and very good he was too. The story that Finney persuaded Ronnie out of retirement was printed in several of the papers, but it was all billhooks, like much of what's in the papers. They got on very well during the filming, but they had never even met before. The man who persuaded Ronnie was the director, Richard Loncraine. Mind you, I don't know how much persuasion you would need to do a cameo role with Albert Finney, Celia Imrie and even, in one short scene, Vanessa Redgrave, who was playing Churchill's wife, Clementine.

The film was very well received, and so was Ronnie's performance, and Richard Loncraine was soon busy at his persuading again. This time Ronnie was offered a bigger role, as a general in the film *My House in Umbria*, an adaptation of a novel by a brilliant Irish writer, William Trevor, which was made in 2003. Here, as so often, there was a delicious irony. The film starred Maggie Smith, with whom Ronnie had acted in several plays in his Oxford Playhouse days, when he had advised her to give the theatre up because she wouldn't be good enough to make it. Now here he was saying, 'I thought I told you to give up this business; you're still at it, aren't you?' Now she was a big star and a Dame, and big enough to greet Ronnie enthusiastically.

My House in Umbria was the story of an ageing English author (why did the publicity material say 'ageing'? We're all ageing, even babies are ageing. It was Gloria Swanson who said, 'All this talk of age is foolish. Every time I'm one year older, so is everybody else'). Let's start again. *My House in Umbria* was the story of a *mature* English author, played by Maggie Smith, who offered solace and shelter to a varied group of people who had survived a bombing of a train by terrorists. Apart from Ronnie and Maggie Smith, it also starred Timothy Spall and Chris Cooper.

The story goes, and I have to say that it's not impossible to believe, that the head of casting at Warner Brothers, having seen Ronnie in *The Gathering Storm*, said, 'How can he play a general? He's a butler.' Hadn't she heard of something known as acting? You can see why actors are afraid of being typecast.

There was speculation – Ronnie had reached a level of fame at which there is speculation about your every action – that it was the fact that these two roles were serious ones that attracted him out of retirement. He denied it, and I believe him. He had never shown any preference for serious roles before, why should he now? They were simply two great roles that were sufficiently tempting to persuade him back for a while. The fact that they happened to be serious ones was irrelevant. End of story.

But it isn't the end of our story. Ronnie's and my paths were still to cross several times.

19

They would cross particularly at award ceremonies, the first of which was given to Ronnie, fittingly, at the very first Comedy Awards, in 1990. The awards were the brainchild of Michael Hurll, who had succeeded Terry Hughes as producer of *The Two Ronnies*. I should also give credit to our other three producers after Michael, who were Marcus Plantin, Paul Jackson and Marcus Mortimer. We were very lucky in them all.

Michael Hurll now had his own television company, and they organized the awards, which were produced by his company for ITV. They were not broadcast live, which was lucky for one of our great theatrical knights, as we will see.

These first awards were held at the London Palladium, and were introduced by Michael Parkinson. The final award in a glittering evening was a Lifetime Achievement Award for television comedy. The award was voted for by the people who write, produce and direct British television, and almost inevitably it was given to Ronnie. Ronnie was introduced by Sir Alec Guinness, who was a great admirer. Ronnie had been astounded to read, in Sir Alec's autobiography, 'I'll tell you who my favourite performer is. Ronnie Barker. Surprised? You shouldn't be. He's really great.'

So this presentation was much more than just another award. It was a rare moment of total sincerity. It was also a meeting between two men who in some ways had very similar natures – they were both known above all for their versatility as actors, and they were both uncomfortable appearing in front of the public as themselves, so there was something really rather appropriate about it.

Sir Alec was clearly ill at ease. 'We've had years of delight,' he said, 'week by week from Clarence, the short-sighted removals man, from Norman Stanley Fletcher, from Ron Glum . . .' (Ronnie played Ron Glum to June Whitfield's Eth in *Six Faces of Jim*, the Glums having come from the classic radio series *Take It from Here*, written by Frank Muir and Denis Norden) '. . . and a host of others all of whom lived happily inside Ronnie Barker, who was a writer, a supreme comic and, for my money, a great actor.'

Sir Alec in fact tried to do a Ronnie Barker joke, which was a shame, as he was a fish out of water. The joke that he tried to do was a news-desk classic – 'There was a collision today outside Newport Pagnell between a van carrying prisoners and a lorry laden with cement. The police are hunting for six hardened criminals.' Unfortunately Sir Alec's mind went blank as he approached the end of the joke. It was extremely embarrassing. As he reached the punchline he said, to stunned silence from a packed Palladium, 'The police are hunting for . . . six concrete men.' Luckily, since the show was recorded, the joke could be edited out, but I don't think Sir Alec would mind my telling it now, after all these years, since he was very game about it at the time, and said he hoped he could come back one day and give another award to Ron and do it properly.

Ronnie's acceptance speech was absolutely typical.

'Sir Alec, ladies and gentlemen,' he began, 'all through my professional life I've been lost without a character to hide behind. "Oh, just go on and be yourselves," they'd say, but to me that was impossible, and tonight is no exception, so my thanks to you all for this prestigious award must also be in character.' ('Yourselves' was an interesting slip of the tongue, and it was interesting that his tongue could slip as himself. It never did in character.)

At this point he adopted the persona of Norman Stanley Fletcher.

'My thanks especially to the governor of this prison for letting me out for the evening to pick up this award. I mean, normally they don't take too kindly to you picking up sharp metal objects, know what I mean, but in this case he said, "OK," on condition that I let him stand it on the mantelpiece in his office next to his autographed photograph of Lester Piggott, and my special thanks must go to the jury, and I never thought I'd ever hear myself say that.'

Next he became Arkwright.

'Secondly, I would like to say, c-c-categ-ca-, I would like to say ca-ca-c, I'd like to say c-c-categ-ca-, but I can't. So thanks to all the customers who over the years have supported us through thick and thin, and in Granville's case, mostly thick, though I must say since my retirement he's been doing quite well, has Granville.' (Here the camera went on to Granville, alias David Jason, who had picked up at least three awards during the evening for *Only Fools and Horses* and *A Bit of a Do*.) 'This award might go far in healing the rift in my social arrangements with Nurse Gladys Emmanuel. I shall give it to her as a b-big peace offering, and, believe me, she's a b-big piece to offer anything to.'

Then it was back to his crisp spokesperson and an old friend of a monologue.

'Finally, as President of the Loyal Sobriety for the sufferers from Pispronunciation, I would like to say how clappy I am to deceive this award. When you have trouble in saying your worms correctly, it is dicky felt to suppress yourself properly when speaking to the general pubic. This can be the case even in such experienced screechers as our late Prim Minister,

Mrs Scratcher, and the bleeder of the opposition, Mr Pillock. So I will merely spray, thank you very much, and a crappy istmas to you all. So it's goodnight from him. Goodnight.'

In 1996 Ronnie received another Lifetime Achievement Award. Not bad, is it, to have one lifetime and receive two awards for it? This was at the BBC Centenary Programme, and again it was being presented by the supreme presenter, the daddy of them all, Michael Parkinson. 'There's one more award to come,' he said. 'This is an actor who retired eight years ago.' Ronnie thought, 'Who else retired eight years ago?' I was sitting next to him, and I said, 'It must be you.'

Everyone stood up, and Ronnie, thinking very quickly, sometimes greased lightning didn't stand a chance compared to his mind, said, 'Thank you very much, ladies and gentlemen, please sit down,' because he wasn't sure if the cameras were showing that everyone was standing up, and he wanted the audience at home to know that they had been!

Not long after that, I did a programme called *An Audience with Ronnie Corbett. An Audience with . . .* was a series in which the studio audience was packed with friends and colleagues of the celebrity who was the subject of the programme. They were primed to ask questions that would lead the star of the show into anecdotes and keep the show buzzing along. Unfortunately, some of the people I really wanted to be there, such as Danny La Rue, David Frost and John Cleese, couldn't make it, they all lead such busy lives. So it was important for me to have Ron there and I just had to ask him to come up from Oxfordshire, even though I knew it would be a lumber. He came, bless him, and of course he didn't want to ask a sensible question, that would have been too much like being himself, so he asked a silly one. 'Who did you most enjoy working with?' 'What'll I say to that?' I said. 'Say Basil Brush,' he said. Well, I'm an obliging, obedient

267

sort of person, so I said, 'Basil Brush.' The little routine went quite well, but it looked strange to everybody to see one Ron on the stage and another in the audience, and somehow everybody began talking about the possibility that Ronnie might retire from retirement, as it were. But no, that wasn't going to happen.

These thoughts were fuelled even more when we actually did appear together in 1997. This wasn't strictly an award ceremony or a tribute programme, but you have to bend the rules in comedy, so I'm including it. It was actually the Royal Command Performance, and they wanted Ronnie to come out of retirement to participate. I'd done a few Royal Command Performances, and I was quite comfortable with them, but they weren't Ron's cup of tea. But then he had an idea, an idea that meant that he could appear on the show in character. It was an idea that we would certainly have been using if we had still been making our shows.

The idea was for a take-off of *The Two Fat Ladies*. These were two lady chefs, Clarissa Dickson Wright and Jennifer Patterson, who did a very popular cookery programme in which they charged round the country on a motorcycle and sidecar combo, cooking high-class meals in high-class accents. They were in the great tradition of English upper-class eccentrics.

All we were to do in the show was introduce the next act, and Ron thought it would be great if we came on to the stage dressed as the two weighty ladies, in a motorcycle and sidecar combo, parked the bike, got off, walked down, took off our helmets, introduced the next act and got off. What could be simpler? Almost anything.

The snag, you see, was that I was going to have to drive the thing, and it involved a gear change, and the stage of the Victoria Palace, where we were to appear, is not large, and beyond the stage is the orchestra pit, and musicians are touchy people: they hate having motorcycles landing on their heads.

I arranged to have the motorcycle and sidecar delivered to the car park at Selhurst Park, Crystal Palace's football ground, and I had to practise three days a week with this damned machine.

I had to drive on to the stage, change gear, put the brakes on, and stop in the middle of the stage. It didn't work too badly, but there was a moment when Ron thought that I *was* going to take him over the edge into the pit. I mean, I've heard of going over the top, but this was ridiculous.

Never mind. We did it. It was all pretty sensational. The sight of the two fat ladies surging on to the stage on their motorbike was pretty amazing, but when we took our helmets off and everyone saw who we were, the place erupted. After all, it was the first time we'd been together for ten years.

We were deeply touched by the warmth of our reception, although I have to say that I always felt that I had too much lipstick on, particularly without the helmet.

Afterwards, in the traditional post-show line-up, Prince Philip said to Ronnie, 'Ah! They've exhumed you, have they?'

But they hadn't. Not yet.

In 2000, Ronnie was the subject of an episode of Channel 4's *Heroes of Comedy*, and in 2004 the BBC showed an hour-long BAFTA tribute to him. Many of the people who paid tribute to him were the same on both programmes, so I will concentrate on the BAFTA one for three reasons – it was the final tribute to him during his lifetime; a BAFTA tribute is a very rare event, given only for the greatest; and I had the inestimable privilege of hosting it.

BAFTA (the British Academy of Film and Television Arts) had their plans, in accordance with their normal way of doing things. But Ronnie, being Ronnie, had other ideas. They wanted him to sit in the audience and watch the show. That was the very thing he didn't want. He felt that if the camera cut to him every two or three minutes, the audience at home would be sick of him before he came on. Also, his self-consciousness about being seen as himself would be tested to the limits. How many modest looks and thrilled expressions could even as fine an actor as Ronnie produce, as person after person sang his praises? No, it was far better that he remain hidden out of the way and come on at the end. This would have a far greater impact, he felt, and, as usual, he was right.

There was an electric atmosphere that night. The audience was packed with stars, real stars, not the so-called celebrities of our times. There was a sense of joy in celebrating a living legend and in celebrating the great gift of comedy.

'Good evening, and welcome to a special BAFTA tribute,' I began, 'a tribute to a remarkable man, an extraordinary actor and a brilliant comedian – and that's not three people, just the one.'

We then saw clips from all sorts of celebrities. 'I think the word that comes to mind in connection with Ronnie is "jolly",' said John Cleese. 'He was capable of total brilliance,' said Michael Palin. 'When I'm with him,' said Richard Briers, 'I feel happier.'

I thought that last quote was about as good as it gets. Wouldn't you just love one of your best friends to say that about you?

'Uncle Ronnie Barker has always had the gift,' I continued, 'of being a star and the man next door at the same time. I often noticed when we were doing the news bulletins, if I came out with a good one, Ronnie would turn to me and just laugh, and that was the only time really in *The Two Ronnies* that you could see Ronnie Barker just as himself, just for the moment. Now later tonight you will be seeing the real Ronnie Barker. He is here tonight, but of course he's shy and retiring – well, he's retiring more than most.'

Peter Kay was the first to come on and sing Ron's praises live to this audience. 'I think he's a fantastic actor, and everything he does, you believe that he really is that person . . . If I make half as many people laugh as he has or mean a quarter as much to as many people as he has, I'll die a confused but happy man.'

Johnny Vegas, recorded on film, said, 'I'm the only bloke, I think, who reads him in the bath . . . I read him with reverence, and I have a special bubble bath I use when I'm reading him.' The picture of Johnny Vegas in a bubble bath was just one of the unforgettable images conjured up during that great evening of laughter and emotion.

One of the most striking tributes was from Gene Wilder, also on film. It was fascinating to hear the take on Ronnie's talent from this most American of comic actors. 'I lived in London for a year doing my first film as a director, and what I looked forward to at the end of each week was going home on a Saturday and ordering in some Indian food and then sitting and watching *The Two Ronnies*, and on one of the shows Ronnie Barker said that he was writing a letter to the Queen, but his typewriter kept jamming on him and every time he hit an "e" it gave him an "o", so it began: "To hor Majosty tho quoon".' It's a lovely thought, that great American actor watching us and laughing at us over his chicken tikka marsala. 'I feel that, no matter how farcical he was, like Chaplin there was always an element of reality to what he did, and when I saw his work I saw the embodiment of what I was striving for in my career.' Phew!

Next Josephine Tewson, the female element in so many of our sketches and of his sitcoms, took the stage and described

Ronnie rather memorably. 'He is the most untheatrical of actors. It's rather like meeting a very, very witty bank manager.'

One of the most extraordinary contributions came from Ben Elton, who recalled, 'I first met Ronnie Barker at a BBC Light Entertainment Christmas party in the early eighties. Stephen Fry and I had been hovering about, hoping that Jim Moir, the boss of Entertainment, might introduce us to the great man. When Jim finally did introduce us, Ronnie nodded at Stephen and said, "I quite like you," before glancing at me and saying, "Don't like you much, I'm afraid." It tells you something of the aura in which I held and still hold this giant of the comic arts that I was just pleased he'd spoken to me at all. If he'd impaled me with his cocktail sausage, I'd have considered it a privilege.'

It's a rare person who never says anything that they regret, and I'm certain Ron must have regretted this uncharacteristic remark, born I'm sure out of the unease he often felt at parties, but the fact that he and Ben became good friends, and that Ben was a regular visitor at his great summer parties in Oxfordshire – Ron and Joy knew how to throw a party – is a lovely ending to a story that began so badly, and a tribute to them both, but particularly, I have to say, to Ben, who took Ronnie's comment so extraordinarily well.

The next man to come on to the set and speak to that audience of the famous was Rob Brydon. 'Growing up as a teenager in South Wales, it was a wonderful experience to know that, come what may, on a Saturday night I would be guaranteed entertainment, and I remember thinking that it would last for ever, and then one day she moved away.' Lovely, but then he added, 'and so it was that I turned to *The Two Ronnies* and if anything had even more fun.'

As I've been writing this book, I've been struck by the

number of people who at various times mentioned the pleasure of those Saturday nights, and I've realized how fortunate we were to perform in an era when a television programme could become a national institution. Those days are past. In the era of a myriad channels, and also of the Internet, television programmes will no longer be events, to be discussed in pubs and offices the next day.

Sir Peter Hall appeared on tape and said, 'You taught me a great deal. You taught me that comedy has to be very serious and has to be very truthful and that it all depends on timing. From the beginning I thought you were a bit of a genius . . . You should have played Falstaff. You are a great actor.'

We did in fact see a short extract from Ronnie's performance in *A Midsummer Night's Dream*, and even in the tiny extract we could see that it was stunning, but if this BAFTA evening proved anything, it was that Ronnie turned his back on the great roles of serious acting not for something lesser, but for something as good, as important, as moving – comedy.

Each speaker was raising the emotional temperature a notch, and the last speaker, Sir David Jason, was no exception.

'To me there has never been anyone with such an ability to make the entire nation laugh so long and so loud as Ronnie B.,' said Sir David.

He spoke of Ronnie's generosity. 'One of the many times I witnessed this generosity as an actor was not long after I first met and worked with "the guv'nor" in the series *His Lordship Entertains*. At the start of my career I was a lowly actor. Mind you, considering my height, I suppose I've always been a bit of a lowly actor.'

He told how he was offered a part in a very funny script, *The Odd Job*, by Bernard McKenna, but thought that he had been offered the wrong part. He phoned the director, Sidney Lotterby, and said, 'Of course I would love to do it, but

273

you've obviously asked me to play the wrong part. Clive is Ronnie's part. Surely you want me to play the husband?'

'No,' said Sid. 'Ronnie wants you to play Clive.'

David told the audience, 'I replied, "But that's the funnier character." "Ronnie knows that," said Sid, "but he thinks you'll do it better." To an up-and-coming young actor, surely that is generosity of the highest order?'

During the evening we did in fact see a clip from *The Odd Job*. Ronnie hires David Jason to kill him. David is astounded and shaken, but agrees. 'When will you do it?' asks Ronnie. 'Leave it to me,' says David, 'and then, when you least expect it . . .' at which point he leaps straight in and tries to throttle Ronnie quite violently. His doing this so immediately, after his initial astonishment and reluctance, is very funny, but what makes it far funnier still is that Ronnie, who wanted to be killed, defends himself equally violently when the moment comes. It's a delicious scene, a very funny and unusual idea played out by two supremely funny men.

David also told one other story about working with Ronnie on *Open All Hours*. They had both just roared with laughter at some invented piece of comic business, and Ronnie said, 'It's amazing, isn't it? It's bloody marvellous. Here we are getting paid very well for making each other laugh. Not a bad life, is it?'

Not a bad life. I'll second that.

The last clip of Ronnie on that night was of a scene between him and David Jason, playing his cameo role as the old man in *Porridge*. Ronnie is telling him a joke. It's an old joke, but it becomes fresh again in Ronnie's superb delivery.

'This old man went to the doctor, you see. He said to the doctor, "My wife and I aren't getting any pleasure out of sex any more." The doctor was a bit taken aback. He said, "How old are you?" He said, "Eighty-one." He said, "How old's your wife?" "Seventy-nine." "Seventy-nine and eighty-one and you're not getting any pleasure out of sex? When did you first notice that?" "Twice last night and once this morning."'

At last it was time for Ronnie to come on. He received a prolonged standing ovation. As it went on and on, he stood there, definitely showing his age, somewhat frail if not yet actually ill, and he shook his head from side to side, as if in bemusement, as if he just couldn't believe that this wonderful moment was real. Surely it must be a dream?

Earlier in the chapter I quoted Ronnie's speech in 1990 at the first Comedy Awards, where he took refuge behind three characters. It was a good speech, amusing and inventive, and yet . . . slightly disappointing, because it cheated the audience of the emotion they craved, because the real Ronnie wasn't there.

I felt that this was different. For the first time there truly was no mask. Ronnie Barker spoke as himself, truthfully, simply and from the heart.

'My lords, ladies, gentlemen and Jimmy Tarbuck,' he began, 'I am naturally overwhelmed by the honour bestowed on me by BAFTA. It's an extraordinary feeling to be the subject of this evening's wonderful show and to be the object of so many kind words from so many talented people. I thank you all most sincerely and humbly. To BAFTA and the BBC a most special thank you for organizing the evening and to all of you for coming here tonight. They say that the party afterwards is going to be better than the show, so that's going to be pretty good.'

Perhaps this is the moment to say that, typically, the hand of Ronnie Barker was even there in the plans for the party. He had been asked what sort of food he wanted and had opted for a hot buffet. As usual with Ron, it was the right decision. The food was excellent, and the party, in the adjoining studio, with black drapes and tiny pinpoints of light so that it looked as if we were eating and drinking under the stars, was worthy of the occasion.

'It's curious, though,' Ronnie continued, 'that on such an important occasion it's very difficult to be funny. Funny, that, isn't it? But I have to tell you that all through my fifty years in the business, two words have always been in my thoughts – these two words are "What luck". What luck to have met, in the far-off days of weekly rep, a marvellous comedian called Glenn Melvyn, who gave me my first TV job and taught me how to stutter. What luck to have been in Oxford rep when a young Peter Hall arrived as director and brought me to London's West End. What luck that James Gilbert saw me do a radio show and put me in *The Frost Report*. What luck that the star of that show, David Frost, put me under contract, that resulted in *Porridge* and *Open All Hours*, and who paired me with the wonderful Ronnie Corbett. What luck to have had a wife for forty-five years who, throughout my television career, sat in the audience of every show and laughed louder than anyone else.

'And finally, standing here before you with this most honoured award bestowed upon me by you, what luck, what wonderful luck, to be flanked on either side by my two best friends, Ronnie Corbett and David Jason.'

Ronnie's voice was beginning to break. At last we were seeing the real Ronnie B. I've watched a recording of the scene, and my face is set in granite, not looking at Ronnie, not daring to, because I still had a small job to do and I couldn't let the emotion take over. Certainly David's eyes were wet, and so were the eyes of many in the audience.

'And I might cry,' said Ronnie, and hurriedly he wrapped a protective joke round the moment. 'Gwyneth Paltrow, watch out.'

'Thank you, Ronnie,' I said, 'and thank you, David, and thank all of you for making this evening so special. Shall we say goodnight, Ronnie?'

'I think we should,' said my old friend. 'It's a very good night from me.'

'And it's a very good night from him,' thundered David and I in unison.

20

At the party after the BAFTA tribute show, Ronnie had a glint in his eye. He had enjoyed a wonderful evening which would have put a glint into anybody's eye. The adrenalin was back in his veins. He talked wistfully of the possibility of bringing back *The Two Ronnies* to mainstream television, and somebody overheard him.

Quite soon he had a meeting with Beatrice Ballard, who had been one of the BBC's executive producers on the BAFTA programme. She had noticed the glint in his eye, and suddenly it seemed that the BAFTA programme had reminded the BBC of what jewels they had in their archives. For many years *The Two Ronnies* had been shown only on cable and satellite, now suddenly everyone seemed to want to bring us back to BBC1. Suddenly the schedulers realized what appeal a family show of that quality could have.

Of course there was no question of our literally making a new series, we were too old for that, and Ronnie certainly wouldn't have had the energy. But they wanted something with a bit more impact than just a series of repeats. The solution, proposed by the BBC, was that we should show six programmes, compiled and edited from all our many shows over the years, with us at the news desk linking the programme and reminiscing over the various items. It would be called *The Two Ronnies Sketchbook*, a title that had been used once before for a book of our sketches compiled by Peter Vincent.

But would Ronnie have the energy even to do this? His

health had deteriorated since the award show, and probably the intense adrenalin on that day had made him appear fitter than he was. His heart problems had returned. The main trouble was basically with a valve, which was growing smaller and smaller. The specialist said that it should be replaced, but that he didn't know if the heart was strong enough.

The glint was still present in Ron's eye that day, but it wasn't shining quite so brightly.

He said that he would be prepared to do the shows if – this was how fragile he really was, how tired he was – it could all be put together in one day, so all the linking material would have to be written and agreed well in advance. He would come in at eleven o'clock, and we'd rehearse for an hour and a half, till half past twelve. Then he'd have a light lunch in his dressing room, and a sleep, from half past twelve till half past two or quarter to three. Then we'd come out and do two or three more runs of the material at the desk, and then he would rest from four o'clock until seven, and in that way he would be able to get his energy up for the evening, but it had to be done in one day with that amount of understanding from the production team, and the production team, under the splendid Sam Donnelly, went out of their way to make things easy.

I must make it clear here, since it's not clear from the name, that Sam is female, our very first and of course therefore our only female producer. We had spent our television careers in a male-dominated world, where, with very few exceptions, women were secretaries, production assistants, and ran the wardrobe and make-up departments. When we returned it was to an industry still dominated by men at the very, very top, but with women well represented at every other level, including being Controllers of channels. This process can only continue. One day a woman will be Director General of the BBC, though maybe not in my lifetime. Will Lord Reith turn in his grave? I don't know, but I know that I won't. What would I be doing in Lord Reith's grave, anyway?

Of course, long before we returned to the studio we had decided which items to show. Only the best. We didn't hold a few good ones back in case we needed them for a later series, because I think we both knew that Ronnie would not be well enough to do another series.

So, we spent many hours watching old shows and being amazed to find how much we had forgotten. Quite often I had no idea what was coming next. I was relieved to find that Ron had been having the same experience. He would watch himself walking round the sofa and doing a bit of business and realize that he had no recollection of having done it.

I think we both approached the task of selection with foreboding, perhaps even fiveboding in some cases. Would a lot of it seem very lame now? Well, I was mightily relieved. There were very few items of which I was ashamed. But we wanted something better than items of which we weren't ashamed. We wanted only items of which we were positively proud. And we were most encouraged when an editor, putting tapes together for us to watch, commented, 'Where is this sort of work now? This standard of words and characters and sets and production costs?'

Ronnie took the lead in this process, marking sketches with two ticks, one tick or a question mark. He was in his element doing that sort of thing. He later admitted that he rejected one or two purely on the grounds that he hadn't been entirely happy with his performance.

Well, there were a few obvious items, like 'Four Candles' and 'Swedish Made Simple' and the duck sketch and the rook restaurant and the *Mastermind* sketch, and the others fell into place fairly easily. We stuck very closely to the original format of the show.

I realize that I haven't actually mentioned the *Mastermind* sketch, which was, I think, one of our most brilliant, due entirely to the script. It was written by David Renwick, and he had such doubts about it that he threw it away as nonsense, then decided that it might not be and retrieved it from the waste-paper basket. This illustrates a truth that is one of the factors that makes writing and performing comedy so difficult. The dividing line between silliness and brilliance is wafer-thin. It's another of those sketches which have an outrageous, contrived premise, but which after that proceed with strict logic. There are a few topical references which may puzzle younger readers, but I think I'd like to give you this one in full. Apart from anything else, it's one where I had the vast bulk of the laughs, so it's nice for me to remember it! And, just as I didn't object to a sketch in which I mainly said 'Hello' and 'What?', Ronnie B. didn't mind doing a sketch in which he was virtually a feed. The success of the sketch was all that mattered to us. We were a true team.

Mastermind set.
RC *is in the chair.*
RB *as Magnusson fires the questions.*
CAPTION: MASTERMIND
RB: So on to our final contender. Good evening. Your name, please.
RC: Good evening.
RB: Thank you. Now, in the first heat, your chosen subject was answering questions before they were asked. This time, you have chosen to answer the question before last, each time. Is that correct?
RC: Charlie Smithers.

RB: And your time starts now. What is palaeontology?

RC: Yes, absolutely correct.

RB: Correct. What's the name of the directory that lists members of the peerage?

RC: A study of old fossils.

RB: Correct. Who are Len Murray and Sir Geoffrey Howe?

RC: Burkes.

RB: Correct. What's the difference between a donkey and an ass?

RC: One's a trade union leader, the other's a member of the Cabinet.

RB: Correct. Complete the quotation 'To be or not to be'.

RC: They're both the same.

RB: Correct. What is Bernard Manning famous for?

RC: That is the question.

RB: Correct. Who is the present Archbishop of Canterbury?

RC: He's a fat man who tells blue jokes.

RB: Correct. What do people kneel on, in church?

RC: The Right Reverend Robert Runcie.

RB: Correct. What do tarantulas prey on?

RC: Hassocks.

RB: Correct. What would you use a ripcord to pull open?

RC: Large flies.

RB: Correct. What sort of person lived in Bedlam?

RC: A parachute?

RB: Correct. What is a jockstrap?

RC: A nutcase.

RB: Correct. For what purpose would a decorator use methylene chlorides?

RC: A form of athletic support.

RB: Correct. What did Henri de Toulouse-Lautrec do?

RC: Paint strippers?

RB: Correct. Who is Dean Martin?

RC: Is he a kind of artist?

RB: Yes, what sort of artist?

RC: Er – pass.

RB: Yes, that's close enough. What make of vehicle is the standard London bus?

RC: A singer.

RB: Correct. In 1892 Brandon Thomas wrote a famous long-running English farce – what was it?

RC: British Leyland.

RB: Correct. Complete the following quotation about Mrs Thatcher. 'Her heart may be in the right place, but her . . .'

RC: *Charley's Aunt.*

RB: Correct. (*Bleeper noise*) And you have scored eighteen with no passes.

The only new element in the show was our linking material. It was no longer closely based on news items, and it did involve Ron being more or less himself. He was less uneasy with this now, but still not entirely comfortable. We weren't aiming at huge laughs, it was quite gentle – the huge laughs were in the old stuff. It wasn't as rich an experience for the studio audience on the night, that was impossible, but we still took care to make them feel welcome.

Ronnie was a proud man, and he took great pains to conceal the extent of his frailty, but I felt that he needed cosseting, he needed careful handling, because he just hadn't got the energy he was pretending to have. When the shows went out, people who knew him well could see how frail he was. He'd lost a lot of weight, and his features were sharper, but he put on such a good show that I think very few members of the viewing public realized how ill he was.

I was sad to see him like that, of course, but I was quite pleased that he was up for it, because I was certain that it would work, and it would be a kind of a little bit of another refreshing burst in our lives and careers, which of course it was, almost more than the originals, because people realized in the vacuum that had gone before how good the stuff had been when it had been shown originally.

This may seem odd, after all the viewing figures the original shows had got, and after the OBEs and the Royal Command Performances and all the various award ceremonies, but I really do believe that it was only when we came to do this compilation that the two of us fully realized the magnitude of our success.

It had been eighteen years since our last series. A man once went up to Barry Cryer in Regent Street and said, 'Didn't you used to be Barry Cryer?', and Ron did toy with the idea of starting the series with, 'Good evening, we used to be the Two Ronnies,' but he abandoned the thought in the end.

We were delighted to be back in primetime viewing on a Saturday night, but even more delighted by the public response and by the reaction of new viewers who had been too young to see us before. It really did mean a lot to us. I couldn't help wondering, though, whether families sat and watched us together as much as they did in the old days. Confucius Corbett, sociologist, he wonder whether in fact families did as much together in the modern era of computer games, the Internet and binge drinking at the weekends.

After *The Two Ronnies Sketchbook*, Ron went back into hospital, for a check-up. It was just before Christmas, and the specialist said that if he didn't have the valve operation, he might not have much more than six months to live. Ron said that he would see how he felt, if there was the right moment, when he felt strong enough, he might have the operation, but then, whenever he did feel strong enough, he persuaded himself that maybe he didn't need the operation. He was frightened of having a stroke, and he didn't want Joy to have to deal with a helpless invalid. He was more frightened of that than of dying. Anyway, he never did have the operation.

Our final show together was a Christmas special compilation. This was recorded in July 2005, with the same format as the *Sketchbook* series, new linking material at the desk and selected items from our Christmas specials. Since this was Ron's very last show, and I've just quoted a sketch in which I had most of the laughs, I would like to remember it by giving you just one extract from it, his monologue entitled 'The Milkman's Christmas Speech to the Nation'.

He was dressed as a milkman, but seated like the Queen at an ornate desk in Buckingham Palace (not really in Buckingham Palace, though that would have been a thought).

'A very merry Christmas to you all,' he began, speaking in a stately way, but also in a milkmanlike way. I'm sure there isn't such a word, but there should be. This was the cleverness of Ron the actor, to be able to seem like a statesman and a milkman at the same time. 'As I think of you,' he continued. (Well, of course he continued. It would have been the shortest monologue in history if he hadn't. Sorry. I'm being facetious to hide the fact that writing this bit is making me emotional.) 'As I think of you, my loyal customers, sitting at home round your firesides this Christmas, it brings home to me very strongly the enormous responsibility I have as your milkman.'

A caption appeared on the screen, giving his name, which was H. M. Quinn.

'And I know that you will appreciate how important it is to me to know that I have your support, and shall continue to have your support, throughout the coming year. The task of supplying milk to a great nation such as ours is, I am sure you realize, not an easy one. Either here at home, or in the colonies – spread as they are, like butter, over the entire globe

– whether home or colonial, it is our express wish that it must be co-operative, uniting dairies across the world. The milk of human kindness must not be watered down. It must flow, not only through the cream of society, but also on to the most humble doorstep in the land, be it black, or white, or gold-top. Let our lives be ordered, and ordered as soon as possible, so as to avoid disappointment, in the years to come. I extend my warmest and most heartfelt bottle to you all.'

It was far and away the shortest monologue that Ron ever wrote or performed, but a perfect little piece, I think, gentle and stylish.

We recorded the Christmas show in July, just three months before he died, so that when it went out it was very much a tribute, a tribute which received the third-highest rating for the Christmas and New Year period.

I knew when we did the Christmas show that he would never be able to work again. He looked so frail. He had a walking stick with him all day. He pretended that he'd pulled something in his ankle and had twisted his foot, but I think he felt shaky on his legs and, rather than worry us all, he made out that he'd hurt himself. He did look very weak and he couldn't even get the voice. Even on the recording you could see the weakness of the delivery, you could hear him pushing the voice out. This time there was no chance of concealing from the viewing public that he was ill, although such was his pride and professionalism that I don't think you would have realized just how ill he was.

When he stood with me and hugged me at the end, tears ran down his cheeks. I didn't dare start myself, otherwise we would both have been blubbing, but he was very emotional. I don't know why he had the strength to be bothered to do it at all, really, but it was marvellous that he did. He knew he would never ever stand there again, or do anything again.

Immediately after the show the BBC gave us a sweet little party. Ron was able to come to it, but by now he was so enfeebled by the day's activities that he had to make straight for a chair and sit down throughout it.

The BBC gave us a most lovely little gift, a book of the photographs of us that there had been in the *Radio Times* over the years, some absolutely splendid photographs, and most beautifully and carefully presented. It was very touching.

This was such a British scene, I think. Everybody knew that it was farewell, the end, goodbye from me and goodbye from him and goodbye from us, but nobody said so. The room was full of emotion, but none of it was expressed. It didn't need to be.

And that was the last time I saw Ron. He began to go downhill very fast after making that supreme effort to do the Christmas show. In fact I later found out that he had told Joy and his daughter Charlotte that he would go downhill fast after the recording. He was living to make this last great professional effort. I think he was ready to go after that. He couldn't enjoy his food. He couldn't sleep. It was time.

I hoped I would see him again. Anne and I wanted to go down and visit him at the mill, but he didn't want us to do that. He thought he looked so tragic and pathetic, which he probably did. He just did not want us to see him in his final frailty.

On Sunday, 22 September 2005, ITV celebrated its fiftieth birthday with a huge three-hour extravaganza. At its centre was the establishment of a British Avenue of the Stars, like the famous American one on Hollywood Boulevard. The British Avenue was the pavement in front of St Paul's Church in Covent Garden, right in the heart of London. This church is always known as the Actors' Church, so it was a suitable location.

One hundred stars were to have themselves immortalized that night. They were chosen, we were told, by 'an independent panel of experts', which didn't leave us much the wiser. Among them were Ronnie and me. I'm glad to say that we didn't have to share a star. We got one each. Thank you, independent panel of experts, whoever you were.

Sadly, Ronnie was by now too ill to attend. His and my stars were to be presented to me, on behalf of both of us, by Richard Briers. He thought this was the only reason for his attendance, but found that he was getting a star himself. Chris Tarrant told the audience that Ricky Gervais had described Richard as 'the greatest living British sitcom actor'.

Dickie seemed almost embarrassingly eager to get off the subject of his star and on to presenting ours. He was a great friend of Ronnie's, and had been ever since they had starred in Tom Stoppard's *The Real Inspector Hound* together.

They showed one or two extracts from our work, including our take-off of Moira Anderson and Kenneth McKellar, which I must say I thought rather good, though it was probably a bit puzzling to the younger members of the audience, and then it was my turn to walk down the huge staircase, grateful that I was long cured of my labyrinthitis.

Dickie Briers read out a letter from Ron, in which he said, 'I'm so sorry not to be with you today for this enormous extravaganza with some of the biggest stars in show business, and also one of the smallest but the best, my dear dear friend Ronnie Corbett. I shall have to ask him to represent us both.'

There was no hint of why Ron wasn't there, and I did a bit of my patter, including those old friends, the Greek restaurant joke and the treadmill only doing widths joke, and I said, 'Thank you. Both Ron and I deeply appreciate this honour and being part of the avenue, so God bless you all who have put us there.' And all the time, in my heart, I was thinking of Ron so ill at home.

Later in the show Sir Richard Attenborough thanked the unknown independent panel of experts for not confining the Avenue of the Stars to the living, and for commemorating so many of the dead. This remark touched a nerve in the audience. There was loud applause.

Nobody there that night could have had any idea how soon Ron would be among that number. Within eight days, to be precise.

The night following that ceremony, I spoke to Ronnie for the last time. James, who works as my chauffeur when I need him these days, was driving me along Ryder Street, which is a side street halfway up St James's, when I got a phone call from home on my mobile, saying that Ron had rung and wanted to speak to me.

We pulled up at a meter and I rang him up, and he said, in a weak voice, 'I just wanted to thank you very much for the way you accepted on my behalf,' and I said, 'How are you?' and he said, 'I'm not well. I'm going. I'm just fading away, and I feel terrible. I *am* going.'

Those were the last words he ever spoke to me, and I can hear them still. In fact I can never pass Ryder Street, and I shall never pass Ryder Street, I shall never pass that parking meter, without thinking of that last conversation.

On the following Monday morning, not long before lunchtime, I was seated at a table of the little house that I suppose I have to call our retirement bungalow. It's a few hundred yards from our old house, and backs on to the same golf course. It's cosy and intimate and private, and has a sensible-sized garden, beautifully laid out with a wonderful orchestration of different shades of green. People love bright flowers, but green is always the favourite colour of gardeners.

Anne and I couldn't believe our luck when it came on the market, and we snapped it up, even though we felt that the move was just a bit premature. Anyway, there we live, with our two miniature Schnauzers and a very old cat, and there I was that morning, busy signing my name opposite Ronnie's.

We had recently done an arrangement with a company that produced a huge, beautiful picture of Ron and me in the 'Four Candles' hardware store, with a quote from the sketch underneath. There were 500 of them, all beautifully mounted, and we were both to sign them all, really sign them with a proper signature. Ron had already signed them all, and I was working my way steadily through them, when the phone rang. It was Charlotte, Ron's daughter, and she said, 'Dad's gone.' He had been in a hospice for the past two days, and there he had just quietly faded away, peacefully. All that energy, gone to nothing.

It wasn't a shock, in itself, but it was a shock that it should happen at that very moment. It was quite uncanny. I thought about Ron, and about Joy, and about his family, and about our times together, and then I picked up my pen. There was a job to do.

I signed, and signed, and signed, and signed, and signed, and each time I signed I saw Ron's signature there beside mine, and I thought, 'He'll never sign anything again. Those people will never be able to get a picture of us together again.'

I still can't get over how strange it was that I should get the news at that very moment. In fact it was a strange day altogether. I had this momentous news, not sad in itself, because I knew that Ron had been ready to go, but very distressing and touching none the less, and Anne and I couldn't share it with anybody, because the news had not yet broken. It wasn't made public knowledge until the following morning, first on the radio and then, shortly afterwards, on breakfast television. I imagine that the family had decided to tell, in private, all those closest to Ron so that they heard it in person, before the news was broken to the media. That was thoughtful.

Despite all the evidence over the years of Ron's great popularity, I must say that I was amazed at the coverage of his death. I was absolutely surprised at the grief of the nation. The impact was enormous. It was the main item on news bulletins and the front-page lead in newspapers. The whole nation seemed to mourn. The *Daily Mail* used the whole of its front page, the whole of page 2, and two other complete pages. The *Daily Telegraph* had a big picture on the front page, a large article on page 2, almost the whole of page 3, an article about him by Jim White on page 26, and a full-page obituary on page 29. Paper after paper used the catchphrase 'It's Goodnight From Him.'

There were only four words on the front page of the *Sun*, and yes, they were those same four words, but the whole of the rest of the page was a giant picture of the glasses Ron wore. Just that. It was amazingly imaginative and moving. And inside was a leading article, which ended, 'We'll light a candle for you, Ronnie. Hang on, m-m-m-make that f-f-f-four candles.'

Other famous comedians and actors had died, and it had been a major news story, but I don't think it had ever been like this. Why did it affect people so deeply?

Doctor Ronald Corbett, Professor of Mass Psychology at the University of Life, has two theories.

The first is that there was something in Ron's personality that made you think he was speaking directly to you, that you knew him, that you were part of his family, and he part of yours. Television is very intimate, and I think people felt that they knew him intimately, which is quite ironic, since he had such difficulty in revealing his real self. But perhaps that very difficulty made people understand him better, and gave him a vulnerability that touched them. I think in the end he was like everybody's favourite uncle.

The other theory is that the more mature generations in Britain are feeling a little starved of subtlety in comedy, and that in a world of increasing violence, rapid climate change and social change, and so many other problems that I won't mention because I don't want to depress you, there is a great hunger for laughter, especially what I would call life-enhancing laughter. In his three great successes, *Porridge*, *Open All Hours* and *The Two Ronnies*, Ron enhanced our lives all right. His funeral was appropriate for the man. It was strictly private, and very modest. It was held deep in the Oxfordshire countryside that he loved, and it was for family only. In fact, since neither Ron nor Joy was religious, it was a humanist funeral. I gather that Ron's son Larry gave a moving and funny picture of the Ron that only his family knew, a man bubbling over, in private, with fun and mischief and affection.

I still had to carry on working. I had commitments. But I found it quite difficult to go out into the streets because everybody knew what was probably going on in my heart, and they didn't know whether to speak, or just to touch me, which was touching Ron really.

But what moved me most, more than all the glowing tributes in the papers and on television, was the taxi drivers in the West End. Normally they'd toot at me and say things like 'How are you, Ron?' very cheerily, and all they were doing now, when they saw me waiting to cross the road or walking along the pavement, was lowering their windows and holding up their hands in a gesture of peace. It was very, very, very moving.

21

On a crisp, late-winter's day in March, with pale sunshine gently lighting up the ancient buildings of Westminster, the great and the good, not to mention the not so great and the not so good, all wrapped up against the chill air, walked slowly and solemnly and with dignity towards the Gothic fifteenth-century west front of Westminster Abbey. Above them, there were ten Christian martyrs, preserved for ever in stone. To either side of them there were at least fifty photographers, taking pictures of the great and ignoring the not so great, to their chagrin. 2,500 people walked into the Abbey that morning, to give thanks for the life of − not another Christian martyr − but a comic actor. Was this appropriate? Oh, I hope so.

The idea of holding the memorial service for Ron in Westminster Abbey was the BBC's. What a contrast to his funeral. But I see nothing inappropriate or hypocritical about it. How I see it is that Ron had been buried in the way he wanted. Now he was being remembered in the way we, the nation, wanted.

Some of the huge congregation that day might never have been into the abbey before. Most would not have been for a long time. But for me, it was my second visit of the morning.

I was to give the final tribute to my great, good friend Ronnie Barker. I'd played Winston's and Danny La Rue's and Margate and Yarmouth. I had never played Westminster Abbey and I was nervous. I had been nervous for quite a long time, waking up in the nights, agonizing over my speech. It was a celebration, but it was also a service. I didn't want to be too cheeky, in the pulpit of Westminster Abbey, but I did rather hope to be funny. And I intended to start with a little visual joke, a joke that would take me back to my very first meeting with Ron, and to the very first chapter of this book. I intended to enter the pulpit, over whose bottom edge I would just be able to see, and then jump on to a hidden box, thoughtfully placed there by the helpful clergy for just such a purpose.

That was why I had gone to the abbey earlier that morning – to check that my prop was in place in the pulpit. It's lucky I did. There was a box, but it covered the complete floor of the pulpit. I could not therefore enter the pulpit and suddenly rise up. The gag wouldn't work.

A box of the right size was found. I tested out my gag. I felt not a little foolish doing this in the haughty silence of the deserted abbey, looking down the Quire to the great nave beyond. The building of the nave had begun in 1376 and had taken 150 years to complete. It made our fifteen years of *The Two Ronnies* seem small and insignificant.

But they didn't seem small and insignificant as the doors opened and the public streamed in. Anybody who was anybody in British entertainment was there, and so were many people from the great British public, who wanted to give thanks for the amount of humour and joy that Ron had brought into their lives.

Of course I was nervous. I wanted to do well by my old friend on this, the very last moment of our lives together. I thought all sorts of thoughts, to take my mind off it.

I wondered if the nave was supposed to have taken 150 years, or had the builders been due to finish in sixty-three years and seven months. What would have been the penalties if they had been eighty-six years and five months late? Was it the Wembley Stadium of the fourteenth century?

I thought about the fact that this was the final resting place of Lord Olivier, whom we had both known just a bit, and of David Garrick, whom we hadn't met, advanced in years though we had become.

I thought about Poets' Corner, where Geoffrey Chaucer, John Dryden, Tennyson and John Masefield lay. So this was an appropriate place for Ron's memorial. After all, he was a poet too.

> Amazing Grace, how sweet the sound
> She played upon a whistle –
> To show you how, she charged a pound
> Behind the 'Dog and Thistle'.

You think I am being irreverent and irrelevant? Irreverent, yes. I'm trying to reflect the mood of that service. Irrelevant? No. I'm getting you into the mood of that service, which was an extraordinary mixture of the reverent and the irreverent.

Here, the full pomp of the church at its most formal mingled with the natural irreverence of humour.

All through the abbey, as the crowds massed, old friends were waving and smiling and reminiscing. Then total silence fell, and everybody stood. The Lord Mayor of Westminster was being met at the Great West Door by the Dean and Chapter of Westminster, and conducted to his stall in the Quire. He sat down, and so did everybody else. Conversation broke out again, as people commented on how much old colleagues had aged.

The service began. We all stood and sang the first hymn:

For all the Saints who from their labours rest,
Who thee by faith before the world confest,
Thy name, O Jesu, be for ever blest. Alleluya! Alleluya!

I cannot better describe what happened during the singing than by quoting the words printed in the Order of Service handed to every member of the congregation: 'THE HYMN, during which the Choir, led by the Beadle, and the Abbey Clergy preceded by the Cross of Westminster and Four Candles, move to places in the Quire and Sacrarium.'

Yes, ladies and gentlemen, four candles. In the midst of all this pomp, a clerical joke, a tribute to the most famous of all our sketches. With that one superb gesture, the mood was set.

There was an address by the Reverend Robert Wright, Sub-Dean of Westminster. There were hymns and prayers, and the choir sang beautifully. There were readings from Richard Briers and Jo Tewson. There were humorous contributions from Michael Grade and Peter Kay. There was a recording of a sermon in rhyming slang by Ron himself. And then it was my turn.

I felt dwarfed by the rather magnificent pulpit as I climbed the steps. I peered over the edge and then rose on to the box. It worked perfectly. I appeared suddenly to be lifted by unseen forces. As with all our ninety-eight shows, the thoroughness had paid off.

Ned Sherrin, producer of *That Was the Week That Was* more than forty years before, wrote in his review of the memorial service, in the magazine the *Oldie*, 'Never before have I seen a eulogist "milk" a pulpit.' He also commented that my box joke was more appropriate than I imagined. 'Bishop William Walsham How, who wrote the first hymn, "For All the Saints . . .", in the 1870s, was less than five foot tall. Being too short for most pulpits, he travelled with a specially built platform wherever he preached.'

Most of my tribute consisted of memories that I have already shared with you: our first meeting at the Buckstone and Ronnie believing that I was standing on a beer crate; Ronnie and Harry dieting and losing my weight between them; the sweet little poem he sent in thanks for the towel and hat in Australia; Ron and I in economy class on the way back from Montreux and Michael Grade sending his message, 'Out front and loving it'; everyone laughing as the doors of the airport bus closed to leave me stranded outside; riding on to the stage in motorcycle and sidecar dressed as the Two Fat Ladies; Ron's triumph at the Saints and Sinners Club – a little collection of our happiest memories. And one incident that I haven't told you about.

It was when Ron was beginning to have worries about his heart, and he'd been sent for a very, very special cardiac examination to a private hospital in St John's Wood, and he was anxious that the whole thing should be kept from the press and remain a total secret, and as he was being wheeled in a chair by a hospital porter, the porter said, 'Oh, you've got no problems here, sir. This is a very, very discreet, private, secret, wonderfully personal hospital. We had Danny La Rue in here on Thursday.' Then I used my old line, 'When we were filming the principle would be that Ronnie would write a sketch, and I would queue for his lunch . . . simple really . . . a very simple formula.' And I ended with my final farewell to Ron. 'He was a dear, dear man, a wonderful friend, a talented artist, and whatever else we could say, you could guarantee that it was always going to be a very, very good night from him.'

As I descended the stairs – very carefully – and was escorted slowly back to my seat with great formality, there was a good round of applause. I'd like to think that it was because, unlike so many tributes at so many memorial services, everyone knew that on this occasion I had meant every single word of it.

22

Several months have passed now since Ron's death, but I feel that he is with me still. Anne and I have, of course, visited Joy at the mill that she loves so much and that Ron loved so much, and it's hard not to expect to find him there, cutting things out of old books or just wandering in the garden, enjoying the kind of peace and quiet that was always so important to both of us. There, in that very private place, Joy faces life without him with her usual courage and humour.

But our house, too, is full of him, just full of him. There is not a corner I can turn without seeing a still of him or a picture on the wall or a book or a biography or a sketch or a little note that he'd written to me.

There were often times, between series and after his retirement, when we wouldn't see each other for a few months, but I haven't seen him now for the best part of a year and I think the reality that I will never see him again is therefore beginning to have a stronger impact on me. I will hear some joke or watch some programme and think, 'I must see what Ron thinks of that,' and then realize that I can't ask him. I have so much of him on tape, of course, and that is a very real consolation. He lives on in the glow of his talent.

I've often thought about the incredible depth of feeling that his death created. He would never have imagined such a thing. He *couldn't* have imagined it. And yet – we don't know – maybe one can know such things when one is gone. It would be good to think so.

I always realized that he was an absolute giant, but because

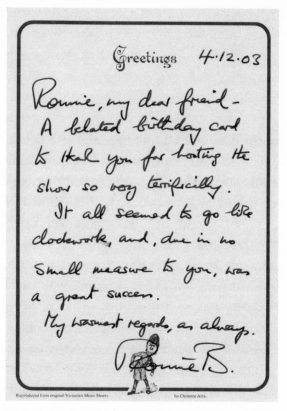

One of many thoughtful cards that Ron sent me over the years.

of his natural modesty as a person, only really after he'd gone did I fully appreciate the library of his work, which was immense. He was an everyday person, day to day. He wasn't a spoilt, chauffeur-driven celebrity. He was a humble man, with huge talents and skills, but because I knew him so well and had so many ordinary, unpretentious moments with him, perhaps it's only now that I can see the whole magnitude of it.

It was an immense privilege for me to work with him. I once said to him, 'I always think to myself, Ron, that I can't be all that bad, otherwise you wouldn't have put up with me.' He said, 'Say that again.' He couldn't believe that I'd said it. He couldn't believe that I felt it. I didn't feel like that all the time; usually I was very comfortable working with him, but there were moments when I sought that consolation. It would have been impossible not to, when working with such a talent.

We were blessed to have been able to create such a legacy of family entertainment, to have been a part of making it, and to have left it. When I walk about I still get warmly thanked, from people that I meet, for all the fun that we have given them. Ron's gone, Eric and Ernie have gone, so many have gone, so I am getting more than my fair share of all this gratitude for what is perceived to have been a golden age for family entertainment.

When I look back over our careers, and think of the ambiance within which we worked, both separately and together, I think that we must have had – how we arrived at it I don't know – well-balanced lives. Our work never took us over, never drove us mad, never turned us to drink or drugs. We enjoyed our grub. We loved and enjoyed our wives and families. Our whole lives were really led in a very calm and measured manner. We were temperate. People find it hard to believe me when I say that we never had rows, never got frustrated with each other, but it's true, and I think a lot of that was to do with the way we each allowed the other space, we didn't intrude upon each other's privacy. It was, truly, a very British friendship.

I know how much Ron meant to me, but when I look back on the last time I saw him, on the day when we recorded the news items for the Christmas special, I can see as vividly as ever his fragility, and I know how difficult it was for him to get through that day; I marvel at the strength of character that he showed, and I think that he made himself do it, for me. He didn't say so, he wouldn't have said so, but I think he did it for me, and that shows me how much I meant to him.

The world has changed in so many ways during our careers, but one thing in particular that has changed is the attitude to our kind of career. Helpful and encouraging though Ron's and my parents were, there was an attitude in the country that if you wanted to act or write or generally be artistic, you were the black sheep of the family. Now everybody wants to do it. Everyone I meet tells me their son is doing media studies at university, or their daughter wants to be a director or has gone on a writing course. It's as if the people who want to be chartered accountants are now the freaks, the black sheep of their families.

I think we were fortunate too, without wanting to sound like a grumpy old man and go on too much about the golden age of television, to work in a young industry that was still fun, and where artistic judgements could still be more important than financial ones.

What luck! That was the message of Ron's acceptance speech on the occasion of his BAFTA award. I have to borrow it off him, and echo it. What luck to have been picked out from Winston's and asked to join Ron in *The Frost Report*. What luck to have won the love of such a wonderful wife as Anne. What luck to have done fifteen years of *The Two Ronnies* together. What luck to feel that, if I was told that I could have my career all over again, and could choose what it would be like, I could with sincerity echo those words of dear Ronnie Barker in the Buckstone Club.

'Same again, please.'

Sources

The author and publisher wish to thank all copyright holders for permission to reproduce their work, and the individuals who helped with the research and supply of materials.

Pictorial Sources

A special thanks to Joy Barker for allowing us access to her photograph collection.

p. 53 'Winning the Golden Rose' © Ben Jones/Rex Features

p. 59 'Ron and me with Josephine Tewson' from *Frost on Sunday*, reproduced courtesy of ITV

p. 60 *Frost on Sunday*, 1968, reproduced courtesy of ITV

p. 64 *Frost on Sunday*, 1968, reproduced courtesy of ITV

p. 106 'Asian Lovelies' reproduced courtesy of Don Smith/ *Radio Times*

p. 125 'As a couple of Welsh miners' reproduced courtesy of Don Smith/ *Radio Times*

p. 126 Nana Moussaka and Charles Azenough, reproduced courtesy of Don Smith/ *Radio Times*

p. 128 'Me and Ron about to burst into song in a sketch called "Ball and Socket" (our version of Hinge and Bracket), from the Saturday night show' reproduced courtesy of Don Smith/ *Radio Times*

Text Sources

Index

Figures in italics indicate illustrations.

popularity of 4, 144, 149, 172, 215, 227

problems getting material 238

and RB as writer 72

RB's monologues 79, 86, 92, 113, 114, 229–32, 242, 248

RC's monologues 79, 86, 92, 113, 114, 135–6, 219–29, 232, 238, 242, 248–51

RC's and RB's lives dominated by the show 95

RC's style 61, 62

recording 122, 123–7

rehearsals 112–15, 122, 129–31

sketches 86, 88, 91, 94, 115, 158, 174–7, 233–4, 234, 238, 240, 242, 245–8, 246

stage version 152, 208–212, 211, 255

title of the show 76–7

two series in Australia 203–7, 240

Two Ronnies Christmas Sketchbook, The (TV programme) 285–7, 301

Two Ronnies Sketchbook, The (TV series) 278–84, 285

Tynan, Kenneth 2

Upper Norwood, Greater London 49

Upstairs, Downstairs (TV sitcom) 103

Usher, Freddie 245

Variety Playhouse (radio show) 5

Vegas, Johnny 271

Victoria Palace Theatre, London 268–9

Victory Club, Edgware Road, London 1–2

Villiers, James 31

Vincent, Peter 61, 82, 112, 115, 157, 174, 229–30, 231, 245, 248, 278

Vosburgh, Dick 6, 9, 53, 61, 86, 107, 123–4, 228, 245

Wall, Max 105

Walton's restaurant, Walton Street, London 187

Warans, Bobby 129

Warner Brothers 263

Water Rats 151–2, 177, 178

Waverley, Ron (Ron Elms) 138, 139–40, 162

We Have Ways of Making You Laugh (TV show) 59

Wentworth, Horace 38

Westminster Abbey, London 293

White, Jim 291

White City, Shepherd's Bush, London 56–7

Whitehouse, Mary 216–19

Whitfield, June 265

Wilde, Brian 150

Wilder, Gene 271

Wiley, Gerald *see* Barker, Ronnie

Williams, Emlyn: *A Murder Has Been Arranged* 38

Williams, Michael 257

Williams, Tennessee: *Camino Real* 45

Wilson, Bill and Mrs 53

Wingfield Hospital, Oxford 40

Winston's Club, London 5, 6, 8, 29, 32, 49, 293, 302

Winters, Mike and Bernie 165

Wise, Ernie 108, 301

Wogan (TV programme) 137

Wolfe, Digby 28–9

World of Sport (TV programme) 59

Wrest Point, Tasmania 196

Wright, Reverend Robert 296